Law Enforcement in a Democratic Society

Law Enforcement in a Democratic Society

An Introduction

Erik Beckman

Nelson-Hall Law Enforcement Series

Nelson-Hall Chicago

Library of Congress Cataloging in Publication Data

Beckman, Erik.
Law enforcement in a democratic society.

(Nelson-Hall law enforcement series) Includes index.
1. Law enforcement—United States. 2. Criminal justice, Administration of—United States. I. Title.
HV8138.B43 364'.973 79-16306
ISBN 0-88229-151-3

Manufactured in the United States of America

10 9 8 7 6 5 4 3 2 1

Contents

CHAPTER **1**

The History of Law and Law Enforcement

Man has had some form of law since the days of the earliest societies, and law has developed through the ages into our modern legal system. In its development the law has retained many influences of the ancient Babylonians, the Romans, and many other civilizations. But the main thrust of our modern law developed directly from the system of law in England.

Along with the development of law went the development of law enforcement. Like the law itself, modern law enforcement philosophy, techniques, and agencies have their roots in history, but they, too, first appeared in modern form in England.

Ancient Law

The Babylonian, Mosaic, and Roman legal systems have had paramount influence on modern law.

Babylonian Law

Although men have had rules or laws governing their lives as long as they have banded together, written law dates back about four thousand years. Since the discovery in 1901 of Hammurabi's code, a compilation of laws written during the reign of Hammurabi as king of Babylon (1704-1662 B.C.), scholars have deemed this code as the apex of early law.

Some scholars believe that the code is a book of instruction for judges or a book of information for the people. As originally promulgated, ancient laws were uniformly theocratic, but this code is distinctly not. Rather than setting forth general precepts, it is a summary of practical measures. It contains the decisions regarding moot points, suggesting that it is an interpretation of the general laws. The code of Hammurabi is not an independent or exhaustive code, but an admininstrative version of a series of general enactments.[1] It seems to deal only with issues that had not been settled previously. For example, the code governed the seduction of a betrothed virgin, but not the seduction of an unbetrothed virgin. Scholars believe that the latter issue had probably already been settled.

The code left no room for lateral movement: things were either right or wrong; justice was absolute and without mercy. The first law in the code is a good illustration—a man who accused another of murder and could not prove it was to be put to death. It made no difference whether the accuser thought he was right or not. The law was just as rigid in its governing of judges. If a judge tried a case, rendered a decision, deposited a sealed document, and later was found to have altered his judgment, he was penalized monetarily and expelled from the bench. So no matter who a person was, he was expected to follow the straight and narrow under Hammurabi's code.

The code contained a great many laws pertaining to wrongs committed by one person against another. The penalty for such acts was compensation, usually in the form of multiple restitution, which in those days was payment in either silver or corn. If, however, the deed committed against a person caused him to lose life or limb, a victim or his relative could demand *lex talionis*—the extraction of an eye for an eye, a tooth for a tooth, a limb for a limb. But because of the class structure at the time, this did not hold for everyone; the right to demand *lex talionis* was a privilege of the dominant, patrician class; the plebeian had to be content with compensation.[2]

Little is known about procedure during this period. In a dispute, the parties would come before a judge and swear their case in the name of their god Shamash, and the judge would decide the case. Whether a private citizen could summon another person before a judge is unknown. In royal correspondence, the king often directed the apprehension of certain persons and their conveyance under custody, but apparently there was no organized police to undertake such a duty.[3]

Although the law was beginning to emerge from primitive custom in some ways, it still retained its archaic character in others. This is shown in the case of a woman who was accused of adultery. She was thrown into the river. If she floated, she was considered innocent. If she sank, she was deemed guilty.

Hammurabi's code had many shortcomings, but it was the first code of laws made for the people and covered vast numbers of possible conflicts they might encounter. It will remain a landmark in legal history.

Mosaic Law

The basis of Mosaic law is the Torah of Moses or the Pentateuch—the first five books of the Bible: Genesis, Exodus, Leviticus, Numbers, and Deuteronomy. The Torah was accepted because of its spiritual significance. As the story goes, it had been given to Moses by God on Mount Sinai. The word *Torah* actually means instruction or doctrine rather than law.

It is believed by researchers that Moses codified the laws that had long been known. In Genesis 26:5, God said of Abraham that he "kept my charge, my commandment, my statutes, and my laws," which indicates that the laws of Moses must have been promulgated long before.[4]

According to Jewish tradition, Moses was given a twofold Torah at Sinai, the first being in writing, and the second orally transmitted. The Torah orally transmitted was at its inception really more than an explanation and interpretation of the Pentateuch. It contained a number of ancient norms that had been followed and practiced from a time whereof "the memory of men runneth not to the contrary,"[5] and which originally may well have been independent of, and without any special relation to, the commandments of the Pentateuch. The written Torah often failed to give any clear direction or even any intimation of what to do in a particular case. The teachers of Israel, therefore, in each generation, by combining Torah and tradition (oral Torah) and by applying scriptural interpretation and ancient custom, made known the "way wherein they should walk and the thing which they should do."[6]

Many interpretations of the Bible developed, and in the third century A.D. these were codified in written form called the Mishnah. Later, scholars commented and elaborated on the Mishnah and created a new book called the Gemara. The Mishnah and Gemara are the two parts of the Talmud, the book of Jewish law.

The Jewish rabbis were aware of the difference between interpreting an existing law and making a new law. But they wanted the laws to fit the needs of their people in a changing society. They felt that the scriptures gave them the right and duty to interpret the laws.

A thoughtful comparison of the penal legislation of the Torah with the penal law of the Talmud demonstrates how the rabbis modified the law in redefining certain capital offenses. For example, "licentiousness" by a priest's daughter was reformed as "adultery while married," thus absolving her from the death penalty for loose conduct while a maiden.[7]

In some instances Jewish law was milder and in others harsher than Babylonian law. Under Babylonian law "Mash-en kaks" and under Jewish law "Gers" were persons who were halfway between free men and slaves (also possibly strangers), each of which had different rights. Under Babylonian law these persons' legal rights were stated, but under Jewish law it was just recommended that they not be wronged or oppressed. Slavery was also considered differently. In Babylonian law a free man could be held in bondage for only three years, while under Jewish law it was six years, and later in the Priests code it was extended to forty-nine years.

The laws governing legal procedure in the early Jewish society were far more advanced than the Babylonian laws. The original rule regarding conviction of an accused person was that two witnesses were necessary to make the proof.[8] An accused person did not have to testify against himself, and even if he confessed, a confession by itself could not convict him. Only direct evidence was allowed, no matter how good the circumstantial evidence. There was no jury, only judges. Witnesses gave evidence, and in capital cases, if the defendant was found guilty, they were his executioners.

The law of Moses, called Mosaic Law, had such an impact on the thinking of both Jews and Christians that a vast amount of it has been incorporated into modern laws.

Roman Law

Roman law can be considered to date back to 753 B.C., the date of the founding of Rome. Roman society at the time was based on clans, which were united into tribes. The heads of these clans ruled the tribes and were the patricians or upper class until the fall of Rome. It was not until 451 B.C., however, that Roman law started to take on the form that affected much of the world. Prior to this time the law was oral and was known only to the patricians. Because the plebeians—members of the lower classes—did not know the law, they often received little or no justice under it. As a result, the plebeians demanded that the laws be put into written form, and in 451 B.C., the Senate finally complied with this demand. The Senate appointed the Decemviri, ten men who were to gather the laws and put them into writing. The result was the Code of the Twelve Tables.

The Romans held the Code of the Twelve Tables in great esteem, for to them it was the basis of equality for all classes under the law. The code as a whole was secular in character and was an indication of the legal genius of the Romans, that they were able, at so early a stage in their development, to separate law so completely from religion.[9]

The code developed in part from the legal customs of people who were not of a clan and therefore had their own laws. It also grew in part from foreign laws, but it came primarily from the clan laws. Although the code covered substantive law, the largest part of it dealt with procedure, or how legal actions can be started. The clan law that was incorporated into the code "ius gentilitatis," was for the patricians only; not until the plebeians fought for and achieved equality did they have any rights.

These clan laws contained many rights—the right to vote, the right to hold legal office, the right of *dominium* (right over property), and many others. Most important was the right to the use of *legis actiones,* the legal methods used to enforce one's rights in court. There were five types of *legis actiones:* (1) *Sacramentum* consisted of a wager by parties in the case before a magistrate. (2) *Manus injectio* provided that if a man owed you money you could seize him while at the same time declaring aloud that he owed you a debt and how it came about. You could then take him before a magistrate and have him locked up for sixty days. During the sixty days, however, you had to take the accused to the open marketplace three times and declare the debt aloud each time. This gave another person the opportunity to come forth and deny the debt. But if no one came forth, and it was found that the debt was real, the accused had to pay double the debt. If the debt then was not paid, you could punish the debtor as you wished, even kill him. (3) *Pignoris capionem* was an attachment of the defendant's body. (4) *Judicis arbitrive postulationem* . . . . a demand for a special arbitrator. (5) *Conditionem* . . . . a demand for a special framing of the dispute.[10]

The magistrates could decide which of the *legis actiones* to use in a specific case. Magistrates, however, did not usually try cases but would prepare a case for a judge to try. The judge acted as the jury and decided the facts, but the rule of law that was to be used in a case was laid down by the magistrate for the judge to follow. If a person was awarded a decision in a case, however, he was usually on his own to collect. Not until later times did the courts help enforce their judgments.

During the Republic (451–31 B.C.), trials by an Assembly of the People were almost totally replaced by *quaestiones perpetuae* (standing jury courts). Each court dealt with a particular statutory offense and had a large jury and a majority verdict from which there was no appeal. The penalties were also standard and not at the discretion of the jury or the president of the court. The juries were drawn from an annual list; they were from the upper class, and the offenses they dealt with were mostly the kind committed by the upper class. It is not known just how crime among the free men and the slaves of the city of Rome was handled. There was probably little real jurisdiction, only summary punishment.[11] The penalties under the *quaestiones perpetuae* were either pecuniary (monetary) or capital. Capital punishment was usually death by a sword, but most persons just left the country and went into exile; in fact, this was usually expected of upper-class citizens.

Although the citizens at this time had procedural rights most of these were never written down, and only the priests knew them. So if a person needed a lawyer, one had to go to the priests. Because the office of priest could be held only by a patrician, a plebeian could never be sure he was getting unbiased advice if the case involved a patrician. This changed about 304 B.C., when plebeians were first allowed to enter the priesthood. From then on a plebeian could get advice from his peers.

In 253 B.C. Roman jurisprudence took a giant step forward when Tiberius Coruncanius began giving public instruction in the *legis actiones*.[12] This produced a profession of lawyers that grew until a great many persons, both plebeians and patricians, knew the law. After about 200 B.C., when one of the first law books was published, the great amount of writing done on the law further increased public knowledge of it. Finally, in 123 B.C., one of the last institutions controlled by the patricians fell, and the office of judge was open to anyone.

The Romans did legislate changes into the laws, but the vast majority of change was brought about by magistrates. Because the magistrates had to decide upon what rule of law a judge could decide the facts, the law was open to change. If the rule did not fit the case, the magistrate often had to bend, twist, or stretch the law to make it fit, thus changing it.

The jurists who gave opinions used the same kind of rationalization the rabbis used in interpreting the laws of the Pentateuch. They would never admit that they were suggesting any change in the law or any variance from it. They somehow fitted old rules of law to new sets of facts, using every trick of rationalization to find a proper answer to a problem without seeming to make new law.[13]

Because of the growth in the number of legal scholars and the growth in the volume of law caused by the interpretations of magistrates, the law became voluminous and confusing. The emperor Augustus (27 B.C.–14 A.D.) decided that he would curb this trend by cutting down on the number of jurists and giving few jurists imperial authority. This system eliminated contradictory opinions, but because the jurists were under the emperor's control, they brought few new opinions forward.

Beginning with Augustus and continuing during the Principate (approximately 27 B.C.–235 A.D.), persons who were accused of statutory offenses were beginning to be brought more and more often before city prefects, provincial governors, and others. Not being governed by any laws concerning the penalties, the officers could do what they wanted with a person. Sending persons to labor in the mines or be gladiators became common. Deaths by decapitation, crucifixion, and burning flourished, although usually only in the lower classes.

In the United States today a foreigner is subject to the penalties of the law if he breaks it, but he is also guaranteed rights under the law. This is called equity. Such was not the case in early Rome. A citizen had rights under civil law, but a foreigner did not. Eventually, however, the Romans appointed a new kind of magistrate and called him the *praetor peregrinus* to distinguish him from the ordinary urban magistrate who administered the civil law. This magistrate determined the law of foreigners—the law applying when aliens were involved and the civil law could not be used.[14] What made this magistrate different from the civil magistrate was that he was left on his own to decide equity. There were no rules of law governing his procedure.

Under the *legis actiones,* the procedure had been very limited because the magistrate had to follow set rules and even the persons in a case had to say and do everything in a prescribed way. Without any guidelines, the *praetor peregrinus* was able to develop what he called a formula. The formula was very simple. The praetor would merely listen to oral pleadings by both sides in a case, then he would put into writing a formula that would be given to the judge. It contained the facts in the case, the issue the judge was to decide, and any pleas that were entered, and it told the judge what to do if the case was decided one way or the other.

The formulary system eventually replaced the *legis actiones* and became the only procedure. The only restriction was that no law of custom could detract from a specific statute; as in our law today, no custom could be pleaded that was contrary to the written law. Thus grew up in Roman law the distinction between *jus* (law in general) and *lex* (law that depended on statute).[15]

The formula system in Rome was eventually replaced by a procedure called *cognitio,* which was merely a simplification of the legal process. The magistrate or praetor still looked into the facts and issues of a case, which now were written pleadings given to him by the litigants. But instead of deciding whether the case should go to a judge, the magistrates simply decided the case themselves according to the law at the time and without holding themselves to any formula in deciding it. Although the magistrates did not generally follow any set procedures, they did follow guidelines called edicts. Before they took office, they would state just how they would apply the law.

Because of the vast number of edicts put forth by the magistrates, great confusion resulted when they conflicted. Emperor Hadrian set out to eliminate the confusion, and so he formed a commission to collect and study the law. The result was the Perpetual Edict, which the magistrates had to follow. Although the magistrates could interpret the edict somewhat, they were really now confined to a set procedure.[16] About this same time citizens gained the right to appeal a magistrate's decision, which in earlier times was impossible.

While the Roman law had many shortcomings in certain areas, it was exceedingly well developed. For example, careful distinction was made between types of liability, and the capacity of the Roman jurists for classifying and distinguishing was truly remarkable. What we today might generally classify as negligence, they divided into several parts. Their category that is closest to our concept of negligence was *improvidentia.* For example, a man who practiced javelin throwing at a place where he knew people might pass was guilty of *improvidentia.* The Romans also discovered contributory negligence. The passer-by who knew that the javelin thrower frequently practiced at a certain place was guilty of contributory negligence if he did not watch out for flying javelins.[17] The reason Roman law worked so well and reached such an advanced state was that unlike law in other societies, it encompassed a system of procedure that could cover almost any incident. It also was able to create a class of lawyers who could administer and shape the law.

In time the barbarians slowly began to capture most of the outermost provinces of the Roman Empire. Eventually the capital was moved to Constantinople, and not long after that, the entire western Roman empire fell. Many of the rulers of the eastern empire, including Justinian I, tried to win back the lost lands, but it was a losing cause, and they eventually abandoned it. The last legal development that was to have an effect on the west was the Justinian Code, 529 A.D., which was a compilation of previous law and innovations on the part of the eastern Romans. [18] This code, however, was not used until many years later—after Europe emerged from the dark ages.

Medieval Law

With the coming of the barbarians—the Germanic tribes—law that had taken centuries to build up was destroyed in a short time. Any remnants of the Roman law that remained were useless, because they were broken up and confusing or simply because few could read them, for literacy had almost completely disappeared. In order to bring order out of the turmoil and social instability, the Germanic peoples imposed feudalism on the citizens. A feudal chief or lord who conquered land would divide the land up among his followers, who in turn could divide their share among their own followers. When the lord made a grant of land to his men, he guaranteed them protection in return for promises by the men to discharge certain duties to him. Some were bound to serve him as soldiers, so an army was always available to the great lords.

At the bottom of the feudal structure were the serfs, who merely worked the land without owning it. The serf was protected by local custom as long as he performed required services, such as working on the lord's land so many days or rendering to the lord certain produce of the land. Next above the serfs were the free tenants. Much like the serfs, they were protected by the rendering of various kinds of service or of rents. Above the tenants were those who held their land based on military service given in behalf of their immediate lord. The gradations continued to the ruler of the state.[19]

The feudal system spread all over western Europe, but it differed somewhat in each country. In England it reached an almost perfect state because William the Conqueror was astute enough, upon conquering England and confiscating much of its land, to demand full feudal fealty from the lords to whom he made his grants, insisting that all land was owned by him and only held in tenure by others, directly or indirectly from him.[20]

The two most important elements of feudal law were first, the return to a state of private war between the holders of land grants, or fiefs, who had no common judge or arbiter, and second, the right of every lord of a fief to hold a court to judge all controversies between his tenants, whether bonded or free.[21] Each fief depended for justice on the will of the lord or on the decision of someone to whom the lord gave jurisdiction. Generally, however, the lord was interested only in the resulting fees. He left the court to his free tenants, who pronounced the judgment of the court.

The lord exercised civil and criminal jurisdiction over his lands and over his tenants, called *vassals,* and held court whenever he wished. The tenants were required to attend these courts as members of juries to try their peers. These local, or *manor,* courts were responsible for most of the great confusion of law in Europe during the Middle Ages, because each manor lord was his own lawmaker.[22] (At this time only the church laid down a single law to be observed for everyone who sought its courts. In all the lay courts the law was whatever the superior forces pronounced it to be in a particular case.)

Alongside feudal law, and in the fields not covered by it, there developed what was called customary law. This law took a strange direction and became class law. The law of the nobles was almost completely feudal, and the peasants were subject to the local law of each manor. Merchants, however, were subject to a separate law that came out of the commercial and trade customs developed by the merchants themselves. The townspeople had a kind of municipal law that was created chiefly by ordinances.

Customary law was administered by judges who applied what they found to be the custom and, if they did not find any, made rulings that became customary after they had been followed a sufficient number of times. But no matter how long the alleged custom had been followed, it was not valid if it was considered to be contrary to the public welfare.[23] The customary law, developing along with feudal law, sometimes changed it; and the remnants of personal law that remained were destroyed by the growth of the feudal and customary law, for everyone in a community was subject to one or both. This was not difficult because, by this time, the various tribal people had mixed to a point where tribal distinctions were almost forgotten. Also, there was now a common religion.

Cases were now tried, not by the assemblies of old, but by judges in the local courts. These lay judges did not determine the issues in a trial. The presiding judge stated the issues and the law that applied, and he gave the judgment, but it had to be assented to by the lay judges in order to become a collective judgment and to be effective. The similarity of this system to the old tribal practice is clear, for the trials of old required the assent of the assembled people to a judgment given by the chief or presiding officer. Another remaining feature of the old tribal system of justice was that the old court sessions were held in the open air; in the feudal era the courtrooms generally were open at one end.

The rules of law remained somewhat primitive: the act of clearing an accused person by the oaths of a certain number of others testifying to their belief in his innocence was still an institution, and ordeal by various methods, decision by combat, and other ancient customs were still employed.[24]

Feudal law declined when new ideas of law and of legal systems came into Europe by way of a renaissance of Roman law. The rapidly strengthened intellectual and middle classes found feudal laws and institutions distasteful after rediscovering the superior codes of old Rome.

English Law

While Europe proper was rediscovering Roman law and changing its legal systems, England began to change, too, in her own way. Crown courts had been in use for some time, although they were few in number. During the reign of Henry II (1154–1189) they were greatly enlarged. King Henry appointed judges who traveled throughout the country trying cases. The circuit courts over which these judges presided were greeted favorably by the people, who felt that they could get fairer judgments from courts that were national and that would therefore be less biased. Eventually, these courts began to incorporate into their jurisdiction a great number of legal actions. These courts went on the concept of the king's peace, which was developed by the Normans. All offenses committed in public places were considered as breaches of the king's peace. In addition, all important offenses were appropriated by these courts.[25]

The church in England had its own courts, which ruled on matters its leaders felt were in the jurisdiction of the church. These courts at one time were the only judicial bodies in many parts of England and therefore ruled on many matters that were outside the church. When a regular court system was formed, the separation into church and lay courts created a conflict of jurisdiction that continued for many centuries. Eventually there came into use a "writ of prohibition" issued by the lay courts to prevent the church courts from infringing on their jurisdiction.[26]

England had for some time a petit jury that sat at trials and decided the facts. Under Henry II, a new type of jury was introduced—a grand jury. It was composed of twelve men appointed by the local sheriff, and it decided whether or not to accuse a person of a crime. If the grand jury decided to accuse a person, he would have to stand trial before a petit jury. The members of the grand jury were called "recognitors," twelve men who were witnesses and who had the duty of finding the facts. They could ask questions or just sit if they wanted to; they could even assume what the facts were. Since there were no real witnesses as such, all the lawyer did was make a pleading of his client's case at the beginning of the trial. When the jurors felt they knew the facts in a case, they could decide on a verdict, which required that all twelve men be unanimous in either an innocent or a guilty verdict. The only feasible way in which such a verdict could be set aside was for another, better-informed body to be called in to say that the former jury spoke falsely. Thereupon, a new judgment could be entered contrary to the former judgment.[27]

The Magna Carta, which King John signed in 1215, stated that a person had a right to a trial by his peers. In reality, however, this was a right guaranteed only to the upper classes or nobles. It was many years before this was recognized as a right of the average man. Not until the reign of the Stuart kings in the 1600s was it granted consistently.

While law in continental Europe was based largely on statutory enactments, England developed common law. Common law was judge-made law, molded, refined, examined, and changed in the course of actual decisions and handed down from generation to generation in the form of reported cases. In theory, the judges drew their decisions from existing principles of law; ultimately these principles reflected the living values, attitudes, and ethical ideas of the English people.[28] One of the important characteristics of common law was that the judges used precedents in deciding their cases. The rule of *stare decisis,* which developed out of common law, meant that when a point of law had been decided by the highest court in the land, all other similar cases that hinged on this point would have to be decided in accordance with the higher court ruling. The theory that common law decisions were drawn from existing principles was really based on the idea that the judges discovered or uncovered the law. When they actually changed the law, therefore, they had to do it in a subtle manner. In deciding a case, a judge might give an incidental and gratuitous opinion as to what the law might be with a different set of facts. Such extraneous opinions are called *dicta,* and while a dictum of a judge does not create law, it can create doubt that is dispelled only when a further case decides the point about which the earlier judge speculated.[29]

The English legal profession dates back to the time of William the Conqueror, who had *serjeants* or servants who later became servants of the king at law. In the 1300s guilds appeared called Inns of Court, where lawyers would go to learn the law and legal pleadings. It was from these guilds that all English judges were drawn. The English bar was an important influence on the shape of English law. Since all English lawyers came out of the Inns of Court, which had no connection with the universities, where the mainstream of thought centered on Roman law, common law was able to survive in England while continental law was based mostly on a rejuvenated Roman law.[30]

Edward I, who took the throne in 1272, brought many changes to English law. In 1295 he developed a model parliament, to which he invited not only the nobles but also two knights from every shire, or district, and two burgesses from every town. This became the basis for the parliament that governs England today. To the court of common pleas and court of king's bench, which had gradually become established since the time of Henry II, Edward I added conservators of the peace, which he appointed to deal with the lawlessness in many areas. These conservators were knights who enforced the laws where other attempts had failed. During the reign of Edward III these conservators became justices of the peace.

After the death of Edward I, parliament began to assume more and more power, and during the reign of Edward III it assumed what was essentially its final character. Though not yet legally broken into two houses, it was divided in fact, and the House of Commons was becoming the more important house. Also during the reign of Edward III, the old system of oral pleading before the court was changed to the present system of written pleading by the plaintiff and defendant. This new sort of pleading was brought about by two factors: (1) the insistence by lawyers that pleadings should be as they wished them and not as the judges on oral discussion decided they ought to be (and the lawyers did not trust the clerks to write out the pleadings as settled upon in the oral discussion), and (2) the recent availability and lower cost of paper.[31]

The English, like the Romans, had courts of equity. Equity courts grew out of the office of chancellor, which was empowered to issue writs to the common law courts. The concept of the king's conscience, which was the duty to change unjust laws or make new ones where there were none, was given over to the chancellor to enforce. Eventually out of this came the equity system. Equity or chancery courts differed a great deal from common law courts in that they were not governed by strict rules of common law; they could and often did use Roman law to decide a case. Yet in many ways common law courts and courts of equity complemented each other. The common law could proclaim duties and rights, but it could not compel any kind of performance other than payment of money. Equity, on the other hand, had a whole battery of other remedies, such as the injunction. Equity courts had power over persons, not over things. They could not render judgments that bound the title to land, for example; they could only act on the parties.[32]

Yet conflict did arise between the two courts. The common law courts were bogged down by the use of juries. Seeing this as disadvantageous, the chancery or equity courts did not use juries but merely executed a judgment if there appeared to be an equitable or fair reason for doing so. This caused bitter resentment on the part of the common law courts. Chancery courts also began interfering in actions that were only within the jurisdiction of the common law courts. Things became so confusing that litigants in an action could receive one rule of law in the common law courts and a totally different one in the chancery courts. Eventually these problems were worked out so that the courts of equity would decide an action only if there was no relief at law. In 1878 it was at last acknowledged that the righteous law must govern England by giving courts of common law equitable powers, and by ruling that where the common law rule differed from that of equity, the rule of equity should govern.[33]

During the reign of Charles I, a reform movement began in England and brought a strong parliament into power. In 1628 this parliament drafted the famous Petition of Right, one of the greatest landmarks in British freedom. It provided that no person could be compelled to pay money to the state without the consent of Parliament, that no person could be imprisoned for any crime without cause and without an opportunity to answer the charge, that soldiers and mariners could not be billeted in the houses of the people, and that no further commissions could be issued to punish persons by martial law.[34] The Petition of Right also gave members of Parliament the right to debate freely. From this Petition of Right have come two of the most valuable rights we have in this country: freedom of speech and the writ of habeas corpus. But for a long time in England the nobility fought against the use of the habeas corpus, and it was not until Parliament passed the Habeas Corpus Amendment Act of 1679 that it became accepted.

A practice to emerge after the Glorious Revolution of 1688 was the permanent tenure of judges during good behavior. The original rule had been that judges held office at the pleasure of the king. Other reforms emanating from this period included the establishment of rules of evidence, and the reform of methods of pleading so that the controversy could be put to the judiciary.

It was left to Jeremy Bentham and others to humanize the law and to do away with archaic laws inherited from the feudal age. For example, the criminal law was still barbaric. A man could be executed for cutting down a tree as well as for over two hundred other offenses. Reforms were also made in laws concerning women. Married women were given the rights to make personal contracts and to hold property independently from their husbands.[35] Thus, the English legal system was able to question existing rules that served no current purpose and thereby discovered that reform can enhance an already stable body of laws.

Influences on American Law

Colonial America during the seventeenth century had a limited legal background. Since the colonies were controlled by England, it was natural that they would draw from her laws, and since the people of the colonies spoke English, the laws needed no translation.

The judicial system in America grew from a simple structure to one as vast and almost as complex as England's. Massachusetts Bay Colony in 1639 had several levels of courts. At the top was the general court, which had legislative-type power as well as appellate jurisdiction. Below this court was the court of assistants, which was made up of judges, administrators, and the governor of the colony. The third type of court, the county court, tried cases and heard appeals from town administrators and justice of the peace courts. The only cases of importance that they did not try were capital cases. The problems with this system were that all these courts had overlapping jurisdiction and that there was no clear division between the branches of government.

During the 1700s the judiciary system had the same form as it had had in the past, but it was more complex because of the additions of vice-admiralty and chancery courts. Court procedures in the regular courts became complex, too, because these colonial courts assimilated all innovations in written pleadings, testimony, and other procedures that developed in England. This was not only because England was the mother country, but also because all lawyers in the colonies had received their training in England.

The Constitution in 1787 created the American system of federal courts, which had power over all federal laws and power to review cases appealed from state courts. The Judiciary Act of 1789 divided the country into districts, each district generally coextensive with a state, each with a federal district court and a district judge.[36] This act also had an effect on the states, which began to arrange their court systems in a more orderly fashion and to draw clearer distinctions between trial courts and appeals courts. The Constitution also gave federal judges tenure for life unless there was good cause to take them off the bench. John Marshall felt that this was a solution to an old problem, because judges could then make and interpret policy without concern for partisan politics. Principle and policy would flow from the logic of law; they would not follow from political expediency.[37]

The single greatest influence on the judiciary, its procedures, and the laws of this country, however, was the Bill of Rights. It was in and of itself a code of criminal procedure. It spelled out the rights of citizens and the duty of the state vis-à-vis these rights. The Bill of Rights was not a singularly American idea that sprang up overnight; it had been influenced greatly by English law. The first, third, and sixth amendments have close similarities to England's Petition of Right.

A more direct English influence on America can be seen in a comparison of the opening lines of the Declaration of Independence with the philosophy of the English philosopher John Locke. Wrote Locke, "The state of nature has a law of nature to govern it, which obliges everyone: and reason, which is that law, teaches all mankind, who will but consult it, that all being equal and independent, no one ought to harm another in his life, health, liberty, or possessions." The first sentence of the

Declaration makes reference to the "laws of nature" as justifying the separation of the colonies from England. That Locke's particular variety of the laws of nature concept is intended becomes evident from other parts of the Declaration. In the second sentence the signers hold it "self-evident" that men have "certain unalienable Rights" and that among these are "Life, Liberty, and the pursuit of Happiness."

Immediately following is Locke's social contract, which is a voluntary agreement among individuals by which organized society comes into existence and is invested with the right to secure mutual protection and welfare and regulate the relations of members. The Declaration says ". . . to secure these rights Governments are instituted among Men, deriving their just powers from the consent of the governed. That whenever any Form of Government becomes destructive of these ends, it is the Right of the People to alter or to abolish it, and to institute new Government. . . ."[38]

Criminal procedure in America began to grow and develop as rules governing evidence and other procedures were defined and redefined. It left us with a unique formula for trial procedure. European law allows almost any evidence to be presented and trusts the judge to separate good evidence from bad. American law reflects distrust of the judge, giving the jury full power to determine facts and, in criminal cases, the final word on innocence or guilt. Yet the law has also embodied a distrust of the jury as well as the judge, and the rules of evidence grew up as a countervailing force.[39]

In 1848 the state of New York adopted a Code of Civil Procedure, which abolished the distinction between actions at law and suits in equity. This meant the end of all special pleadings, forms of actions and writs, the closing of the chasm between equity and law. Although New York eventually discarded this code, it was accepted throughout the West and Midwest, and by 1861 twenty-four states had adopted it.

The essential difference between the civil and common law lies in the generating force of authority. In the common law it rests wholly in the decisions of the courts; in the civil law it rests on legislation. A code is not intended to provide for every contingency that might arise. It is a statement of general principles to be applied by deduction or analogy to particular cases. It is the function of the common law jurisdiction to make the law. In the civil law the function of the court is one of interpretation.[40] Codified laws put a damper on judges in that they are no longer able to define new crimes out of the law but are still able to define the meaning and application of old crimes.

England was not the only source from which this country drew its laws, however. Before becoming a state, Louisiana, with a predominantly French population, had a mixture of Spanish and Roman, but mostly French, civil law. In 1825 the state legislature adopted a civil code that was taken almost entirely from France's Napoleonic Code and that remains in Louisiana even today.

America was fortunate to be able to form such a unique and democratically workable system of laws. The country was small at its inception but had a goodly number of educated men. Unlike other countries, we did not have an existing complex social and economic society that could not survive for long without an equally complex legal system. As we grew, we were able to assimilate into our legal system only those things we wanted. Our ability to sift through laws and discard what was bad has enabled America to seek justice under laws of men.

The History of Law Enforcement

Men have always had some kind of laws guiding their lives, but such laws are meaningless without enforcement. Enforcement began with self-enforcement by social groups and has progressed through the ages to our modern system.

Preliterate Societies

Man is a social animal; he has lived in groups since his ancestors lived in trees. But if a society is to survive, it must provide for certain needs. These needs or prerequisites were described by anthropologist John W. Bennett and sociologist Melvin M. Tumin as the following:

1. to maintain the biologic functioning of the group members;
2. to reproduce new members for the group;

3. to socialize new members into functioning adults;
4. to produce and distribute goods and services necessary to life;
5. to maintain order within the group and between itself and outsiders; and
6. to define the "meaning of life" and maintain the motivation to survive and engage in the activities necessary for survival.[41]

To provide the prerequisites, society creates rules, some of which inhibit undesirable behavior and others of which encourage desirable behaviors. Through enculturation, an individual learns which responses his society encourages and rewards and which ones it frowns on and punishes. When a person has internalized all the desired characteristics of his society, he is said to be mature.[42]

Because history was not recorded for many years, the behavior and life style of early man must be inferred from present living styles of primitive cultures and from evidence found by archeologists. Early man lived in family groups. As the family flourished, the extended family or clan evolved. The oldest male in the clan was usually the clan leader. Clans sometimes merged to form tribes, and tribal leaders were given authority to protect the tribe from external sources, such as other tribes, and to maintain tribal regulations. Tribal leaders therefore performed both military and police functions.

Trade centers developed through which tribes exchanged goods with one another. When man learned to domesticate plants and animals, fewer people were needed for the task of providing food for the tribe. Some members, therefore, moved to the trade centers, which grew into the first cities. The surplus crops and animals of the farmers and herders were adequate to maintain the urban dwellers. Formal religions and governments sprang up in the centers of population. As civilization advanced, rural dwellers were taxed by the government and were, in turn, provided with protection. The advent of writing then opened up a whole new era in law enforcement.[43]

Law enforcement up to this time had been in the hands of the family, clan, or tribe. The head of the group had been the executive and judicial officer, but the people were the police force. Early justice was retaliatory in nature. Mutilation and branding were often used as punishment and were the first form of criminal identification. The rules were made by the society to enable it to survive. The laws were not formal; they developed from custom.

Early Literate Societies

Hammurabi's code is the earliest known codified set of laws. They were inscribed in stone and were found by modern archeologists; the inscriptions are still legible today. As discussed earlier, crimes and punishment were standardized, the responsibilities between the individual and the state and between two individuals were prescribed. Hammurabi's code prescribed both physical punishment and the first known civil restitution. The police force at the time consisted of messengers who were obliged to see that the laws were obeyed. Punishment was often brutal, but, because it was standardized to the crime, the code still was considered to be a great step in the furthering of lawmaking and law enforcement.

Ancient Egypt. Egypt, as early as 1500 B.C., developed sophisticated laws and court systems to hear transgressions of the law. A century later, custom houses were established and a marine patrol was created to assist them in enforcement.

Ancient Greece. As the people of Greece began to move to cities, they also developed policing practices. The Athenian Pisastratus, known as a tyrant, had guards who were responsible for the protection of his person, his property, and the highways. The city of Sparta had an authoritarian ruler. Because of this, its police force was considered to be the first secret police force. This police body consisted of five ephors, who faced yearly election. Their power was limitless. They governed each other's conduct and had both executive and judicial powers. Ephori were often corrupt but maintained their office because the people feared retaliation for voting against them. Greek philosophers held serious discussions on what we consider to be the criminal justice system. One philosopher, Plato, believed that the criminal should not only be punished, but should also be given the means for rehabilitation.

Ancient Rome. Augustus, the first emperor of Rome, created several law enforcement units, one of which was the urban cohort. It was a military unit, composed of members of military legions.

The urban cohort had the responsibility of keeping the peace in the city of Rome. It was later replaced by the Vigiles of Rome, whose duties were to keep the peace and fight fires. The Vigiles were the first police unit composed of nonmilitary personnel. Because they had both police and fire duties, they are considered to be the forerunners of modern, integrated, police/fire departments. Augustus also formed the Praetorian Guard, which was composed of the elite military legionnaires. Their duties were to protect the emperor and his properties. Their duties were much like those of our present Secret Service, which protects the president.[44]

This period was known for codified laws and punishments and utilized seeds of modern enforcement practices including courts, marine patrols, fire patrols, and nonmilitary police.

Feudal Societies

After the fall of the Roman Empire, law enforcement was at a standstill due to the frequent wars and invasions of the period. Europe was a ravaged continent.

Early England. In England there were new developments between 700 and 900 A.D. Various systems were developed to discover the guilt or innocence of an accused criminal. Trial by ordeal was one of these methods. Trial by physical combat between the parties involved was another. During this period, too, the fine, restitution, rendition, and involuntary servitude had their beginnings.

Capital punishment was rarely used. Instead, serious criminals were branded so they could be easily recognized. An elaborate system of fines was also set up, and punishment was created to fit the crime. These penalties were enforced by the community as a whole.

In the latter half of the ninth century Alfred the Great united all of England. In order to force the people to comply with his laws, he established a national police force. The means he used was the tithing system, which not only established a police force but insured local justice, maintained the peace, protected the community, and required close adherence to the rules of society.[45]

Under the tithing system the head of each household was responsible for the actions of the members of his family. If the head of the household was landless, it was necessary for him to group with nine other landless families to form a tithing. In the case of a landed proprietor, his dependents comprised a tithing. All men over twelve years of age were required to belong to a tithing, and all members were armed. Each member of a tithing was responsible for the acts of the other members.

The head of the tithing was called the chief tithingman and was elected by the other landless members of the tithing. He was responsible for raising the "hue and cry," apprehending criminals, and meting out punishment. The "hue and cry" was an order to form a "posse comitatus," or power of the county, in which every able-bodied man assisted the shire reeve or one of his assistants, the chief tithingman, to apprehend criminals. If a criminal escaped, his tithing was obliged to make restitution for his crime.

Ten tithings were grouped together to form a hundred, headed by a reeve. Several hundreds were united into a shire, which was a geographical area equal to a county. The shires were under the direct command of the shire reeve (later sheriff), who was appointed by the king or a nobleman and served at the king's or nobleman's whim.[46] The shire reeve served the functions of both the executive and judicial branches of government at the local level, and he represented the state in all matters of national importance. The next step in the tithing system was the ealdorm, which was under the direct control of the ealdorman. An ealdorm was a grouping of several shires. The ealdorm was directly responsible to the king.

The purpose of the tithing system was to diffuse the responsibility for obeying the laws among the people. Each person in the tithing was obliged to help control the behavior of the other tithing members or face the responsibility for their errant acts. One defect of the system, which hampered its effective use, was the fact that crime was often covered up by fellow tithing members to save one or all members from making restitution. Tithing worked well in emergency conditions and in rural areas. It was not very effective when people began moving to cities, because its bonding power declined.

England began forming its court system during this period. The court of the *pied poudre* (dusty feet), so called because it was held in the county market, tried minor matters. The hundreds courts, or courts of the shire, were also formed, and the ealdorman, shire reeves, and other officials sat in judgment. Judicial innovations included suspended sentences, release on personal recognizance for rich or well-known persons and the use of bail by suspected criminals.

In 1066 the Norman king William the Conqueror invaded and conquered England. He divided England into fifty-five separate military areas and placed a commander in charge of each. This military commander was the shire reeve, who also kept his powerful civil position. King William placed England under a very repressive police system and established martial law. He believed that the security of all was more important than the rights of a few. He took the judicial power away from the shire reeve and in 1072 created the position of vicecomes, who were traveling judges and were the forerunners of today's circuit judges. The vicecomes were not well liked because, like the justices of the peace today, the public believed their sole purpose was to collect fines. The shire reeve still remained the chief law enforcement officer on the county.

During the early Norman period (1066–1285) the office of comes stabuli (constable) was created. The constable was hired on a full-time basis to assist the shire reeve in performing his duties. The constable was the forerunner of the modern town constable or chief of police. This office still exists today, but it has relatively little power.

Prior to the year 1116, law enforcement concerning state matters such as land and tax problems was in the care of the shire reeve and his constables. Private guards were needed by shop owners and individuals to protect their persons and property because shire reeves and constables did not deal with individual victims and crimes. Police forces existed only for the state.

In 1116 the son of William the Conqueror, Henry I, issued his Leges Henrici. Through these laws, England was divided into thirty judicial districts and the laws defined the types of crime. "There will be certain offenses against the king's peace, arson, robbery, murder, false coinage, and crimes of violence. These we deem to be felonious." The king stated that all other crimes would be considered misdemeanors. The crimes against the king's peace were the basis for laws concerning disturbance of the peace. These laws also placed authority to punish in the hands of the state instead of in the hands of the victim or victims. A "felon" was considered to be a most vile person, and "misdemeanors" were acts of bad behavior. Criminal law enforcement now became a public matter.

Henry II, in his Assize of Arms, required that every freeman bear arms to protect his country and keep the peace. (An assize is a court sitting or in session.) During his reign, the courts began keeping judicial records. Common law dates from this time and a division was made between criminal and tort law. Torture was often used to gain confessions and as punishment after conviction. Henry II also introduced the jury system.

In 1194 King Richard I created the office of coroner, but the duties of the office were very vague. In 1195 he appointed knights to get oaths of allegiance from all males over fifteen years of age. This was the first formal loyalty oath. These knights later became known as peace wardens and conservators of the peace. They became powerful persons as power was slowly taken from the shire reeve. Eventually, they were given judicial powers.

During the twelfth century new offices and new courts were created. The people in these offices and courts supervised matters pertaining to forests, game, and game protection. The Norman system of game management was established in England:

> Verderers were judicial officers; agisters supervised the grazing land of the deer; regarders were responsible for the registration and declawing of dogs; and foresters and rangers were sworn to preserve the game and forests by enforcement of the law. Forest courts—Woodmote Court, Court of Regard, Court of Suranimote, and Court of Justice Seat—made inquiries, judged, and convicted.[47]

These laws and officers of justice were very unpopular with the people. The feudal nobles were able to stalk the game in the forests—a right denied to the commoner. Many bands roved the forests, much like the fictional Robin Hood and his men.

In 1199 King Richard I died and his brother, John, became king. He was very unpopular with both the populace and the nobles. On June 15, 1215, King John was forced to sign the Magna Carta (Great Charter) on the plain of Runnymede. This charter guaranteed "due process of law" to the populace and nobles by protecting their rights and liberties. Articles 13 and 39 were important to law enforcement. Article 13 stated:

> and the City of London shall have all its ancient liberties and free customs. Moreover, we will grant that all other cities and villages shall have all their liberties and free customs.[48]

Article 39 stated:

> No freeman may be taken or imprisoned or disseized or outlawed or banished or in any way destroyed . . . except by the lawful judgement of his peers, or by the law of the land. To none will we sell or deny or delay right or justice. We will not make men justiciaries, constables, sheriffs, or bailiffs, unless they understand the law of the land, and are well disposed to observe it.[49]

Article 13 separated the national and local governments. It returned the right of the people to manage their local cities. Article 39 guaranteed a trial by jury and due process of law. Also, some type of selection process was to be used to choose better persons for law enforcement offices.

By 1250 the tithing system had lost any efficiency it had during its prime. In 1252 Henry III organized a national militia. All men were ordered, and had to take an oath, to bear arms for maintaining the public peace. Each person was required to serve as a watchman on a rotation basis, but substitutes could be hired because the duty was unpopular. Often the substitutes were inefficient, dishonest, and lazy.

In 1285 King Edward I issued the Statute of Winchester, which created a watch and ward system.[50] Hundreds were again made responsible for offenses committed by their members. Guards were posted by city gates from spring to fall to protect the property of farmers while they were working the fields. Persons rotated on the watch and were punished if they failed to serve. Bailiffs were commissioned to inquire about and keep track of strangers in the towns. Today a bailiff is a court officer. The assistants of the bailiff were referred to as sergeants, a term still used by police today.

Edward III, in 1361, created the office of justice of the peace. This officer had both judicial and executive power. His duties were "to restrain offenders, rioters and other barrators, and to pursue, to arrest, to take and to chastise them according to their offense." In certain places this office exists today, but it has been abused in the past and may soon be abolished.

Because the people felt the king was too powerful, Henry VI created the office of state informer. The person placed in this office was given a monetary reward if he could expose any activities against the king. This was a last-ditch effort to retain the awesome power of the crown.

In the first part of the sixteenth century, England dealt heavily in world trade. Wool was in short supply at the time. Because the farmers did not own their lands, they were expelled from the rural areas and the landowners raised sheep because of the huge market. The dispossessed farmers by necessity moved to the cities. Because many were poor and had no way to earn a living, they resorted to crime.

Merchants began to hire private police forces to protect their property and apprehend violators. This private police force was called the Merchant Police. The people also wanted better police protection and formed a Parochial Police in each parish. Cities were divided into parishes, and each member of the parish was required to serve in rotation on the force. Later, the rotation method was abandoned and replaced by a system of paid parish constables.

In 1641 Charles I abolished the Court of the Star Chamber, which used torture to obtain confessions and required cruel and inhumane treatment for persons found guilty.

Civil war broke out in England, and in 1655 Oliver Cromwell seized power. He used military personnel to hold the people in line. England was divided into twelve districts, each headed by a military commander who served as an executive and judicial officer.

In 1663 the "shiver and shake" or "Charlie" watch was formed by King Charles II. One thousand bellmen were to be on duty from sunset to sunrise. These watchmen were ineffective and lazy and were publicly ridiculed.

In 1668 England was again faced with a revolution, and James II was deposed as king. Parliament passed an act in 1689 that gave citizens the right of free speech and protection against self-incrimination. These are two of the basic rights in our Bill of Rights. American colonists realized that these rights were necessary for a free society.

Crime was still increasing at a rapid rate. A system of rewards was initiated, but it failed miserably. Persons were wrongly accused of crimes so their accusers could get the reward, and others were punished without being proven guilty. In 1737 George II passed a law allowing cities to levy taxes so they could pay for a police force.

In 1748 Sir Henry Fielding was appointed magistrate in the town of Middlesex. He proposed a new type of police force. His police officers were called "Bow Street Runners" or "Thief Takers." He stated that police personnel should be well paid and swiftly dispatched to the crime scene. He utilized both foot and horse patrols. His police force is considered to be the first detective unit, because it was mainly concerned with the investigation of crime

In 1777 George III proposed some improvements in the night watch. Watchmen were given the duty of checking doors and arresting loiterers and disorderly persons. These watchmen received pay and were required to carry rattles, staves, and lanterns while on duty. They were also required to cry out the time of night at periodic intervals.

The industrial revolution replaced many men with machines. More people became jobless and poor, and crime was rampant. Stiff penalties were established for crimes, but these penalties failed to deter criminals. Many of the people had to commit crimes to survive or to support their families. They were in a hopeless situation, dead if they did not break the law and dead if they were caught in the act.

In 1796 Dr. Robert Colquhoun made several recommendations for improving the police forces. He recommended that police organizations maintain records. He also stated that the police should be centrally located, receive training, and be vigilant.

Early France. During the reign of Charlemagne (in the eighth and early ninth centuries A.D.) France was divided into geographical areas known as *contes* (counties) and each was headed by a *conte* (count). The count was a feudal lord and represented the king in all legal matters.

France also developed the seeds of the modern trial—the inquest, which was a hearing to establish an opinion on a legal matter, and the jury, those sworn in to express their opinion. The jury's statement to the king was called the *veredictum* (verdict, or true saying). The inquest was initially used in disputes over royal property, but later its use was expanded to other areas.[51]

After Charlemagne's death his kingdom was split among his heirs. The new king established the Marshals of France to protect the security of the country. France also developed an organizational system that was the model for the English tithing system. It worked in much the same manner, diffusing the responsibility for enforcing and obeying the law among the people.

Peelian Reform

In 1829 Sir Robert Peel, a member of the English Parliament, proposed a bill that would establish a new police force for the metropolitan area. His recommendations were based on a study, conducted by Dr. Robert Colquhoun, that established that the present police service was inadequate. Peel stated that the watch and ward system should be termed the "shiver-and-shake" watch because its force shivered half the night from the cold and shook the other half out of fear. His suggestions were adopted by Parliament, and formal operation began on September 29, 1829.

Twelve principles of modern law enforcement were stressed by Peel. These principles are still applicable to modern police officers:

1. The police must be stable, efficient, and organized along military lines.
2. The police must be under government control.
3. The absence of crime will best prove the efficiency of police.
4. The distribution of crime news is essential.
5. The deployment of police strength, both by time and area, is essential.
6. No quality is more indispensable to a policeman than a perfect command of temper. A quiet, determined manner has more effect than violent action.

7. Good appearance commands respect.
8. The selection and training of proper persons are at the root of efficient law enforcement.
9. Public security demands that every police officer be given an identifying number.
10. Police headquarters should be centrally located and easily accessible to the people.
11. Policemen should be hired on a probationary basis before permanent assignment.
12. Police crime records are necessary to the best distribution of police strength.[52]

Two commissioners were put in charge of the new organization. Both were disciplinarians, and they managed to mold the force into a workable unit. At the outset, their headquarters was in the Home Office. Later, it was transferred to the place from which it took its name—Scotland Yard.

Out of approximately 12,000 applicants for the new police positions, 1,000 were immediately screened, hired, and grouped into six divisions. One-third of the force was drawn from the ranks of unskilled laborers. A probationary period was used to weed out persons who did not meet the high standards set by Peel, resulting in a very large turnover; within the first eight years, 5,000 men were dismissed and 6,000 resigned. Employment could be maintained for life if the officer was productive and lived up to Peel's requirements, but in 1850 only one man, a Charles Pierce, remained on the force from the original members.[53] Each man was furnished a uniform consisting of blue cloth clothing, a black chimney-pot hat, a high stiff-neck collar, which was securely fastened by a buckle, a rattle for requesting aid (replaced in 1880 by a whistle), a baton labeled "police officer," a striped armlet to show that the officer was on duty, a number to distinguish the officers, and a letter to show the officer's division.

As divisions were created to cover a given area, the police agencies in that area were disbanded or absorbed by the Metropolitan Police. A major reorganization occurred in 1830. Seventeen divisions were created, each controlled by a superintendent and responsible for a population of approximately 80,000. Each division was divided into eight patrol sections which in turn were divided into eight beats. The entire force consisted of

3,314 men with the following ranks: 17 superintendents, 68 inspectors, 323 sergeants, and 2,906 constables—1 policeman for every 410 individuals.

Day and night rotating shifts were created. At any one time, two-thirds of the force was on night duty and one-third on day duty. The individual officer was on night duty for eight months of the year and on day duty for four months.

The primary duty of the "Peelers," as they were called, was crime prevention. In the words of Sir Robert Peel:

> To this great end every effort of the police is to be directed. The security of person and property, the preservation of public tranquility and all the other objects of a Police Establishment will thus be better effected than by detection and punishment of the offender after he has committed the crime.[54]

A detective division was not established until 1842. In 1878 Howard Vincent, a lawyer, was named director of the Criminal Investigation Division (CID). Initially, he had a force of 250 officers; later the force had 800.

The "Peelers" were very effective in preventing crime, but they also drove criminals to the outer fringes of England where crime prevention was not very effective. This caused the counties and burroughs to abandon their ancient police systems and organize them better, although still not very efficiently. The inefficiency was due to the fact that local governments wanted to retain local power. England was well covered by local police agencies by the end of the nineteenth century. Each area had local control, but help was available from Scotland Yard upon request.

The English people had a great dislike for authority and at first resisted Peel's proposed system. Their fears were due to the fact that this system was unknown and therefore scared them. Peel's officers were victims of much abuse and name-calling. Not until the new force gained the respect of the people did they receive such honorable nicknames as "Peelers" and "bobbies" (after their founder). The nickname of "bobby" is still retained today.

Peel's new force was accused of many evils, such as beating suspects and invading privacy. There were even rumors that the department was an advance force for the invasion of England by the Duke of Wellington. An example of the contempt of the people toward the police was that when a constable was stabbed to death while helping disperse a crowd at a political rally, a jury ruled the murder a justifiable homicide. The jury was escorted home and each member received a medal for the verdict. Most of the English people later learned to respect their police, and Sir Robert Peel eventually became an English hero.

England passed a law in 1856 that required all counties to develop a paid police force. This was another great step by England to provide its people with effective law enforcement.

The United States

Europeans coming to America settled on the Atlantic Coast. The great majority of the colonists were of English ancestry. Some came to America voluntarily; others had no choice, having been deported by royal proclamation. In either case they had observed in England the evils of a government with strong central authority and wished to have local control of government in this new country. Strong central government was looked upon with suspicion and contempt.

Colonists settled in two general areas—New England and the South. Southern colonists lived by agriculture and developed a rural life style. They established a county type of government in which, as in England, the sheriff was the chief law enforcement officer. In 1634 the first sheriff's office was established in America, in the state of Virginia. This sheriff had all the powers of the shire reeve in England. In New England, agriculture could not provide an adequate livelihood. The area became a center of industry and commerce and developed an urban life style. The office of constable was established in these urban areas. Due to the fear of central authority, both the sheriff and the constable were elected and served for short periods. The citizens believed that if a person stayed in office for an extended period of time he would amass too much authority. This principle backfired, however, because the person placed in charge of the police could not gain enough knowledge during his tenure to run the police department efficiently.

Local Police Agencies. Most cities with fairly large populations in early American history had some type of night watch.

The duty of persons on this watch was to patrol and, while patrolling, shake a rattle to discourage would-be thieves.

As in England, these watchmen were lazy and inept. Some men served on the watch for minor crimes they had committed; others slept during their watch to prepare themselves for their daytime jobs, thus getting extra money.

In certain cities, service on the night watch was the duty of all citizens on a rotation basis. Many people refused to serve, however, and it became evident that a police force was necessary and that it needed more power.

In 1800 New York established the first paid daytime police force. The day force controlled crime when the night force was not operating. Philadelphia in 1833 and Boston in 1838 established their own daytime police forces.

New York City was very impressed with Peel's London police—so impressed, in fact, that a delegation was sent to England in 1833 to examine the London force. The purpose of the delegation was to see whether this method of policing would work in New York City. After the visit, New York City reorganized its police department. It resembled the English system, but the form of control was different. In America the citizens maintained control of their police departments; in England the government exercised central control.

In 1844 New York City consolidated the day and night watches into one department, and in 1845 the first New York chief of police was appointed. Other large cities began to follow the lead—Chicago in 1851, New Orleans and Cincinnati in 1852, Baltimore and Newark in 1857, and Providence in 1864. The snowballing effect stimulated the modernization of American policing.

Most early police officers felt that wearing a badge was a sign of degradation and servitude. Any effort to make police officers wear a badge was met with stiff resistance. The first city to adopt a full uniform for police officers was New York. Each ward of the city, however, was allowed to choose the style of uniform for its own officers.

The era during which modern policing came of age in America was known as the "spoils era." Political corruption was at its peak, and police departments often became tools for corrupted officials. Enemies of the administration in power were fair game for the police. Also, positions as officers could be filled by supporters of the winning office-seeker. Discipline became almost impossible within the department.

To overcome these problems, it was suggested that people elect police officers, but this only increased the level of political intervention. Newly created police boards also failed to stop the political interference. The final straw was the assassination of President Garfield in 1881 by a person who believed he should have received a favored office for his work during the election. The American people were disgusted, and public clamor was responsible for the passage of the Pendleton Act in 1883. This act created civil service on the federal level. Cities and states followed suit and began using the same system. Slowly this act eliminated outright political manipulation of police departments. Although it did not wipe out interference altogether, it reduced the level so that departments could operate more effectively.

State Policing Agencies. In America's early history, there were some problems that local law enforcement officials could not overcome because of corrupt governmental officials, jurisdictional boundaries, or lax law enforcement. State police forces were needed to overcome these weaknesses. One by one the states instituted such departments, particularly after World War I. This was due to increased mobility of the public by motor vehicle and huge outlays by the national government for building new highways.

Today all states have some type of state police, although their duties vary. In some states, such as Michigan, the state police have general police powers. In others, such as California, they are highway patrols and only have authority pertaining to motor vehicle codes. State police may also maintain central identification, criminalistic, and investigative units that can be utilized by local jurisdictions that usually do not have the funds to support such units of their own.

The state police are not the only law enforcement personnel in the state government. Other agencies with authority in specific areas include liquor control boards and commissions, conservation agencies, departments of motor vehicles, state bureaus of narcotics, state fire marshals, and state gaming commissions. Some of these will be discussed in detail in Chapter 6.

Federal Policing Agencies. Most federal agencies have some type of regulatory powers, but most do not have any enforcement power as such. The two main federal government police units are the Justice Department and the Treasury Department. These will also be discussed in Chapter 6.

Conclusion

Law has always been with man, developing from unwritten tribal customs to our modern system that is based on both common and written law. Our system has been heavily influenced by that of England but has roots in all law and law making in history.

Law enforcement also has ancient roots, but it has its modern beginnings with Sir Robert Peel and his English police force. The United States has progressed since Peel's time to a complex system of integrated local, state, and federal law enforcement agencies.

CHAPTER **2**

The Crime Problem in America

The issue of law and order has assumed tremendous importance in America today, as crime and delinquency are widely recognized as among our most pressing problems. Not only has crime itself increased, but the fear of crime, especially in large cities, is significantly affecting many aspects of our life style. As the Commission on Law Enforcement and Administration of Justice observed in its 1967 report, "the existence of crime, the talk about crime, the reports of crime, and the fear of crime have eroded the basic quality of life for many Americans."[1] An obvious example of such erosion is the number of people who are afraid to venture out of doors after dark. A Gallup Poll in April 1972 reported that about 67 percent of the women sampled were afraid to leave their homes at night, compared with about 44 percent in 1968.[2]

It is not always easy to tell how much of the reported increase in crime represents actual facts and how much reflects improved reporting. Since national crime statistics were first published in the 1930s, the use of computers and the development of new techniques have led to a considerable increase in general statistical sophistication. In addition, the categories into which crimes are divided in the reports have been somewhat altered. Hence, it is of dubious value to compare old statistics with more recent ones. Furthermore, it has never been possible to measure the degree of organized crime with any substantial accuracy. The Uniform Crime Reports of the FBI show a rise in the crime rate over the past several years, and it seems likely that crime has indeed increased in prevalence and perhaps in seriousness. The extent to which this is true, however, must remain a matter of conjecture to some degree.

Although the public and law enforcement officials generally agree that crime is a growing problem, they do not agree about what should be done to counter it. Crime, particularly violent crime, which is what one usually thinks of first, is frightening, and people naturally tend to react to it with demands for violent repression, stricter laws, harsher penalties, and stronger prisons to protect "honest citizens" from the depredation of "criminal elements" in society. Yet repressive measures have not proven effective against crime in the past, and there seems no reason to suppose that they will be any more so today.

What Is Crime?

If crime is a problem and something is to be done about it, a definition of crime is necessary first. There are several ways of looking at crime and criminology. Some psychologists feel that crime is the outer expression of an inner conflict that a person cannot resolve; he therefore explodes in violence toward his fellow man. Another viewpoint is that of sociologists who feel that crime is a product of society and that a society produces areas that breed and feed crime. This could be expanded to a belief that an individual is not responsible for his acts, as he is only the product of his environment or society. These two views will be expanded and discussed in more detail later. For now, it suffices to say that neither is completely correct nor completely wrong.

Definitions

For a definition of crime, however, we must also look to the criminal justice system, which defines crime in the legal sense. Legally, crime is any act or omission to act in violation of law, without justification, with a penalty attached. This definition clashes in some respects with the generally accepted sociological definition of crime as any act that is harmful to society.

In comparing these two definitions, one can see that the legal definition would cover only crimes that have been written into law. Written laws include many that are outdated and outmoded, some of them passed in the heat of legislative passion. In other words, due to a great public outcry over some real or imagined evil, a law was put on the books to satisfy the public and alleviate the uproar. Even when the whole matter came to seem less important, the law remained on the books. The sociological definition is of course more flexible. As attitudes change, the nature of offenses would change, and an outdated set of prohibitions would not apply. The problem with the sociological approach is that there is no way to enforce laws of this type through a legal system, as a system of laws must be reasonably stable in order to provide the protective cover for all of society. If laws were to become fads and change with every whim, the entire system would collapse.

While some laws are outdated and should be repealed, social changes produce new situations and opportunities for new kinds of activities that could be considered crimes. Students of crime have suggested that some such activities should be defined as crimes when they are obviously harmful to society: engaging in shady business practices, taking advantage of the ignorant, and exploiting impoverished people. Defining such activities as crimes would bring the sociological and legal definitions of crime closer to each other. The law enforcement officer must know the written law, but he should also be aware of activities that are not illegal in themselves but that are socially harmful in that they can lead to illegal actions.

The legal definition of crime can be analyzed and examined in more detail. First, the entire definition is *any act or omission to act in violation of law, without justification, with a penalty attached.* The first phrase, "any act," means any actions taken by one person against another or by a person against property. For the sake of law, "any act" could also be considered to include what one person does to himself, such as using narcotics or alcohol. The second phrase, "or omission to act," means failure to perform an act that is required by law—for example, failing to file an income tax return or refusing to obey a police officer when told to act. The third phrase, "in violation of law," means that either the unlawful act or the unlawful omission must have been written into law—by a legislature, by a court ruling, or by executive order of the president of the United States. If a prohibition or requirement to act is not written, or codified, it is not law and therefore cannot be violated. The next phrase, "without justification," means that some otherwise unlawful acts can be committed that, because of a set of circumstances, are not crimes. One example is justifiable homicide, which is the taking of life for reasons of self-defense or defense of another; a second is being forced to commit a crime one would not normally commit. The final phrase, "with a penalty attached," is rather self-explanatory, as all written criminal laws have penalties attached, either specifically with each statute or as a blanket penalty that covers a whole act or group of statutes.

Classification of Crimes

The next step toward understanding crime and criminality is an explanation of the different levels of criminal statutes and their origins and a discussion of the different types of crimes. Crimes are divided into two major classifications—felonies and misdemeanors. Both have their origins in English common law. The felony was considered a crime that was *mala in se,* meaning the act in and of itself was clearly bad. This concept is carried through today in that a felony is more serious than a misdemeanor and generally carries a sentence of a year or more in a state or federal prison. Felonies today include such crimes against the person as murder, rape, robbery, and aggravated assault and such crimes against property as burglary, grand larceny, and arson.

The second classification is misdemeanors. Under the old common law system, these were considered crimes that were *mala prohibita,* or crimes not necessarily bad in and of themselves, but acts that were simply prohibited by statute. Today this concept is generally carried over in that misdemeanors are considered less serious than felonies and usually carry maximum penalties of a five-hundred-dollar fine and/or six months in jail. Misdemeanors are those crimes that are considered petty in nature—traffic violations, drunkenness, disorderly conduct, and the like.

A third classification that tends to bridge a gap between misdemeanors and felonies is the **high misdemeanor** or **circuit court misdemeanor,** a category recognized in some states, such as Michigan, yet unknown in others, such as California. This crime carries up to a year in jail or prison and covers such crimes as assault on a police officer and certain types of assaults and larcenies.

Types of Crimes

In addition to being classified by seriousness, crimes can also be classified by type—street crime, crime against the person, crime against property, white-collar crime, organized crime, and victimless crime. Although these classifications of crimes are listed separately, one crime could fall into one or more categories. A mugging, for example, could be considered a street crime or a crime against the person or both.

Street Crimes and Crimes Against the Person. Let us begin more detailed explanation of these categories with street crime. This is the crime most feared by the general public. It can take the form of either crimes against the person or crimes against property, although it generally refers to crimes against the person. Street crime is one of the most frequently reported, studied, and classified of crimes. It is usually the target of civic organizations and is highly deplored by all "law-abiding citizens." Generally, politicians running for election on "law and order" platforms refer to street crimes. What, then, is street crime? It is just what the name implies—those crimes that occur in the street. Street crimes of course include crimes in all other categories. The mugging previously mentioned is also a crime against the person; the stealing of a car is actually a crime against property but takes place in the street and could be classified as a street crime.

Street crimes often consist of murder, rape, assault, and robbery, which are also considered the four index crimes of violence according to the FBI's Uniform Crime Reports. Briefly, murder is the unlawful taking of the life of another and is further categorized according to premeditation, heat of passion, and negligence. Rape is sexual intercourse by use of force or threat of force. Assault is an attack on a person with intent to injure but not kill. Robbery is the taking of the property of another by force, either with a weapon (armed robbery), or by using physical force (strong-arm robbery).[3] Generally, the fear of street crime is fear of robbery in the form of mugging. The other three categories, however, are more serious in their consequences and cannot be overlooked by overemphasizing muggings.[4]

Crimes Against Property. Crimes against property are divided according to the FBI's Uniform Crime Reports of index crimes into three categories: burglary, larceny, and auto theft. These are generally considered crimes of stealth. They are usually the most difficult to solve due to their very nature—usually no one sees the perpetrator. Burglary is the breaking into the business or home of another with intent to commit a crime, usually larceny. Larceny is the taking of the property of another with intent to deprive the owner of his property. Auto theft is the unlawful taking of an automobile. However, it should be noted that the majority of cars stolen are not taken with intent to deprive the owner of its use permanently, but rather for the purpose of obtaining transportation. This lack of intent reduces the crime of auto larceny to a misdemeanor of joy riding.

The fact that these three categories—street crime, crime against persons, and crime against property—do not have clear divisions and do in fact overlap makes them difficult to tabulate and record as separate groups. As will be seen later, improperly classified crimes can put the whole picture out of focus and cause too much emphasis in one area and too little in another where emphasis is more needed.

Of the three categories, street crimes arouse the most fear in the public and bring forth the greatest emotional response. The public calls for drastic action to suppress this type of crime without taking into consideration its true nature and causes, when in fact only by understanding the causes can an effective fight be launched to eliminate them and thereby reduce crime. In addition, the heavy emphasis on these crimes diverts attention from other areas—such as white-collar crime and organized crime—that go on silently undermining the effectiveness of law enforcement.

White-Collar Crime. When the word *crime* is mentioned, most people think of a junkie mugging someone on the street. They seldom think of the business executive who leaves for work every morning or the clerk who works regularly day after day, year after year. Yet crime is not restricted to the "depraved degenerate"; the business executive or the clerk may steal an amount that makes the street criminal look like a piker. What, then, is white-collar crime? Edwin H. Sutherland defines it as "that committed by a person of respectability and high social status in the course of his occupation."[5] In general, he holds, white-collar crimes consist of violation of delegated or implied trust, and most of them fall into two categories: (1) misrepresentation of asset values and (2) duplicity in the manipulation of power, better known as fraud. Under this definition white-collar criminals would include the businessman who misuses inside knowledge of the market to sell large blocks of stock at a tremendous profit, the accountant who juggles the books to conceal several thousand dollars of company money he has pocketed, the store that raises the list price of a twenty-dollar dress to forty dollars in order to offer it as a "sale" item at twenty-eight dollars, or the firm that makes false statements about its profits in order to avoid paying taxes or to attract investors. These are but a few examples. It has been conservatively estimated that white-collar crime causes at least three times the loss of the index crimes of robbery, burglary, larceny, and auto theft combined.

The white-collar criminal is the most difficult criminal to detect and apprehend. There is a fine line between shrewd business practice and white-collar crime. And when crime is detected, the violators are generally excluded from criminal prosecution, as they are processed through state and federal regulatory agencies. The white-collar criminal is thus protected from going through the process of the criminal courts with the resulting humiliation and criminal label. He is allowed to keep on functioning in a society where he has committed crimes.

The average American has only recently been exposed to white-collar crime. Recent intense studies of crime and criminality have revealed that although most people fear street crimes, white-collar crime actually does more harm and affects almost everyone from slum dweller to suburbanite. Many Americans have been made aware of this through the media, which until recently did not want to dig too deeply to expose this type of criminal lest they ruin his "good name." Increased public awareness should stimulate demands to enforce the laws and regulations that are designed to control and deter white-collar criminality. Moving some statutes from the realm of regulation to the realm of criminal law would deter many present white-collar criminals. Nothing can or will be done, however, until the public is made fully aware of the extent and damage of white-collar crime. For white-collar crime, like organized crime, is extremely difficult to detect, and, once detected, difficult to prosecute. This brings us to the next type or classification of crime: organized crime.

Organized Crime. Generally, people have a stereotyped view of organized crime as a tightly knit group of gangsters with secret codes who drive big black luxury cars and go to meetings guarded by men with machineguns and heavy Italian accents. The crimes are assumed to be confined to importing and selling heroin to slum dwellers and organizing rings of prostitution and gambling, also in the slums. In actuality, however, organized crime is a business operation that has only one goal—to make as much money as possible with the least amount of risk. Organized crime includes any type of illegal activity from labor racketeering to importing and distributing heroin. Organized criminal groups are, in fact, composed of many different people from all walks of life who share the common goal of obtaining money regardless of the law or damage to other people.

Only recently have studies shown that where organized crime exists, it corrupts. Police, courts, and elected officials must be bribed in order for this type of crime to flourish. Organized crime is not perpetrated by a tightly knit group from coast to coast as was believed for many years. Although organizations from city to city do cooperate when necessary, they are usually more or less autonomous.

Only when a complacent public does not bother to keep an eye on officials, when people demand and pay for illegal services, and when people resign themselves to saying that the problem is too big to do anything about, will organized crime exist.

Victimless Crime. The final area to be considered is victimless crime,[6] which consists of illegal actions that in most cases do not involve a complainant. Victimless crimes include gambling, homosexuality, intoxication, drug abuse, and prostitution, to mention only a few. These crimes are in reality offenses against the norms or morals of society, and criminologists and law enforcement officials have been questioning whether or not these acts should be criminal. Because victimless crimes are so difficult to control, arguments concerning them range from legalizing these activities under government regulation to increasing penalties for engaging in them. In a few arguments it is noted that enforcing these laws takes up a good deal of time by law enforcement personnel that could be better spent in fighting more serious forms of crime.

Of the total arrests in the United States, it is estimated that two-thirds are victimless crimes—drunkenness in particular. The expense of processing this number of cases should in itself be incentive enough to develop alternative methods for handling intoxication offenses, for drunkenness is considered by many to be a social problem rather than a law enforcement problem. If drunkenness were decriminalized, law enforcement officials would be free to devote more time to areas where they are more needed.

Crime Data

Besides defining and categorizing crime, it is important to tabulate and record crime and specific crime trends.[7] Although one must remember that statistics can give only a general idea at best and can completely distort at worst, they are still necessary to attempt to record what is happening in the area of crime. Through the use of statistics, high-crime areas can be identified and trends in crime can be analyzed. These figures are necessary in order to carry out an effective program to combat crime.

Uniform Crime Reports

Various agencies and schools of thought have their own methods of recording and tabulating crime and crime trends. However, the most generally recognized for its thoroughness and completeness is the annual Uniform Crime Report, or UCR, collected and tabulated by the FBI. The UCR is a comprehensive report of the total reported crime picture in the United States. It is released once a year in total and in quarterly editions, and it can give a good idea of trends based on crimes reported to police.

The UCR is the result of a generally recognized need for a national and uniform method of tabulating law enforcement statistics. A national program was started in 1930 by the Committee on Uniform Crime Records of the International Association of Chiefs of Police (IACP). At the same time, the FBI was established as the national clearinghouse for this information.

The first step was to establish definite crime classifications that would apply throughout the country. Crime was divided into two parts. Serious crimes with the greatest likelihood of occurring and being reported to police were listed as Part I crimes. Less serious and less likely reported crimes were listed as Part II crimes (see Table 1). The next step was to decide where these statistics would be collected and which would be used. The FBI decided that they would be based on all offenses reported to police, with consideration given to clearance rates, convictions, and disposition of offenders.

Statistics were compiled by local agencies and forwarded to the FBI on a strictly voluntary basis. The program to date includes areas in which about 93 percent of the total population of the United States resides. Recently, the FBI has advised states on how to set up their own crime reporting system to coincide with the FBI and forward these to the FBI, thereby eliminating the need for all local agencies to report directly to them. States could force compliance from local jurisdictions, which would make the report even more comprehensive.

Uniform Classification of Offenses

Part I

1. Criminal homicide
   (a) Murder and nonnegligent manslaughter
   (b) Manslaughter by negligence
2. Forcible rape
3. Robbery
4. Aggravated assault
5. Burglary—breaking and entering
6. Larceny—theft (except auto theft)
7. Auto theft

Part II

8. Other assaults
9. Arson
10. Forgery and counterfeiting
11. Fraud
12. Embezzlement
13. Buying, receiving, possessing stolen property
14. Vandalism
15. Carrying, possessing weapons
16. Prostitution and commercialized vice
17. Sex offenses (except forcible rape and prostitution)
18. Violating narcotic drug laws
19. Gambling
20. Offenses against the family and children
21. Driving under the influence of alcohol or narcotics
22. Violating liquor laws
23. Drunkenness
24. Disorderly conduct
25. Vagrancy
26. All other offenses
27. Suspicion
28. Violating curfew and loitering laws (juvenile)
29. Running away (juvenile)

U. S. Department of Justice, Federal Bureau of Investigation, Director Clarence M. Kelley. *Crime in the United States* (annual). U. S. Government Printing Office, 1976, pp. 6–7.

Fourteen states now operate their own Uniform Crime Reporting Programs: California, Kentucky, Rhode Island, Illinois, Pennsylvania, Michigan, Minnesota, New Jersey, Nebraska, Florida, Wisconsin, West Virginia, North Carolina, and Delaware.

The original Committee on Uniform Crime Records, IACP, continues to act as an advisory panel to the FBI and plays an active and effective part in quality control through surveys of police records and crime reporting systems. In June 1966 the National Sheriffs' Association, NSA, established a Committee on Uniform Crime Reporting Programs, which actively encourages sheriffs throughout the country to participate in this program and acts in the same advisory capacity as the IACP.

The main purpose of the UCR is to tabulate a reliable set of crime statistics on a national basis for use by local agencies in assessing their crime problem and analyzing crime trends. This information is also available to other professionals and scholars with an interest in crime, and the report is important to the general public as an indicator of the extent of crime in society. To accomplish its objectives, UCR attempts to do the following: (1) measure the extent, fluctuation, and distribution of crime in the United States and present this through Part I crime, (2) measure the total volume of serious crime known to police, and (3) show activity and effectiveness of law enforcement through arrest counts and clearance rates.

The UCR attempts to bring the entire area of crime into focus for use by local agencies. However, it is clear that a city with a population of 25,000 cannot be compared with a metropolitan area consisting of millions, and so a method of comparing the two was developed by use of the crime index. Simply put, this index is based on the number of Part I offenses per 100,000 population. Thus a city with a crime index of 600 would have had 600 reported index crimes per 100,000 citizens. It could be a city of one million with 6,000 such crimes or a city of 50,000 with 300. To put it another way, a city with a population of one million and a count of 47 index crimes might seem to have more crime than a city of 50,000 with 6 index crimes, but in terms of the rate per 100,000, the larger city has a crime index of 4.7 while the smaller city has an index of 12.0. This example also shows how easy it is to misinterpret statistics and why they must be viewed skeptically.

Yet the advantages of crime statistics outweigh the disadvantages. It has been recognized for over forty years that some method of tabulating crime is necessary to aid law enforcement officials in combating it. Because it draws on a wide base, the UCR can be considered largely valid. Because UCR reports the crime rate, local areas can compare themselves with other areas, both larger and smaller, and recognize the degree of severity of their problem and attempt to rectify it.

To be able to use UCR to its fullest advantage, one must remember that disadvantages are inherent in any form of statistics.

One of the major disadvantages of UCR is that it is limited to those offenses actually reported to police. Thus, it can be safely assumed that all figures stated are in reality too low.[8] Crime statistics are often used to evaluate the effectiveness of a local law enforcement agency. If reported crime drops, it is assumed that the local agency is more effective. Conversely, if the crime rate climbs, local agencies are considered less effective when in fact just the opposite may be true. If a local agency is very good, the community will have more faith in a department to solve crimes and therefore will more readily report offenses. By the same token, when a community has an ineffective agency, citizens will feel that it is useless to report crime. The figures will therefore decrease and, in effect, make the poor agency look efficient.

Another disadvantage is that the UCR program is voluntary and does not cover almost 7 percent of the population. Local agencies, in order to create a favorable impression, can adjust the classification of certain crimes to fit categories of lesser crimes. By establishing state mandatory reporting systems and standardized categories, this disadvantage can be controlled.

Another major disadvantage is that the UCR is related to population and does not take into account social pressures caused by population density, racial makeup of an individual population, economic status, behavioral standards, and stability of a population, climate, or many other effects of social interaction that can lead to higher or lower crime rates.

However, as long as all these disadvantages are kept in mind and these statistics are not twisted to suit personal motives, the yearly Uniform Crime Report can be said to be the most complete and reliable set of crime statistics available today. From the UCR we can objectively look at the crime picture with an eye toward changing and updating law enforcement to combat crime more effectively.

Table 1.

Crime Rate by Region, 1975

[Rate per 100,000 inhabitants]

Crime index offenses	North-eastern States	North Central States	Southern States	Western States
Total	4,931.9	5,081.3	4,847.8	6,823.7
Violent	535.4	416.8	460.8	547.1
Property	4,396.4	4,664.6	4,387.0	6,276.6
Murder	7.6	8.1	12.7	9.0
Forcible rape	21.0	24.1	25.8	37.6
Robbery	300.4	207.3	168.6	216.5
Aggravated assault	206.4	177.2	253.8	284.0
Burglary	1,448.0	1,322.2	1,475.1	2,029.4
Larceny-theft	2,295.7	2,911.0	2,582.2	3,708.2
Motor vehicle theft	652.8	431.4	329.8	539.1

U.S., *Crime in the United States* 1976, p. 11.

Table 2.

National Crime, Rate, and Percent Change

Crime index offenses	Estimated crime 1975		Percent change over 1974		Percent change over 1970		Percent change over 1960	
	Number	Rate per 100,000 inhabitants	Number	Rate	Number	Rate	Number	Rate
Total	11,256,600	5,281.7	+9.8	+8.9	+39.0	+32.6	+232.6	+179.9
Violent	1,026,280	481.5	+5.3	+4.4	+38.9	+32.5	+255.8	+199.3
Property	10,230,300	4,800.2	+10.3	+9.4	+39.0	+32.6	+230.5	+178.1
Murder	20,510	9.6	−1.0	−2.0	+28.2	+21.5	+125.1	+88.2
Forcible rape	56,090	26.3	+1.3	+.4	+47.6	+40.6	+226.3	+174.0
Robbery	464,970	218.2	+5.1	+4.3	+32.9	+26.8	+331.2	+263.1
Aggravated assault	484,710	227.4	+6.2	+5.4	+44.7	+38.0	+214.1	+164.1
Burglary	3,252,100	1,525.9	+7.0	+6.1	+47.5	+40.6	+256.6	+200.0
Larceny-theft	5,977,700	2,804.8	+13.6	+12.7	+41.5	+34.9	+222.2	+171.1
Motor vehicle theft	1,000,500	469.4	+2.4	+1.6	+7.8	+2.8	+204.8	+156.5

Crime Rate by Area, 1975

[Rate per 100,000 inhabitants]

Crime index offenses	Total U. S.	Metropolitan areas	Rural	Other cities
Total	5,281.7	6,110.5	1,997.2	4,437.2
Violent	481.5	580.8	167.3	269.1
Property	4,800.2	5,529.7	1,829.9	4,168.1
Murder	9.6	10.6	8.1	5.5
Forcible rape	26.3	31.3	12.0	13.5
Robbery	218.2	284.0	23.5	57.8
Aggravated assault	227.4	254.9	123.7	192.2
Burglary	1,525.9	1,747.9	785.9	1,103.3
Larceny-theft	2,804.8	3,195.6	941.6	2,849.2
Motor vehicle theft	469.4	586.2	102.4	215.5

U.S., *Crime in the United States* 1976, p. 11.

Table 3.
Index of Crime, United States, 1960–1975

Population[1]	Total Crime Index	Violent[2] crime	Property[2] crime	Murder and non-negligent man-slaughter	Forcible rape	Robbery	Aggra-vated assault	Burglary	Larceny-theft	Motor vehicle theft
Number of offenses:										
1960–179,323,175	3,384,200	288,460	3,095,700	9,110	17,190	107,840	154,320	912,100	1,855,400	328,200
1961–182,992,000	3,488,000	289,390	3,198,600	8,740	17,220	106,670	156,760	949,600	1,913,000	336,000
1962–185,771,000	3,752,200	301,510	3,450,700	8,530	17,550	110,800	164,570	994,300	2,089,600	366,800
1963–188,483,000	4,109,500	316,970	3,792,500	8,640	17,650	116,470	174,210	1,086,400	2,297,800	408,300
1964–191,141,000	4,564,600	364,220	4,200,400	9,360	21,420	130,390	203,050	1,213,200	2,514,400	472,800
1965–193,526,000	4,739,400	387,390	4,352,000	9,960	23,410	138,690	215,330	1,282,500	2,572,600	496,900
1966–195,576,000	5,223,500	430,180	4,793,300	11,040	25,820	157,990	235,330	1,410,100	2,822,000	561,200
1967–197,457,000	5,903,400	499,930	5,403,500	12,240	27,620	202,910	257,160	1,632,100	3,111,600	659,800
1968–199,399,000	6,720,200	595,010	6,125,200	13,800	31,670	262,840	286,700	1,858,900	3,482,700	783,600
1969–201,385,000	7,410,900	661,870	6,749,000	14,760	37,170	298,850	311,090	1,981,900	3,888,600	878,500
1970–203,235,298	8,098,000	738,820	7,359,200	16,000	37,990	349,860	334,970	2,205,000	4,225,800	928,400
1971–206,212,000	8,588,200	816,500	7,771,700	17,780	42,260	387,700	368,760	2,399,300	4,424,200	948,200
1972–208,230,000	8,248,800	834,900	7,413,900	18,670	46,850	376,290	393,090	2,375,500	4,151,200	887,200
1973–209,851,000	8,718,100	875,910	7,842,200	19,640	51,400	384,220	420,650	2,565,500	4,347,900	928,800
1974–211,392,000	10,253,400	974,720	9,278,700	20,710	55,400	442,400	456,210	3,039,200	5,262,500	977,100
1975–213,124,000	11,256,600	1,026,280	10,230,300	20,510	56,090	464,970	484,710	3,252,100	5,977,700	1,000,500
Percent change 1960–1975[3]	+232.6	+255.8	+230.5	+125.1	+226.3	+331.2	+214.1	+256.6	+222.2	+204.8

Table 3.
Index of Crime, United States, 1960–1975

Population[1]	Total Crime Index	Violent[2] crime	Property[2] crime	Murder and non-negligent man-slaughter	Forcible rape	Robbery	Aggra-vated assault	Burglary	Larceny-theft	Motor vehicle theft
Rate per 100,000 inhabitants:										
1960	1,887.2	160.9	1,726.3	5.1	9.6	60.1	86.1	508.6	1,034.7	183.0
1961	1,906.1	158.1	1,747.9	4.8	9.4	58.3	85.7	518.9	1,045.4	183.6
1962	2,019.8	162.3	1,857.5	4.6	9.4	59.7	88.6	585.2	1,124.8	197.4
1963	2,180.3	168.2	2,012.1	4.6	9.4	61.8	92.4	576.4	1,219.1	216.6
1964	2,388.1	190.6	2,197.5	4.9	11.2	68.2	106.2	634.7	1,315.5	247.4
1965	2,449.0	200.2	2,248.8	5.1	12.1	71.7	111.3	662.7	1,329.3	256.8
1966	2,670.8	220.0	2,450.9	5.6	13.2	80.8	120.3	721.0	1,442.9	286.9
1967	2,989.7	253.2	2,736.5	6.2	14.0	102.8	130.2	826.6	1,575.8	334.1
1968	3,370.2	298.4	3,071.8	6.9	15.9	131.8	143.8	932.3	1,746.6	393.0
1969	3,680.0	328.7	3,351.3	7.3	18.5	148.4	154.5	984.1	1,930.9	436.2
1970	3,984.5	363.5	3,621.0	7.9	18.7	172.1	164.8	1,084.9	2,079.3	456.8
1971	4,164.7	396.0	3,768.8	8.6	20.5	188.0	178.8	1,163.5	2,145.5	459.8
1972	3,961.4	401.0	3,560.4	9.0	22.5	180.7	188.8	1,140.8	1,993.6	426.1
1973	4,154.4	417.4	3,737.0	9.4	24.5	183.1	200.5	1,222.5	2,071.9	442.6
1974	4,850.4	461.1	4,389.3	9.8	26.2	209.3	215.8	1,437.7	2,489.5	462.2
1975	5,281.7	481.5	4,800.2	9.6	26.3	218.2	227.4	1,525.9	2,804.8	469.4
Percent change 1960–1975[3]	+179.9	+199.3	+178.1	+88.2	+174.0	+263.1	+164.1	+200.0	+171.1	+156.5

[1] Population is Bureau of Census provisional estimates as of July 1, except April 1, 1960 and 1970, census.
[2] Violent crime is offenses of murder, forcible rape, robbery, and aggravated assault. Property crime is offenses of burglary, larceny-theft, and motor vehicle theft.
[3] Percent change and crime rates calculated prior to rounding number of offenses. Revised estimates and rates based on changes in reporting practices.

U.S., *Crime in the United States* 1975, p. 49.

Table 4.

Economic Impact of Crimes and Related Expenditures
(Estimated in Millions of Dollars)

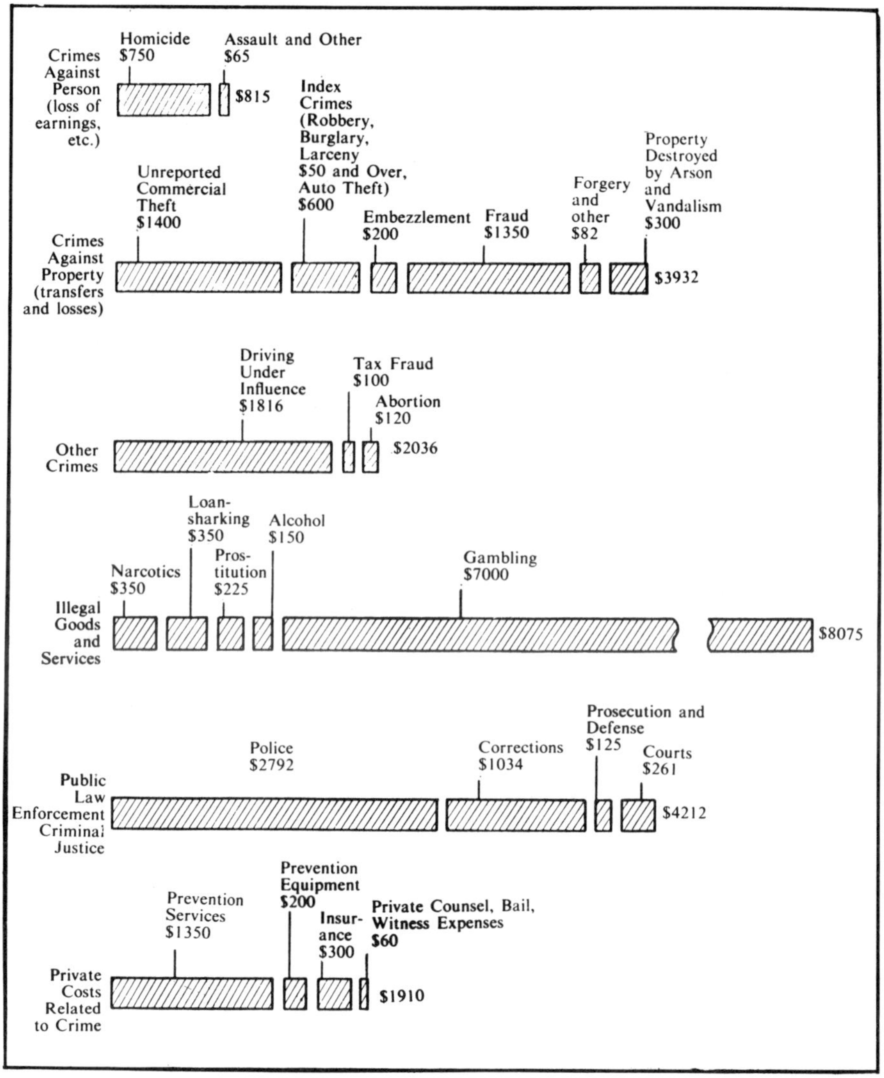

President's Commission on Law Enforcement and Criminal Justice, *The Challenge of Crime in a Free Society*. Washington, D.C.: U.S. Government Printing Office, 1967, p. 33.

Table 5.

Crime and Population

1970–1975

PERCENT CHANGE OVER 1970

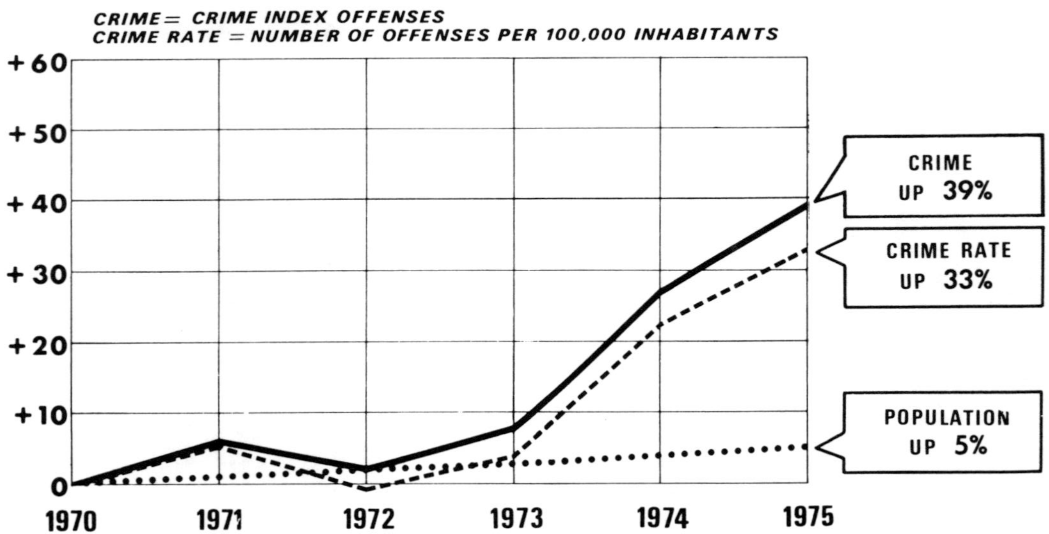

U.S., *Crime in the United States* 1975, p. 12.

Table 6.

Crimes of Violence

1970–1975

PERCENT CHANGE OVER 1970

LIMITED TO MURDER, FORCIBLE RAPE, ROBBERY AND AGGRAVATED ASSAULT

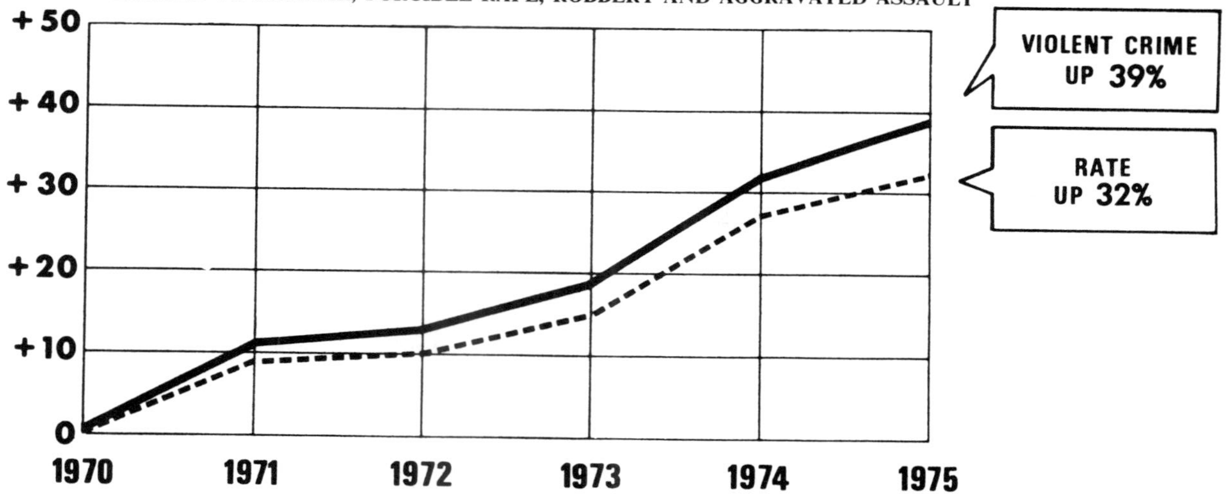

U.S., *Crime in the United States* 1975, p. 13.

Table 7.
Crimes Against Property
1970–1975

PERCENT CHANGE OVER 1970

LIMITED TO BURGLARY, LARCENY–THEFT AND MOTOR VEHICLE THEFT

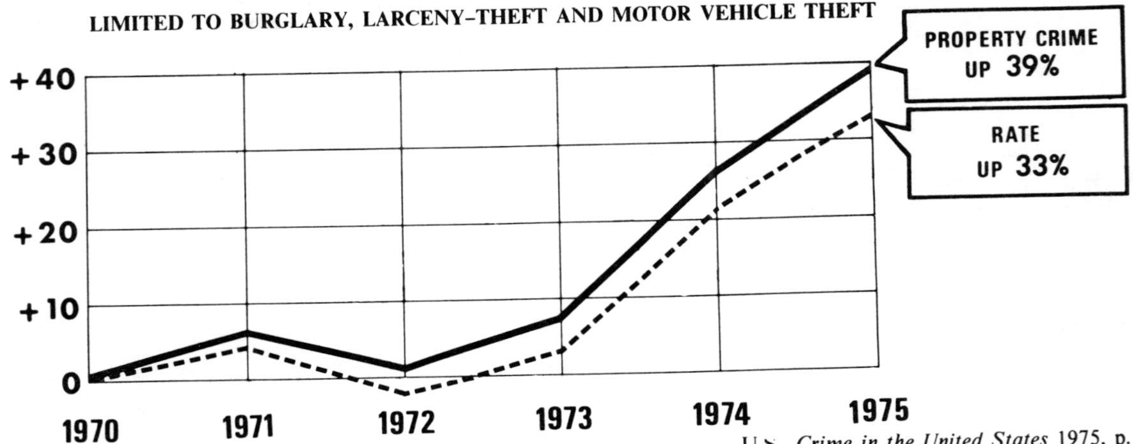

U.S., *Crime in the United States* 1975, p. 14.

Table 8.
Murder

1970–1975

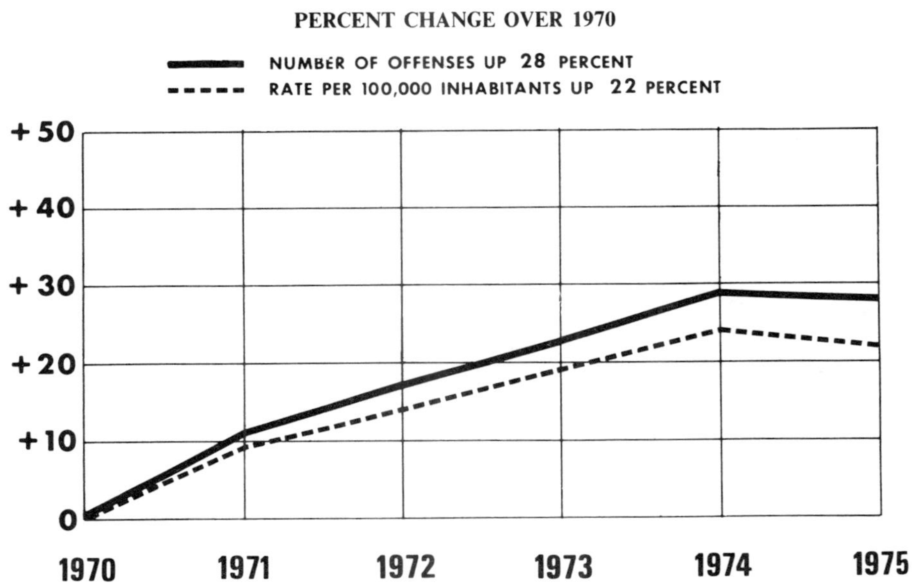

U.S., *Crime in the United States* 1975, p. 16.

Table 9.
Forcible Rape
1970–1975

PERCENT CHANGE OVER 1970

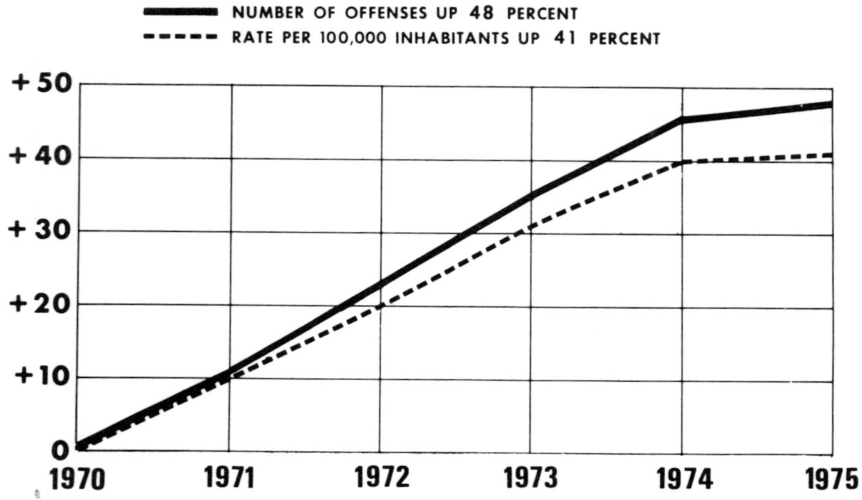

U.S., *Crime in the United States* 1975, p. 23.

Table 10.
Robbery

1970–1975

PERCENT CHANGE OVER 1970

NUMBER OF OFFENSES UP 33 PERCENT
RATE PER 100,000 INHABITANTS UP 27 PERCENT

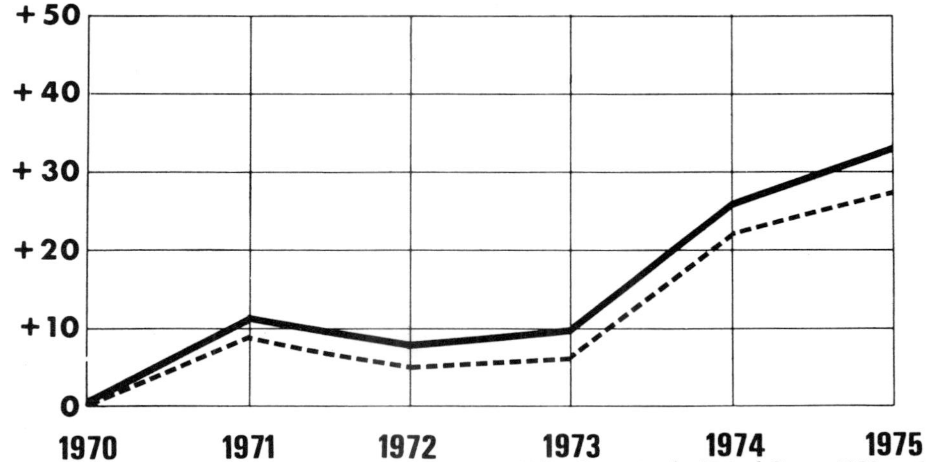

U.S., *Crime in the United States* 1975, p. 25.

Table 11.
Aggravated Assault
1970–1975

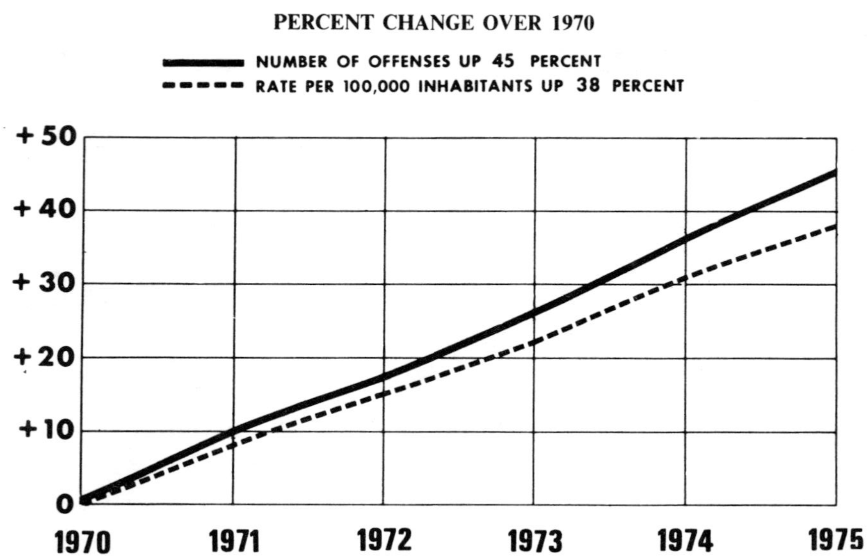

U.S., *Crime in the United States* 1975, p. 21.

Table 12.
Burglary

1970–1975

PERCENT CHANGE OVER 1970

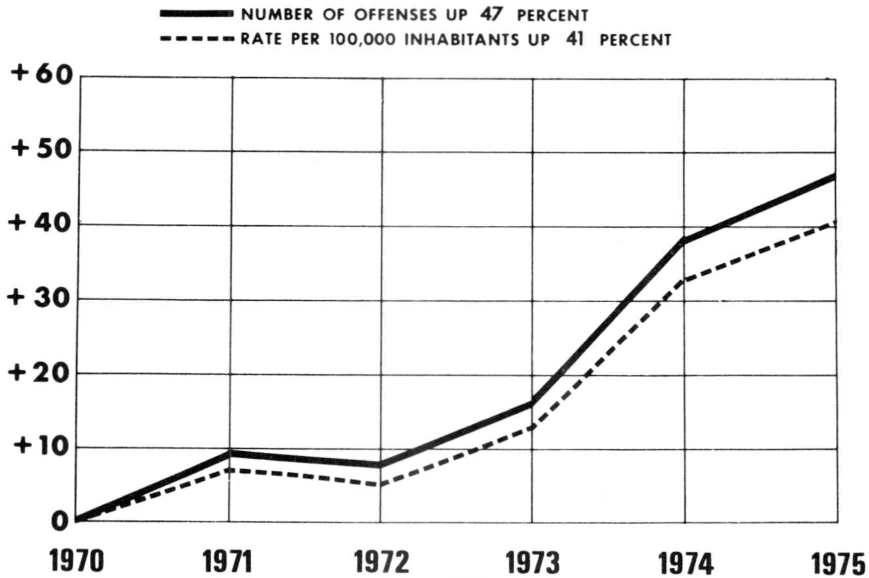

U.S., *Crime in the United States* 1975, p. 29.

Table 13.

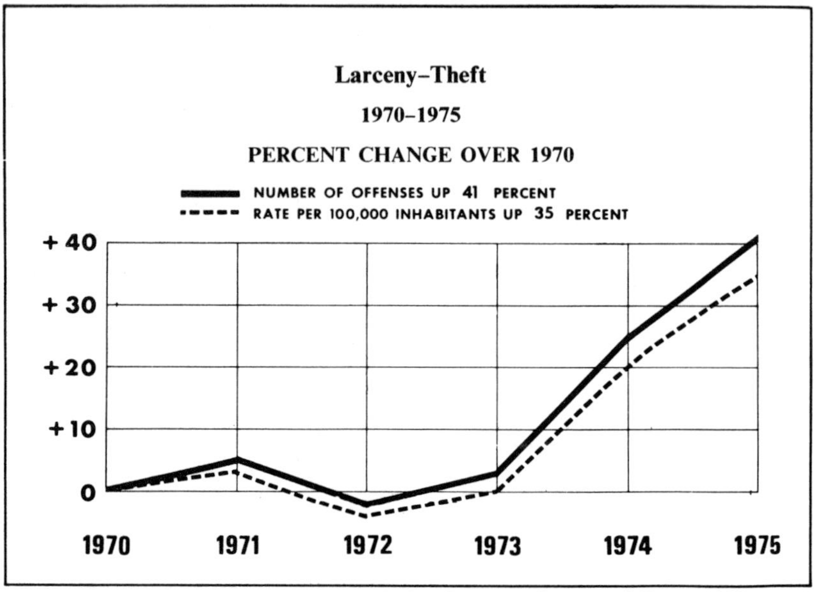

U.S., *Crime in the United States* 1975, p. 36.

Table 14.

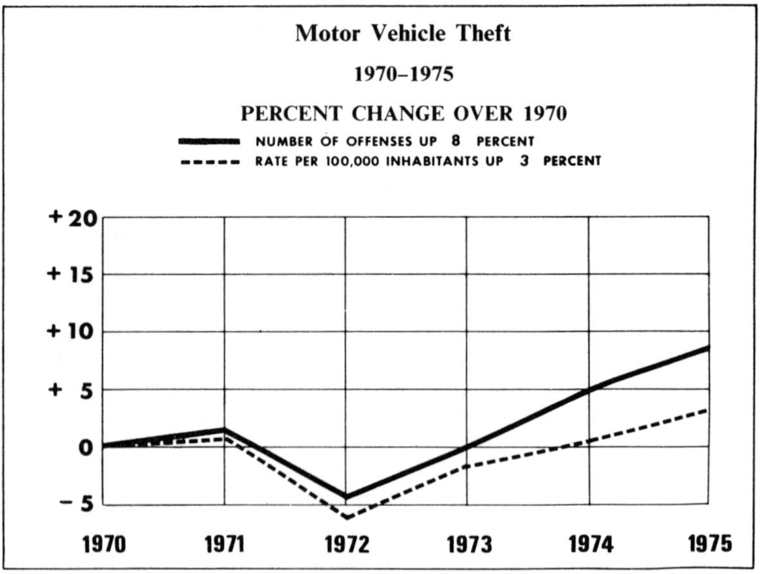

U.S., *Crime in the United States* 1975, p. 32.

Table 15.

Crimes Cleared by Arrest

1975

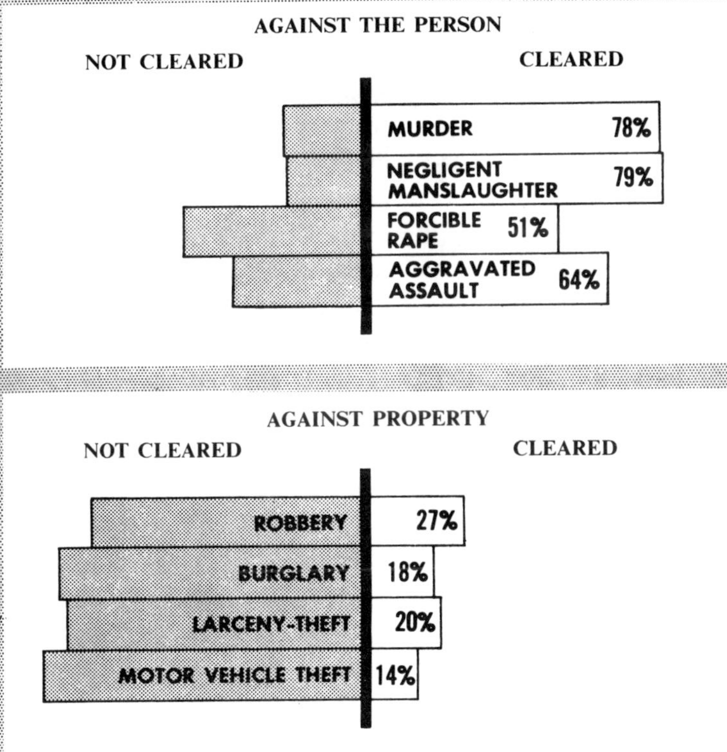

U.S., *Crime in the United States* 1975, p. 400.

Crime Figures

Table 2 illustrates the number of total index crimes in the United States during 1975. The same figures are shown broken down into violent and property crimes, and finally they are listed according to each of the seven index crimes. The table also provides the same information according to area: metropolitan, city, and rural. The crime index is, as expected, higher in metropolitan areas (6110.5), lower in other city areas (4437.2), and lowest in rural areas (1997.2).

Table 3 gives information similar to that in Table 2 but is particularly helpful in showing the changes in the crime picture between 1960 and 1975. The crime statistics in Table 3 are again divided into the two categories of violent crime and property crime. Violent crimes increased in number from 288,460 in 1960 to 1,026,280 in 1975 and in index rate from 160.9 to 481.5. Property crimes increased in number from approximately 3 million in 1960 to over 10 million in 1975 or an index rate increase from 1726.3 to 4800.2.

Table 4 shows an estimate of the economic impact of crime in terms of expenditures and losses. When the totals are added, the estimate of the loss due to criminal activity is $14.8 billion annually. Added to the cost of prevention and apprehension, estimated at $6.1 billion, the total estimate of crime cost is over $20 billion annually.

It is tempting to assume that the crime increase is simply due to an increase in population. However, as shown in Table 5, while the population increased 5 percent between 1970 and 1975, crime increased 39 percent—a crime index increase of 33 percent. It is obvious, therefore, that crime is increasing at a much higher rate than can be justified by the population increase.

Needless to say, this huge cost is passed on to every American through increases in insurance premiums to cover a great deal of this loss, and through taxes that support the criminal justice system, which attempts to keep the loss to a minimum. This total economic loss does not take into consideration the pain and suffering involved in violent crimes nor the mental anguish caused by losses of property nor the fear involved on the part of those who cannot walk the street in safety. And even though this is a general estimate, it still shows that crime is costly and affects everyone.

Tables 6 and 7 show the percentage changes in crimes of violence and crimes against property between 1970 and 1975. From Table 6 one can see that the total number of violent crimes reported was up 39 percent with a crime index increase (allowing for population trends) of 32 percent. This big jump in crime occurred during a period when population increased only 5 percent.

Likewise, crimes against property increased in total reported and rate (see Table 7). However, as this chart shows, there was a decrease in 1971-72. It must be remembered that this decrease could amount to nothing more than the decrease in crimes reported to police and could, in fact, be hiding a greater increase. Only time will tell whether this is a lasting trend in the overall crime picture.

Murder. In reviewing the index crimes individually, several observations can be made. Murder increased 28 percent from 1970 to 1975 with the murder rate (allowing for population) increasing 22 percent.

Forcible rape. The number of reported rape offenses in 1975 increased 48 percent over 1970, (see Table 9). The rate increased 41 percent.

Robbery. The third category of violent crime is robbery. The 1975 figure for robbery shows an increase of 33 percent over 1970, or a rate increase of 27 percent (see Table 10).

Aggravated Assault. The final area of violent crime is aggravated assault (Table 11). The total picture shows an increase of 45 percentage points over 1970 or a 38 percent rate increase.

Crimes against property can be categorized and analyzed just as violent crime is.

Burglary. In comparing the crime of burglary in 1975 to 1970, we see an increase of 47 percent and a 41 percent rate increase (see Table 12).

Larceny. Larceny, the second category of crimes against property, previously included only losses of fifty dollars or more but now disregards monetary value. Between 1970 and 1971 there was an overall increase of 41 percent, and a 35 percent rate increase (see Table 13).

Auto theft. The final area of major crime to be analyzed in this manner is motor vehicle theft. Comparing figures of 1970 to 1975 shows an overall increase of 8 percent and a rate increase of only 3 percent (see Table 14).

Although the UCR lists many types of crimes, these seven are considered the most serious, the most frequent, and the most likely to be reported. The FBI and others believe that these index crimes give some idea of the scope of the crime problem in this country. There are those who feel that on the average, the crime rate has not increased considerably over the years, that only the methods of reporting have improved. Whatever theory is advanced, its proponents still recognize that crime in America is a major problem. At least by tabulating reported crime, we can develop some idea of the size of the problem.

Arrest and Clearance Rates

The FBI not only tabulates crime by many and varied categories with several divisions and subdivisions to show crime by type, population area, geographic location, and age and type of victim; it also gives statistics on arrest and clearance rates. These figures show how the field of law enforcement is reacting to the climbing crime rates. These statistics are broken down into areas and types of offenders by age, sex, and race and are contained in the annual issues of the Uniform Crime Reports.

As can be seen from Table 15, there is a distinctly higher clearance rate for violent crimes than for crimes against property. This is because in most violent crimes, the perpetrator is known to or at least seen by the victim or by witnesses, while crimes against property are primarily characterized by stealth.

Causes of Crime

The history of criminological thought over the last two centuries is commonly divided into three schools. The classical school is associated with Cesare Bonesana, (Marchese) de Beccaria (1735–1794), an Italian nobleman and mathematician. The *Neoclassical* school modified classical theory in light of the practical experience of applying it to the administration of criminal law. The *positive* school is associated with Cesare Lombroso (1836–1909), an Italian professor of legal medicine with a strong interest in criminological anthropology.[9]

Early Schools of Thought

Beccaria felt the law was cruel, arbitrary, and corrupt. He originated his theory in an attempt to demonstrate systematically the faults in the laws and at the same time to suggest ways to determine crime. He wanted the power of judges to be limited and the penalties imposed to be based on the amount of harm caused to society by an offender. His theory included the concept that the individual and the state have a social contract in which the individual gives up some rights in exchange for protection and security from the state.

Thinkers in the neoclassical school modified the classical theory as they recognized that extenuating circumstances exist when many crimes are committed. For example, neoclassical theorists introduced the concept of limited responsibility for the commission of crimes by children and mentally ill persons.

In the late nineteenth century the positive school rose largely through the work of Lombroso, Enrico Ferri (1856–1928), and Raffaele Garofalo (1852–1934). Lombroso urged the study and treatment of the offender as an individual, rather than focusing attention on the abstract crime in the classical manner. He generally supported reformatory treatment of all prisoners except "born criminals." He accepted Beccaria's emphasis on deterrence, replacing it with a more general theory that society must be protected through punishment of offenders.[10] Lombroso considered the born criminal to be a person who has evolved only to a low level of development.

Ferri believed that crime resulted from geographical, anthropological, psychological, and economic forces. He developed a positivistic school of "social defense." His theory had three fundamental concepts. First, he wanted offenders incarcerated under indefinite sentences, the length of which would be determined by the subject's power to do harm and the possibility of his readapting to society. Second, he wanted the victims of crimes to be paid for their losses and suffering by the state. Third, the means of social defense would vary depending on the type of crime. Ferri believed in a system of legal and social responsibility. Anyone would be subject to the consequences of his acts if he violated the law.

A number of theorists believed that criminality was related to physical or genetic characteristics. They believed that persons engaged in crime were organically inferior or that the tendency to commit crime was inherited. No consideration was given to the environmental factors that shape a person's personality. Some believed that the shape of parts of a person's body had something to do with crime. Some characteristics associated with criminals were a low, sloping forehead, thin lips, thin beard and body hair, and thick red hair. These physical and biological theories do not appear to have factual bases and are not presently used to explain the causes of crime.

The psychoanalytic theory of human behavior was originated by Sigmund Freud. He believed that all human behavior is caused by subconscious, inner feelings. He coined some terms for what he believed to be the various parts of a person's psychological makeup:

> Largely unconscious in operation, the *id* is the source of basic biological drives present at birth. The *ego* is the conscious personality that represents the growth of attitudes, habits and ideas through contact with the material and social world. Arising out of relations of the *id* and the *ego*, the *superego* reflects the mores of the groups shaping the individual's social experience.[11]

It is believed by Freudians today that psychiatric disorders are caused by conflicts between the id, ego, and superego, and that some of these disorders can predispose a person to commit crimes. Some psychiatrists believe that criminals are physically healthy but socially abnormal. The acts they commit are but symptoms of their disorders, and in order to cure a disorder the inner motivation must be discovered.

Neurotics may commit crimes that are symbolic in nature. They may subconsciously feel a need to be punished. These "guilt feelings" result in acts designed to call attention to their real problems.

Psychopaths or sociopaths are people who commit crimes because of what might be described as an underdeveloped conscience. The reasons vary, but among the psychological explanations is the belief that such persons suffered a lack of love during childhood. Persons displaying psychopathic or sociopathic characteristics may show either insensitive aggression toward people or display outward charm and docility. However, they have a gross and callous indifference toward people and no emotional attachments. Intolerance of authority is one characteristic that can make these people antisocial.

Current Theories

The current explanation of crime causation appears to center around a multiple factor approach. This means that no one reason or group of reasons causes an individual to commit crimes. The person who develops a delinquent personality is usually handicapped by many factors. Most people can overcome a few handicaps, but when they become overwhelming, a person may turn to some deviant form of behavior.

The theory of differential association put forward by Edwin H. Sutherland explains crime causation in a different manner. He believes that people learn to be criminals by associating with criminals. A greater amount of time spent with criminals will increase the probability of choosing a criminal career. This theory is succinctly explained in this passage:

> A person becomes delinquent because of an excess of definitions favorable to violation of law over definitions unfavorable to violation of law. This is the principle of differential association. It refers to both criminal and anti-criminal associations and has to do with counteracting forces. When persons become criminal, they do so because of contacts with criminal patterns and also because of isolation from anti-criminal patterns.[12]

Among other famous theories of crime causation is Gresham Sykes and David Matza's theory of neutralization. It suggests that the offender "neutralizes" (or rationalizes) the effects of his actions in one or several of these ways:

1. Denial of responsibility. In this instance the delinquent deflects blame from himself by rationalizing that he was really not responsible for his acts.
2. Denial of injury. Through rationalization the delinquent denies that he hurt anybody, cost anyone his property, or engaged in any major delinquent or criminal activity.
3. Denial of the victim. In this instance, the delinquent accepts the fact that his act may have caused harm or injury, while arguing that the victim deserved such injury for his previous acts committed against others.
4. Condemnation of the condemners. Focusing upon the motives and shortcomings of those who sit in judgment, he shifts blame from himself to his accusers. In exposing their shortcomings, he silences his own sense of guilt or qualms concerning his deviance.
5. Appeal to higher loyalties. Ties and commitments to companions, family, or primary groups supersede other loyalties and take precedence over conformity to laws and social norms.[13]

Any experienced policeman will readily recall several juvenile and even adult offenders who have employed such rationalizations during the course of a police interview.

Another classic theory of crime causation is Robert K. Merton's theory of conflict between goals and the means of achieving those goals.[14] This can be expressed in the following illustration:

Modes of Adaptation		Culture Goals	Institution-alized Means
I.	Conformity	+	+
II.	Innovation	+	−
III.	Ritualism	−	+
IV.	Retreatism	−	−
V.	Rebellion	±	±

While most Americans share the culture goals of achieving material wealth, status, and success, they may or may not have the institutionalized means such as education, stability, job training, and so on.

The person who has both the goals and the means is labeled a conformist. He is not a criminal problem. Others have the goals but reject the means. They become innovators in that they engage in alternate or sometimes criminal behavior. The ritualist rejects the traditional goals but goes through the process of the means (the boring job, the meaningless education); in short, he plays the game. The retreatist rejects both goals and means. He sees the traditional goals as worthless and refuses to live in pursuit of such goals. He in effect "drops out" and becomes a deviant, but not necessarily a criminal. The rebel accepts and rejects part of the goals and part of the means. He may become a political activist, for example, either within or outside the law, depending upon the circumstances.

Causative Factors

The conditions under which a person lives have much to do with his personality. People have fundamental needs that must be filled. Food, clothing, and shelter are the basics. A person who believes that he is being deprived of any of these requirements will question his chances of survival. He may turn to criminal means if his needs cannot be filled by any other method. Some of the conditions to be considered are as follows:

Unemployment. Unemployment in itself will not cause a person to turn to crime. If a person has been employed regularly and finds himself out of work, he will probably wait until he is called back to his job or seek work elsewhere. Unemployment of an individual over a long period of time, however, may contribute to the crime problem. The chronically unemployed person will have to find other ways to fulfill his financial needs. He will find himself with much time on his hands and will generally associate with others in the same predicament. Such persons may be concentrated in parts of town known as areas of congregation. These areas are often run-down and sometimes have a large population of indigent persons. These sections of towns often have the highest rates of crime.

Education. Education is another factor that has no exclusive bearing on the crime problem but must be considered. The fact that a person is uneducated does not in itself mean that he will turn to crime, but it does mean that he may have more difficulty finding suitable employment. People who are underemployed may be dissatisfied with their condition. The life style they adopt and the acquaintances they make as a result of that life style may predispose them to commit criminal acts. An uneducated person may be more easily persuaded by others to do things that he would not otherwise do.

Housing. Housing and neighborhoods have been shown to be important factors in explaining crime. Clifford Shaw studied neighborhoods in Chicago. He used maps to pinpoint the residences of juvenile delinquents and adult criminals. He found that some neighborhoods had a disproportionately high percentage of offenders:

> Those neighborhoods were characterized by disorganization and congestion and anomie, and absence of social influence or controls. The neighborhoods were in the center of town, adjacent to industry and commerce.[15]

These neighborhoods are generally found in slum areas, where serious crime is frequent and the victimization rate is very high. The residents of these areas often belong to minority groups, thereby adding other sociological problems and stresses.

Most serious crimes happen in the urban slum. "For example, crimes related to physical violence (murder, aggravated assault, weapons) occur at a much higher rate in the ghetto than in the rest of the city."[16] Family and social disorganization also appear to be concentrated in such areas.

> Crimes related to social difficulties, family disintegration, and broad psychological problems are more prevalent in the ghetto (prostitution, narcotics, drunkenness, offenses against the family).[17]

In addition, psychological disorders and the accompanying problems are more prevalent among slum dwellers than among residents of the greater society. Decaying physical conditions, poverty, and family disintegration tend to infect people with a tendency toward violence or other outlets for their deep-seated problems.

The question appears to be whether people cause the conditions found in slums or whether the slums influence people to behave the way they do. The attack on crime in the ghetto appears to have two fronts. The social ills affecting the people must be attacked, and at the same time something must be done about the physical environment.

Poverty. Economic conditions are distinctly related to crime. Poverty in itself does not cause crime, but problems arise when one group of people sees that they have very little and that everyone else appears to be much better off. Advertisements promote the "good life." Our society as a whole creates the desire for material wealth. When the desire for wealth is implanted in a person and he does not have the money to obtain the things he wants, he may resort to criminal means.

Many people consider personal prestige to be based on wealth. Some will rob, steal, and cheat to get the things they want. This desire is not only inherent in people of limited means. People with some degree of wealth will at times resort to illegal means through their business or profession to get the extra wealth they desire. (Ironically, during periods of depression, crime does not rise as might be expected. It may actually decline because there are less significant differences between people of different classes.)

Race. Race must be considered when discussing the causes of crime. It is a statistical fact that blacks are involved in reported crime to a higher degree per capita then whites.

> The offical statistics of arrest per 100,000 population of the same race fifteen years of age and older for the entire United States suggests that blacks have arrest rates about three to four times those of the white population.[18]

One explanation of this fact is that Negroes have been trapped by all the vicious circles that block opportunity for poor people. In addition, their problems are compounded by prejudice and discrimination. It is safe to predict that blacks will continue to be involved in crimes disproportionately to their numbers until the conditions under which they live change and improve.

Community Stability. Cohesiveness and stability of the community are other factors that influence the crime picture. In a closely knit community where people know each other or are related, the conduct of the individual is controlled by his family and neighbors. When this closeness breaks down, as it often does in large population centers, people become anonymous. They do not know their neighbors and often care little about what other people do. There are few standards for behavior in such a neighborhood. Therefore, crimes will be committed that might not have happened in a cohesive neighborhood.

In a disorganized community, bookies and prostitutes can work with little or no community opposition. If they are apprehended, little will happen, because there is no community demand for their removal. Generally they are returned to the community to continue their work.

Mobility. Our present era is sometimes called the "jet age." We have the ability to travel vast distances in short periods of time, but we have discovered that the great increase in mobility has some side effects. Due to the ease of travel, many people no longer consider the family to be their primary reference group. Communications and mass transportation have made men a part of a wider society. A person has the ability to work and play where he wants to. Mobility has also given people the opportunity to commit crimes far away from home. A person can cover great distances rapidly, making it very difficult for law enforcement to operate effectively. Part of the reason is that police techniques have not kept abreast of the times. Small, uncoordinated efforts cannot deal with the problems of crime on a countrywide scale.

Weather and Climate. The climate, weather, and changing seasons bring with them differences in crime.[19] Hot summer weather brings people out of their houses and into more contact with others, precipitating an increase in crimes of violence. Winter creates the conditions necessary for different types of crimes. Burglaries and other property crimes increase substantially during winter months, when there are long periods of darkness. The Christmas season brings large numbers of people to shopping areas, and as a result, shoplifting and larcenies increase significantly.

Crimes of violence also increase during the holiday season. People get together at parties and reunions and usually drink a fair amount. The result can be fights, family disorders, assaults, and more serious forms of violence. Drunk driving arrests also peak during the holidays.

Personal Needs. A person has certain emotional and physical needs that must be filled in order for him to live a useful, well-adjusted life. If a person feels that some of these needs are not being filled, he may react in a socially unacceptable manner.

> Psychological needs include love, recognition, affiliation, prestige, popularity, self esteem, a feeling of well being, security, and a general freedom from mental and emotional pressures. Social needs might include luxury and comfort, better homes, newer and bigger automobiles, more and costlier clothing, jewelry, and more money to buy the items that serve those needs. Other social needs might be the need to dominate others or a need for power.[20]

There is an order of needs that has been identified by Abraham Maslow:

> In sequence, from lower to higher categories, Maslow's hierarchy appears in the following sequence: (1) Physiological: thirst, hunger, sex, relaxation, body integrity. (2) Safety: orderly, safe, consistent, just. (3) Love and belongingness: human relationships. (4) Esteem: achievement, competence, independence, freedom, reputation, prestige. (5) Self-actualization: exploitation of talents, capabilities, and potentialities.[21]

It is not possible for people to satisfy all their needs; they must compromise. Because people do not always want to respect the rights of others, rules are set up, and agencies are created to enforce them. The person who feels his needs have been filled will not likely enter a life of crime. If our society were able to fill more of the needs of its people, some of the causes of crime could probably be eliminated.

Drug Abuse. The drug problem can be a direct cause of crime. People may get involved in drugs casually, and their habits may gradually increase. After a person becomes addicted, life itself is a perpetual series of law violations. It is unlawful to purchase or sell drugs without proper licensing. Addicts pay a high price for their poison. Some estimate that the daily cost of heroin ranges between twenty-five and sixty dollars in New York City. Three to five dollars' worth of merchandise must be stolen to get one dollar in cash. If an addict had no other source of money, a fifty-dollar-a-day habit could require him to steal about two hundred dollars' worth of merchandise a day. Some people have much more expensive habits. Drug addiction is both physical and psychological, and the addict will do almost anything to get enough money for a "fix." In most urban areas, drugs must be considered one of the major causes of crime.

Emotional Disturbance. Mentally disturbed people also contribute to the crime problem. The psychopath is believed to be one of the more dangerous types of offenders:

> The terms psychopath, psychopathic personality, and constitutional psychopathic inferior are used with little or no differentiation to refer to persons who are regarded as emotionally abnormal but who do not manifest the break with reality that characterizes psychotics.[22]

There appears to be no standard method of identifying this type of behavior. Some psychiatrists argue that psychopaths make up no more than 5 percent of the prison population while others say they make up more than 90 percent of it.

A psychotic is severely mentally ill and is identified by his loss of touch with reality. A person manifesting psychotic symptoms can be very dangerous. He may, for example, be guided by "voices" that tell him to kill. People with such disorders account for only a small percentage of offenders. It would be difficult to establish that a person manifesting psychosis is responsible for his actions.

Family Stability. The family is very important to a young person; it provides the environment where one gets the first experience of social living. It is believed that a deficient family background is possibly the most significant factor in the development of juvenile delinquency.

> The early life experiences of the child in the family lay the ground work for the type of future behavior and the development of attitudes, values, and a life style. Parental hostility, rejection, and inconsistency can all contribute to delinquent behavior.[23]

Without the aid of the family, a child loses most of his psychological support. Without parental love, affection, and guidance, a young person may turn to outside groups, frequently deviant groups. Early emotional deprivation can also be directly associated with later psychological and emotional problems. There is generally a reason why young people commit delinquent acts.

> Delinquency signifies more than mere misconduct, it is the expression of desire, drives, urges, and motivations which have been greatly influenced by the youngster's early experiences in the family.[24]

It has been found that the majority of offenders come from deteriorating neighborhoods near the center of a city. The area is characterized by general social disorganization and a concentration of minority and foreign-born persons.

It is true that not all children who grow up in bad surroundings become delinquents. And in many cases children from "good" homes have become delinquent. The family is not the only cause.

Delinquency appears to be a multifaceted disorder. Many pressures are brought to bear on a young person, and the family is the greatest defense against those forces. Parents who are willing to try to understand the difficulties that young people must face can do much to prevent delinquent behavior. Control and guidance are essential in the family.

If the family fails to keep a young person from going astray, then the community and government step in. Community controls can take the form of probation, placement in halfway houses, and detention. By the time outside forces are brought to bear, it may be too late for many kids. Efforts to prevent delinquency must take into account the family, neighborhood, peer groups, and community.

Alleviation of the Crime Problem

Alleviation of crime requires the involvement and cooperation of various groups and institutions—the family, various organizations, the community, the police, the courts, the corrections system, and the legislators. Each has its own role and its own area of responsibility and control.

The Role of the Family

The family is the first institution with which an individual is in contact. From the day he is born a person is taught the customs, language, and accepted behavior of his society. It is considered the responsibility of the family to teach children the proper way to act in their world. Parents not only teach but become models that children imitate. Parents who provide an unstable home pass their attitudes and habits on to their offspring. A stable, model home life serves to teach the youngster the behavior considered proper in his society.

The Role of Organizations

People join service organizations, unions, and social clubs to organize for various purposes. Their goal may be to increase the number of their friends, to bargain for better working conditions, or to work for another cause. It does not matter what the specific goal is. Just the fact that people are united in a common effort for the general good of the membership gives such groups a positive value. The energy of organizations can be channeled into activities that will help combat crime. The leadership can try to promote the concept of citizen involvement, which includes reporting crimes when they are observed and not being afraid to get involved.

Service organizations can collect funds to start a "secret witness" or "silent observer" program that will reward persons for reporting crimes they might not otherwise have reported. The person who reports a crime under such a program does not have to be a witness in court if he does not wish to do so. These organizations can also instigate programs to stop prejudicial hiring practices by employers or to support bond issues that will encourage better education.

Certain organizations can sponsor recreation programs for children and teenagers. If youngsters are kept busy and have quality leadership in recreation programs, they will be less likely to be tempted into unlawful activities.

The Role of the Community

The community has a great responsibility in controlling crime. Most of the social factors that predispose a person toward a life of crime originate there. The people and their government cannot be separated because they are interrelated. People elect representatives to run their local governmental machinery. This machinery, to a large degree, determines what programs will be undertaken to better the lives of the people.

Local government is responsible for most of the public services—police, fire, garbage collection, maintenance and construction of streets, street lighting, building inspection, and public welfare. All these agencies have something to do with the quality of life in a community. It is not known whether any particular failure in public services will breed crime, but it has been established that people are the product of their environment.

The people in the community are partially responsible for the incidence of local crime. They can do something about the conditions of life, although it is not an easy task after years of neglect. Citizen pressure exerted at the proper place and time can bring about improvements. People can demand better police protection. They can force building owners to bring housing up to lawful standards. The community must want to better its conditions before anything will ever be done. Before changes are made, apathy must be replaced by involvement.[25] Methods of reporting crime and suspicious activities should be stressed. People should be told that they need not be witnesses if they do not want to be. The important thing is to report incidents.

Juveniles commit a large percentage of crimes, and the community can step in and help in this area. A variety of programs have been tried and found to be of value with youthful offenders. Halfway houses are quite beneficial. An offender is taken out of his home environment and put into a more structured and orderly one. Trained caseworkers help him deal with his problems. The youth is under close supervision, but he can be allowed some freedom. The community must not only help pay for such a program, but if it is to work they must believe in it. It is often difficult to find a suitable location for a halfway house because the area residents fight its establishment.

Another method of community help to juveniles with problems is the "drop-in center." Centers are usually staffed by trained volunteers under the supervision of a trained counselor. Young people with problems or no place else to go can stop by at any time. They find someone with whom they can share their problem and maybe get some help or guidance on what to do about the situation. Drop-in centers can help refer young people to other agencies if their problems require professional help. Drop-in centers, like halfway houses, often meet resistance by residents, and a suitable location may be hard to find.

"Hot lines" staffed by trained volunteers can do much to help people in crisis situations. Those in trouble dial a number that connects them with a person who is trained in dealing with crises, ranging from suicide threats to drug abuse. The phone counselors try to help the caller talk out the problem or refer him to someone who is more able to help. Just having someone to talk to can do much to alleviate stress in people with emotional problems.

Funding for all such projects can come from charitable organizations, through separate donations, and in part from local government.

All of these are community-based projects that can help lower the incidence of crime and at the same time benefit the individual in trouble. It takes both time and money to make such projects successful. If the community members seriously want to do something about their problems, they can put both their money and their personal efforts where it will do some good.

The Role of the Police

The police, among their many roles, act as teachers. In order to help reduce crime, police agencies must take it upon themselves to inform the public of the facts of crime. Most people never have any contact with the police or any other agency in the criminal justice system. These people are the ones footing the bill for law enforcement services. If properly informed, people will not rebel when they find their taxes going up, especially when they believe the money is spent for worthwhile purposes. Police can educate people by various means. Speakers from law enforcement agencies can speak at such functions as PTA meetings, Rotary and Kiwanis Clubs, community groups, social change organizations, and so on. They can also turn to the mass media. Newspapers, TV, and radio are always eager to print or disseminate information that can help lower the crime rate.

One of the valuable teaching services of the police is to tell people what they can do to protect themselves against criminal acts. If people are informed of what they can do to reduce crime, many will follow the advice given. For instance, installing sturdy locks on doors, locking their windows, and being generally security-conscious can help reduce a person's chance of being burglarized. In case of a robbery, citizens should be told how to act in such a way as to reduce the possibility of injury. Good descriptions of suspects and the getaway vehicle will help in apprehensions; therefore, the potential victim should know how to look for identifying characteristics of the person or persons committing the crime. A good public education program can yield surprising results.

Store owners are especially vulnerable to crime; they are victims of robbery, larceny, and burglary. Their losses on one incident can run to thousands of dollars. These losses are felt by everyone in the community because they are reflected in the costs of all the goods and services people buy. Police officers can make it a point to talk with store owners on their beat. These people are more than happy to share their problems with patrolmen. When they do, that is a good opportunity for an officer to help correct situations that may be contributing to criminal problems.

In the case of burglary, the owner can be informed of the value of sturdy doors and locks. Many businesses are operated in old buildings that are very easy to break into. The policemen point out that the cost of improved security may be cheap compared with the losses that could result from a burglary. Many merchants keep large sums of money in their stores overnight. This practice should be discouraged, as it only invites burglary. Safes and vaults are not burglarproof, but many storekeepers do not know that. Alarm systems have both apprehension and prevention value, and installation of such a device might be recommended. The store owner can be made aware that robbery losses can be minimized by having less money on hand at any time. In the case of high-volume or high-value stores, making two or three bank deposits a day may be cumbersome, but it would certainly cut the loss if a robbery occurred.

Larcenies can be prevented by removing temptation. Putting small pocketable articles out in plain sight may be good merchandising, but it is very poor crime prevention. The policeman can also point out that many of the losses due to larceny are the result of employee thefts, so better hiring and supervision could help reduce them. Employees should also be instructed what to do if a robbery occurs and how to get a good description of the suspects and the getaway vehicle.

The police can help reduce crime by working harder and more efficiently at what they do best—prevention, detection, and apprehension. Every available means of doing the job should be put into effect. Innovative methods should be tried; old methods that do not work well should be discarded. The police are not the only ones responsible for the prevention of crime, but they are the most visible. If it becomes apparent that they are doing a good job, then other sectors may follow.

Cooperation with other government agencies is important to attack poor housing, poor education, slums, filth, poverty, racism, and other social problems. The police can stimulate the community into positive action, and the results may be well worth the effort expended.

The Role of the Courts

The courts, which will be discussed in Chapter 4, are responsible for trying persons suspected of crimes. They must decide whether or not a person is guilty and then bring sanctions against the person if he is convicted. Courts also protect people's constitutional rights by insuring that the accused is granted all his privileges under the law.

A system must be developed in which people of similar backgrounds who commit similar crimes do not receive widely differing sentences. Background information is obtained through presentence investigations. The judge may make his sentence on the basis of the findings; therefore, the report should be factual and not biased.

Probation is a tool used in lieu of incarceration. The guilty party is subject to controls for a determined period of time. Reducing caseloads by hiring more officers could have a beneficial impact on the crime problem. Parole is similar to probation. Persons released from prison before the expiration of their sentences are usually on parole. Again, reducing the number of people an officer has to see increases the effectiveness of the program. Effective probation and parole can do much to make useful citizens of persons who may otherwise be in and out of jails and prisons for the rest of their lives.

The Role of the Corrections System

When all other measures have failed to keep a person from a life of crime, the corrections system comes into play. Defendants placed in "short-stay" institutions—for persons with sentences of a year or less—come out no better than they were when they went in. These institutions offer no programs of benefit to the offender or to the society to which he will eventually return. The suggested solution would be the elimination of local jails and their replacement by a regional institution staffed by people schooled in modern correction methods—medical doctors, psychiatrists, and social workers who would make a serious attempt to determine offenders' problems and correct them.

State and federal prisons have a somewhat better reputation than local jails, but many of them are little better. Inmates come out hardened and educated in the ways of crime. Large sums of money must be appropriated to replace old structures and methods. The goal should be total rehabilitation of all sentenced offenders. It may be an impossible goal, but administrators must try their best to do the most they can to make offenders into responsible citizens.

Sentencing procedures must be changed to align to a greater degree with these goals. The wide use of indeterminate sentences would be a start. People should not be released if they show no inclination to change. Something must be done to stop the revolving-door process by which a large percentage of released felons engage in criminal acts soon after they are released, are rearrested, tried, and sent back to prison.

When the day comes that prisons truly treat offenders in the same manner as doctors treat patients, then the recidivism rate will decrease.

Society must learn that what has to be done in these areas is costly, but the cost is less than the cost of continuing crime.

The Role of Legislators

Legislatures, too, have a responsibility for reducing the crime problem. Almost every unpopular act has been legislated against.[26] The problem that law enforcement people must face is not too few laws, but too many for any person to comprehend. Law-making bodies continue to pass new laws that have to be enforced. What is needed is a simplified code of laws. Laws must be understood and supported by the average citizen and law enforcement officer. The penalties for similar violations should be uniform and should be proportionate to the actual amount of harm caused by the unlawful act.

Archaic laws that no longer have meaning should be repealed, as should laws that legislate morality. The laws should reflect the ideas of our society today. Constant updating is necessary to keep up with changing times.

CHAPTER 3

The Police Function

A modern police department has many functions to fulfill, and these are fulfilled both by individual officers and by specialized divisions. Because so many duties must be performed, allocation of police services is a major problem.

The Police Role

The police officer wears many hats and assumes many roles and subroles while carrying out his duties. He is a father-confessor to the youngster who has made his first mistake, a referee in a family or neighborhood quarrel, an actor in the drama of pursuit and capture of a wanted felon, an investigator at the scene of a crime or accident, and a director of pedestrians and vehicles on the street. He seldom has time or opportunity to vie for popularity among the people he serves, and he settles for at least a little tolerance for himself and the role he fills. Some people learn to respect the policeman; some learn to fear him; and others are taught to despise and sometimes openly flout him and his authority. The most significant characteristic of the unique role the policeman plays in the community is that very few people actually know exactly what that role is.

Policemen today serve the same function as law enforcement officials through the ages. The primary differences between the past and the present are in the multiplicity and complexity of the laws and the intellectual level of the enforcers, now known as peace officers. The ideal policeman or peace officer of today is not only strong and trustworthy; he is also expected to be intelligent, diplomatic, and charismatic.

The traffic summons, the curfew arrest, and the field interview are just a few of the police procedures that involve a daily confrontation between peace officers and law-abiding citizens. Because of the negative connotations these contacts engender, they do not tend to endear the police officer to the people he contacts. The purposes of and the procedures involved in these citizen-police contacts, and a great many other police processes as well, need explanation:

The police officer's role is more complex than it appears. Inherent in police procedures and processes is a fact that is scarcely discussed in lawbooks and is seldom recognized by the public: Law enforcement policy is made by the policeman, for he cannot and does not arrest all the offenders he encounters. (It is doubtful that he arrests *most* of them.) A criminal code, in practice, is not a set of specific instructions to policemen, but a more or less rough map of the territory in which policemen work. How an individual policeman moves around that territory depends largely on his personal discretion.

That a policeman's duties compel him to exercise discretion many times every day is evident. Crime does not look the same on the street as it does in a legislative chamber. How much noise or profanity makes conduct "disorderly" within the meaning of the law? When must a quarrel be treated as a criminal assault—at the first threat, at the first shove, at the first blow, after blood is drawn, or when a serious injury is inflicted? How suspicious must conduct be before there is "probable cause"—the constitutional basis for an arrest? Every policeman, however advanced or limited his education, is an interpreter of the law.

Every policeman, too, is an arbiter of social values, for he meets situations in which invoking the criminal sanctions is a questionable line of action. It is obvious that a boy throwing rocks at a school window is committing the statutory offense of vandalism, but it is often not at all obvious whether a policeman will better serve the interests of the community and of the boy by taking the boy home to his parents or by arresting him. Who are the boy's parents? Can they control him? Is he a frequent offender who has responded badly to leniency? Is vandalism so epidemic in the neighborhood that he should be made a cautionary example? With juveniles especially, the police exercise great discretion.

Finally, the manner in which a policeman works is influenced by practical matters—the legal strength of the available evidence, the willingness of victims to press charges and of witnesses to testify, the temper of the community, the time and information at the policeman's disposal. Much is at stake in how the policeman exercises this discretion. If he judges that a person's conduct is not suspicious enough to justify intervention, he may lose a chance to prevent a robbery, rape, or murder. If he overestimates the seriousness of a situation, he may hurt or kill someone unnecessarily. His actions may even spark a riot.

The term *police work* conjures up in some minds a dramatic contest between a policeman and a criminal in which the stronger or the craftier will prevail. To be sure, there are heroic moments in police work, but the situations that most policemen deal with most of the time are of quite another order: poverty, racial antagonism, family breakdown, the restlessness of young people, and other problems that are associated with American crime, delinquency, and social conditions. During the last twenty years, these conditions have been aggravated by such profound social changes as the technological and civil rights revolutions and the rapid decay of inner cities into densely packed, turbulent slums and ghettos.

The police are the primary civil agency of government responsible for the regulation of conduct and protection of life and property. They are responsible for assuring that orderly activities of society may proceed. Their purposes are to control and/or apprehend those members of society who do not conform and to assist other duly constituted agencies of government in the creation of an orderly environment. The extent of police activity is prescribed by laws, court decisions, and customs in the society in which they operate.

The Patrol Division

A primary police function is to prevent unlawful acts. Crime and misconduct of any type occur when two factors exist: (1) the desire to commit the misdeed and (2) the belief that the opportunity to do so exists. When either factor is absent, criminal acts will not be committed. The presence of one factor alone, regardless of how strong it may be, will not result in crime. The elimination or reduction of these two factors, therefore, is a basic police duty. One task is to prevent or eradicate criminality in the individual; the other embraces all security measures designed to hamper or prevent criminal operations.

The apparent likelihood of arrest influences the degree to which the potential offender is convinced that the opportunity for successful misconduct exists. Patrol helps reduce the apparent opportunity for successful crime more than any other branch of police service. An impression of omnipresence is created by frequent and conspicuous patrol at all hours and in all sections of the community. Proper patrol depends on a reputation for quick and certain apprehension, and this reputation is reinforced by newspapers, radio, and word of mouth. The potential offender is thus persuaded that the police patrol is a detriment without the necessity of personal experience. Patrol is indispensable; it is the only form of police service that directly attempts to eliminate opportunity for misconduct.

The patrolman is the ultimate example of decentralization of municipal service. He is a mobile city-hall information service and a complaint counter for distressed citizens who are disgruntled by the inconvenience of trips to city hall, unsatisfactory telephone calls, and sometimes apparent lack of attention to their complaints. The constant availability and mobility of the patrolman make his services useful to other city departments, and he improves both public and interdepartmental relationships by attending more immediately to citizen needs. The extent to which patrol officers will provide such nonpolice services is determined by the chief executive of the city and his department heads.

The patrol division is the largest police division and is responsible for the performance of all primary police tasks. It provides complete coverage of the city and command at headquarters every hour of the day and night. The patrol division must take immediate action in the absence of members from a special division, and during certain hours, the patrol command may supervise the records section, jail staff, and dispatchers regardless of the division to which these areas may regularly be assigned. The proportional strength of the patrol division and the special branches will depend on the services performed by each.

In each department, a patrol method must be selected based on its purpose—to provide called-for services or inspection or to cover the area routinely. Factors that influence the choice of patrol method include the density and distribution of the population in the area, the kind of crime that occurs there, the frequency and nature of action required of the patrolman, light conditions associated with the time of year and the adequacy of illumination provided by street lights and lights on private premises, the surface and condition of the streets and sidewalks, the usual weather conditions during the various seasons, the racial characteristics and behavioral standards of the population, and the character of business establishments and residences.

The automobile is viewed by O. W. Wilson as undoubtedly the most effective and economical type of patrol when operated conspicuously by one man using superior patrol methods. To insure effectiveness and safe operations, however, procedures must be adopted for stopping suspicious cars and for dispatching patrolmen to assist.[1]

Other police administration experts comment:

> Preventive enforcement falls under the heading of protection, and involves the prevention of crime through the noticeable presence of police vehicles and personnel.

It has proven its value and continues to do so in the area of accident prevention. It is a statistical fact that where the police have purposely made their presence known by parking their patrol vehicles at or near hazardous intersections, or by heavily patrolling critical areas, a reduction in offenses occurs. The California Highway Patrol has found this technique quite effective by parking "dummy" vehicles that are painted to simulate regular Highway Patrol vehicles, in critical spots along the highway.

Preventive enforcement as a criminological philosophy was first presented by Sir Robert Peel just prior to 1829 when he suggested the formation of the Metropolitan Police to Parliament. It was Peel's contention that when London criminals saw a group of able-bodied, uniformed policemen patrolling the streets, they would throw up their hands in fear and run off to the nearest form of honest employment. Peel and his associates had little real understanding of the true and basic causes of crime, and they believed that all criminals were criminals solely by choice. They failed to comprehend the sociological implications of the industrial revolution. Although the resulting effect of the Metropolitan Police fell quite a bit below the high expectations of Peel and the members of Parliament, it still showed positive results and proved the value of preventive enforcement.

Prevention of crimes is the soundest of all criminological theories. It is much easier to patch a crack in the dike than it is to repair the wall after it has broken.[2]

The Crime Investigation Division

The basic purpose of the detective division is to investigate certain designated serious crimes in order to arrest and convict the perpetrators and recover stolen property. To this end, the detective should undertake a staff supervision of investigations by patrolmen and a continuing investigation of all felonies, all incidents that may be felonies, and all thefts except those categories of crimes that are assigned by department regulations to the traffic, vice, and youth divisions. Detectives should also, however, report to each appropriate division all facts regarding violations in its special field that come to their attention and take immediate action when necessary to prevent a failure of police duty in any area.

The success of investigations is heightened by active patrol participation. Suitable coordination of the patrol and detective divisions multiplies the effective strength of detectives without commensurate loss to the patrol division. Each patrolman should serve as the eyes and ears of the detective division and otherwise assist in the investigation of crimes and suspicious persons. Some tasks relating to the investigation of crimes that detectives are responsible for clearing by arrest may be performed to best advantage by patrolmen. Patrol division duties concerning a reported crime may be classified as noninvestigative (direct action) and investigative (preliminary investigation). Direct action consists of the care of injured persons, apprehension of a criminal at the scene or in flight, protection of the crime scene pending a search for physical evidence, and finally, the recovery of stolen property. The preliminary investigation is that part of a criminal investigation which may be conducted up to the point at which temporary postponement of further investigation of the case does not jeopardize its successful completion.

When the preliminary investigation results in the arrest of the criminal, the detective's responsibility is limited to the recovery of stolen property, the preparation of the case for presentation in court, and the investigation of other crimes, either reported or unreported, that the offender may have committed. When the perpetrator has not been arrested, the detective should analyze and integrate the information contained in reports by patrolmen and continue the investigation with the assistance of the patrol division. The skill and ability of the detective, his background and experience, and his possession of many facts from similar or related investigations qualify him to continue the investigation until the criminal has been apprehended or further effort seems futile. He may utilize the facilities of the patrol division in additional routine searches for witnesses, physical evidence, and suspects, and thus save his own time and energy for more difficult phases of the investigation. The detective may reinterview the victim and the principal witnesses in the hope that closer and more skillful questioning may uncover additional information to that acquired in the preliminary investigation.

Each detective, while on duty, should be notified of reports of major crimes that his detail is responsible for investigating. He may then participate in their investigation to the extent warranted by the seriousness of the crime and his own availability. When the preliminary investigation is conducted by a patrolman, the detective's immediate attention is not usually necessary. This applies more to crimes against property than to offenses against persons. Immediate attention by a detective is required only when his special skills, knowledge, and freedom of movement are needed and when the investigation should be conducted without delay.

The head of the detective division must make certain decisions concerning policy. First, he must decide which types of crimes occurring during detective off-duty hours should be reported immediately to him or to the detective assigned to that type of crime. Second, he must decide how far the investigation of the patrol division should proceed before conferring with the detective division. These decisions are influenced by the competence of the patrol force and particularly by the ability, judgment, and experience of the commanding officer in charge of the preliminary investigation.

The exact limits to patrol investigations are difficult to establish because of the variables involved, but a general policy may be worked out between the commanding officers of the patrol and detective divisions, and occasional informal conferences will make possible the definition of these limits to the satisfaction of both divisions.

The Youth Division

If real and permanent progress is to be made in the war on crime, the police must develop and promote a program designed to prevent the intellectual-emotional conditions in children that may result in criminal behavior and to correct unsatisfactory conditions that exist. The development of a favorable public attitude toward law enforcement, especially on the part of youth, is an important aspect of this task.[3]

It is vital for all departments to provide delinquency-prevention services, and departments of any size will find it necessary to establish a separate division for this purpose. Certain characteristics of philosophy of service, attitudes of personnel, and relationships outside the department will distinguish this division from the others in the department. The number of persons to be assigned to the youth division depends on the size of the department, the degree of specialization that is needed, the nature of the delinquency-prevention program, and the facilities that must be provided by the police because they are not available through other community agencies.

The methods and objectives of the youth division differ from those of other branches of police service. In large police departments the youth division usually includes qualified adjustment officers who are trained in social work and in the application of psychology in diagnosis and treatment of maladjustment. If the adjustment section is to accomplish its purpose, it must really be a child guidance clinic, although it may not be called by that name. The extent of the clinical facilities will depend on the availability and adequacy of other such services in the community, although the youth division staff should be qualified to diagnose and treat minor cases of maladjustment without outside assistance.

Organized Crime and Vice Control

Morals law constitute a particularly difficult problem for the police because of the frequent resistance to their enforcement by the public and sometimes by city officials. Although violations of the laws regulating or prohibiting prostitution, gambling, and the sale, possession, or use of narcotics and liquor are referred to collectively as vice, the police officer must weigh the seriousness of the offense before deciding how to deal with it. Gambling for charity is fashionable; drinking to excess is socially acceptable when it involves no injury to another person; and prostitution is widely accepted by various segments of society. Vice offenses are characterized by the absence of direct harm to anyone except the willing participant, although in some cases the person's family and associates are indirectly injured. Many citizens and some public officials believe, therefore, that even though a given participant is a weak person who cannot control his appetite, he should be free to indulge in his vice in spite of injury to his health, the dissipation of his property, or the destruction of his own life so that others may taste enjoyments that do them no apparent harm.[4]

Traffic Administration

Traffic control overshadows in magnitude every other police regulatory task and brings the police into contact with practically every person in the community. Automobile drivers and pedestrians, rich and poor, young and old, criminal and noncriminal—all are inevitably affected by the diverse problems arising from the continuously increasing use of the automobile. More people are injured and killed in automobile accidents than as the result of all other acts under police control combined. The economic loss from automobile accidents is greater than all other losses the police are charged with preventing. In every community this loss exceeds the total police budget. Furthermore, a greater number of people are disgruntled with traffic control than with police effort in any other field[5]; traffic control causes the police more annoyance and subjects them to pressure from a greater number of sources than any other problem.

Police control of automobiles and pedestrians is intended to facilitate their safe and rapid movement. To this end police try to alleviate the inconveniences, dangers, and economic losses that arise from the movement, congestion, delay, stopping, and parking of vehicles. Accidents and congestion are evidence of failure to provide safe and rapid movement. First attention should be given to accident prevention because of the pain and sorrow incidental to injuries and death; inconvenience and cost, however, force police to give attention to congestion and parking problems also.

Control of traffic is accomplished in three steps: (1) The causes of accidents and congestion are studied; facts are gathered and analyzed for this purpose. (2) Police and others try to remedy these causes by changing physical conditions that create hazards and enacting legislation to regulate drivers and pedestrians. (3) Police try to educate the public as to the provisions of traffic laws, train motorists and pedestrians to drive and walk safely, and enforce compliance with regulations—by giving tickets or making arrests if need be. The police should initiate action and coordinate the efforts of other agencies that are also concerned with these activities—the highway department, driver education programs, and traffic planning operations.

Statistics indicate that the human factor, the willingness of drivers and pedestrians to take unwise risks, is the cause of the large majority of automobile accidents. Defects in roadways and automobiles, physical defects of motorists and pedestrians, and lack of driver and pedestrian skill are contributory factors in some traffic accidents. The majority occur, however, when there is no defect in the driver equipment or roadway; they involve the skilled rather than the unskilled driver. The contributing factor in these accidents—and in congestion problems—may be called attitude, a state of mind that influences conduct. An aggressive, inconsiderate, or reckless attitude can be said to cause over 80 percent of all accidents, since it is a cause that overlaps many other causes.

The Problem of Allocating Police Services

Quite a bit has been written in the last few years about the allocation of public services. The problem of allocating police services has been ranked high among the public service allocation problems. Large cities throughout the nation are being plagued by the shortage of resources necessary to deal with many of their problems, including a rapid rise in the crime rate.

Before anything can be said about allocating police services, the objectives or outputs of police departments must be defined. Some typical objectives include:

1. Minimizing total index crime within a city
2. Providing an average minimum time within which police respond to all calls
3. Providing equal protection to all parts of the city—defining "protection" in terms of resource inputs
4. Providing equal protection to all parts of the city—defining "protection" in terms of safety outputs
5. Creating equal workloads on all operating units
6. Developing an effective capacity to respond quickly with "massive" force needed to confront large-scale violence such as riots.

With one or a combination of these objectives in mind, police administrators must be able to operate within the constraints placed upon them. Some of these constraints are as follows:

1. The much higher incidence of reported crime and certain other calls for service in low-income neighborhoods than in middle-income and high-income areas
2. The concentration of calls for service in certain periods of the day—probably 4:00 P.M. to midnight
3. The concern of police with a great many services in addition to fighting crime
4. The legal constraint of providing services for everybody
5. The political constraint of city administrators' having to allocate services in such a manner as to be reelected and receive a larger budget the next year.

Police departments have multiple objectives and multiple constraints. Different cities have different combinations of objectives depending on the composition of their populations, their size, and other variables. A solution to the problem of allocation will have to satisfy the greatest possible number of objectives within the given constraints.

The Monopoly Approach

The monopoly approach to allocating police services is essentially an argument for centralization. Advocates of a monopoly approach argue that services can be provided at a lower cost once the size of the local government or the group of governments over which a single police force has its jurisdiction is increased. Several arguments have been presented in favor of centralization of police activities. George Berkley points out that centralization encourages such practices as standardization, advanced education, crime prevention, public relations, trade unionism, representativeness, and impartial treatment.[6] According to Berkley, impartial treatment and the ability to handle national emergencies are the key points.

Many administrators see the need to improve the services of their department, yet they disagree with the completely centralized arrangement. They feel that certain aspects of centralization are logical. The problem of records, for example, could well be handled through a central records office. The President's Commission on Law Enforcement and Administration of Justice listed these points in favor of centralized records:

1. A person seeking information needs to check only one source rather than several.
2. Duplication of effort and the possibility of errors are decreased.
3. The speed of obtaining information is increased.
4. Reporting and documentation can be reduced.
5. An accurate overview of crime in an area can be obtained.
6. Related files are eliminated.
7. Fewer personnel are needed to operate the system.

Records systems could be centralized on a local, state, or national level, depending on the units involved.

The study by the commission also cited radio communication as another example of the need for centralization. It suggested the sharing of all network frequencies in an area to improve the probability of transmitting a call at any given time.

While much attention has been focused on physical inputs of police services, attention also should be devoted to the human inputs. The quality of the output of police services will be no better than the quality of the input. If the officers lack training and skill, it will be reflected in their output. Small towns lack the necessary finances to sponsor extensive training, while large cities in many cases lack the time. What can be done to secure better-trained personnel for police protection? The President's Commission on Law Enforcement and Administration of Justice points out the need for a uniform system of training policemen—some arrangement to provide all policemen with similar training. This could be provided through a state training institution that could supply communities, counties, cities, and towns with policemen according to their preferences and needs.

An example of the monopoly approach to allocating police services is the Toronto metropolitan area. The unification of the Toronto area's thirteen police forces caused quite a bit of debate at the time. The arguments against unification were based on community preference and the effectiveness of the present arrangement.[7] The arguments for unification were more numerous and quite detailed. They were as follows:

1. Duplication of police services would be eliminated.
2. A central communications department would eliminate delays in emergency and critical situations where speed is an important factor in apprehending the offender.
3. A properly equipped crime laboratory could be established to provide expert witnesses for court action.
4. A proper system of centralized records of offenders would be available to the entire area and would eliminate delays caused by searching of several police files.
5. Uniform control of traffic would result from direction received from a central traffic bureau.
6. Specialized bureaus could be established to operate over the entire metropolitan area and release personnel for very important and too often neglected duties of foot patrol.
7. The entire metropolitan area would have the benefit of central morality branches, traffic branches, criminal investigation, criminal identification branches, training schools, and transportation of prisoners.
8. Substantial saving to the taxpayer would result from central control of purchasing.
9. Policing the metropolitan area would be efficient, and the cost of such policing would be equalized over various municipalities.
10. A unified police force would provide better control over criminals who operate as receivers and disposers of stolen goods by making it possible to provide adequate surveillance of such persons.
11. The number of unsolved crimes in the metropolitan area indicated that a change in police organization was necessary.
12. Differences in wage schedules for police officers doing similar work in different municipalities would be eliminated.
13. Local councils would no longer attempt to direct and administer the activities of a local police force.
14. Adequate finances would be available to properly equip a unified force.
15. One police commissioner would administer the entire metropolitan area in an impartial manner, resulting in a uniform enforcement of police regulations and the criminal code, free from the responsibility of local interference.

16. Unification and modernization of police departments by the formation of a metropolitan police force would result in greater benefits to every municipality.[8]

Even though some very convincing arguments for the monopoly approach exist, citizens must consider seriously the preferences of the political units involved. Such an arrangement could lead to a police state if not carefully organized and controlled.

The Federated Approach

The federated approach combines features of centralized and decentralized police organization and recognizes the importance of community preferences for police services. The model for the federated approach divides police services into two categories—personal and impersonal—to be provided by two police units. Services that reflect community tastes or depend on strong personal contact and knowledge of the community should be carried out by local units. On the other hand, services with whose operation the community has no direct concern should be delegated to a larger or higher political unit. For example, if the federated approach were applied to traffic, the enforcement of traffic between communities should be handled by the larger police unit, which would provide standard procedures. Community traffic problems would be handled by local police units, since speed limits, parking, and so on are of local concern only. The approach also provides the necessary tax base for each unit and keeps each one reliant on its respective base.

The approaches discussed thus far have dealt with only one aspect of a multifaceted problem. The federated approach clearly recognizes the problem and makes a realistic attempt to keep the citizens' preferences in mind while attempting to solve the problem. The decision made by one police unit will definitely have a bearing on other units.[9]

Community Service

A community's attitude toward the police is influenced most by the actions of individual officers on the street. No community-relations or recruiting or training program will avail if policemen in their contacts with citizens do not show courteous and cool-headed conduct. The officer must remember that there is no law against making a policeman angry and that he cannot charge a man with offending him. Until the citizen acts overtly in violation of the law, the officer should take no action against him, least of all lower himself to the level of the citizen by berating and demeaning him. The officer who withstands angry verbal assaults shows his own character and maintains the standard of the department.

Policemen are citizens of the community too. They are not only restricted by the same laws as other citizens, but they are protected by the same Bill of Rights and Constitution. Although their on-duty action must be impartial and in the best interest of the community as a whole, they may have their personal beliefs and freedoms, too. Enforcing the intent of the law while being aware of the letter of the law is a responsible task to be performed by intelligent and objective peace officers.

CHAPTER **4**

Prosecution, Defense, and the Courts

The Constitution of the United States assures that every person who comes in contact with the criminal justice system by way of arrest and/or trial will be afforded equal protection under the law. In order to actualize this idea, two opposing sides face each other in criminal proceedings. They are represented by the prosecuting attorney and the defense attorney.

Prosecution

The origin of the public prosecutor's office was in thirteenth century England; it is believed that the prosecutor started as an agent or representative of the king or some other power who was interested in maintaining community peace.[1] This representative was the forerunner of the present-day attorney in England prior to

1879. Earlier, legal prosecutions were mostly private, and not until the establishment of a director of public prosecutions in England in 1879 was the system changed to any great degree. This, then, was the forerunner of today's prosecuting attorney.

Officers of the court, as the prosecutor and defense attorney are often called, have at least one basic goal in common—the search for truth. This goal, though common to both, is approached in a different way by each attorney. Although both are responsible to the public in that they must see that justice is done, the prosecutor's job is generally to construct or build a case against the accused person, whereas the defense attorney's job is to defend the accused against all charges and to diminish the prosecutor's case. Because in the American criminal justice system the defendant is presumed innocent until proven guilty beyond a reasonable doubt, the defense attorney may advise his client to remain silent, and while the defense attorney may withhold evidence by refusing to put his client on the stand, the prosecutor is bound by legal ethics to present all material evidence.

The duties and responsibilities of the prosecutor are endless. For this reason, all fifty states have written into their constitutions the areas in which the prosecutor may be involved. In general, a prosecutor and his staff may engage in activities ranging anywhere from the actual prosecuting of a case to assuming the investigative duties of the local sheriff in small communities to surveillance of other local law enforcement agencies to ensure that they are acting properly in their enforcement area.

Generally, a prosecuting attorney has the authority to participate in three types of investigations. First, he may initiate investigations of suspicious individuals believed to be involved in illegal activities (usually, though, this is handled by local police). Second, he is authorized to investigate in order to gather additional information necessary to his case, and third, he is empowered to investigate whether or not the police are properly performing their prescribed duties. Whether he is called assistant attorney general, county attorney, circuit court attorney, circuit solicitor, commonwealth attorney, county solicitor, criminal district attorney, district attorney general, prosecuting attorney, solicitor general, or state's attorney, his duties are generally the same.[2]

Usually prosecutors are elected by the public, and except in a few states they may simultaneously have a private practice. In many areas prosecutors are so poorly paid that they must and are expected to engage in private practice. This inevitably causes a conflict of interest between the demands of the office and those of individual practice. The President's Commission on Law Enforcement and Administration of Justice, also known as the National Crime Commission, recommended that localities should revise salary structures so that prosecuting attorneys and their assistants need not engage in outside practice and that an effort should be made to raise the quality of the office so that highly talented lawyers will seek it.[3]

The prosecutor in most states can and usually does handle both civil and criminal matters. His position gives him great discretionary power that is limited only by the courts, the attorney general, and the pressure of public opinion. Usually the prosecutor has the power to (1) either prosecute or not prosecute, (2) select the actual charge, (3) recommend sentence, (4) bargain for a lesser plea, (5) request the court to dismiss the action, and (6) obtain the assistance of a special prosecutor.[4]

Because he has these powers, the prosecuting attorney has more control over an individual's liberty and future than any other public official or public body and, except for the judge, is the most influential court official. In addition to having the discretionary powers just listed, he is responsible for the organization and presentation of evidence before the court. As a politician, the prosecutor is usually eager to continue in his position or advance to a higher office (the prosecutor's office is often used as a steppingstone). He must, therefore, in the eyes of the public, do the best job possible. Whether or not it is a fair standard, the quality of his effectiveness is measured by the number of cases he wins and the severity of punishment he recommends.[5]

The decisions the prosecutor makes have profound effects on all cases brought to him by the police. His practices and decisions also significantly affect the arrest practices of the police, the volume of cases in the courts, and the number of offenders referred to correctional departments.[6]

Although the prosecutor does not make a final determination as to guilt or innocence, he must satisfy himself that a crime has been committed. Once he has done this, the actual charge is submitted and the trial process begins. As with any adversary battle, the combatants must at one time or another come face to face and fight it out. After the charge is formally submitted, the two combatants "lock horns" in the form of the initial interaction between prosecutor and defense attorney. This is the first in a series of steps that will lead to a final disposition of the case.

The prosecutor may dispose of a criminal case in one of two ways—by way of a criminal trial or by a process known as plea bargaining, commonly called the "negotiated plea." From available sources, it is known that some 95 percent or more of criminal cases are disposed of by the plea bargaining process. The negotiated plea takes three forms: (1) a sentence recommendation, (2) a plea of guilty to a lesser offense, and (3) dismissal of charges. In making a sentence recommendation, the prosecuting attorney suggests to the court a sentence favorable to the defendant or seeks a lesser penalty.

Inherent in our criminal justice system is the desire to individualize punishment, to make the system fit each individual rather than making the individual fit the system. Because neither side can dominate, plea bargaining offers a chance for a reasonable compromise. Though some people consider this process to be unethical and contrary to Anglo-American ideas of criminal justice, it nevertheless benefits both sides—the state is spared the work and expense of a trial, and the defendant is given a second chance.

Naturally, there are both pros and cons to the plea bargaining process. In addition to the benefits to both sides just mentioned, the quality of justice could be improved if time and talent were reserved for the most important trials. Plea bargaining also relieves the defendant and the prosecution of the inevitable risks and uncertainties of a trial.

The dangers of plea bargaining are also evident. In jurisdictions where courts are hard pressed for time and manpower, dangerous offenders may receive an unjustifiably light sentence.

A great deal of significance is attached to the criminal trial process because it sets standards that affect all other stages of the criminal justice process from arrest to corrections. The following steps are those involved in the trial process; however, for purposes of distinction and clarification, the first four steps may be seen as the pretrial process:

1. Arrest and Booking
2. Arraignment (district court or municipal court)
3. Preliminary Hearing (district court or municipal court)
4. Arraignment (circuit court or superior court)
5. Trial (circuit court or superior court)
6. Appeal (optional; not a part of every criminal trial)

In order for a trial to occur, no step can be bypassed; each one must be completed before the following one can take place. (At any point in the process, however, the accused can be released and possibly have all charges dismissed.)

By the very nature of their office, prosecutors alone cannot handle the enormous volume of work that is required to prepare for all the criminal cases they prosecute. For this reason, they employ assistants.

Assistant prosecutors perform a vital function in the efficient and expedient handling of cases. They often investigate, interview, research, and compile information for use in the prosecution of a criminal trial. Although it may seem that they do all the work, the prosecutor also does pretrial investigations. In many cities, the prosecutor must handle an enormous number of cases with a small staff of assistants. In large communities, the prosecutor has a relatively large staff of assistants, as many as 216 in Los Angeles County or 153 in Chicago. Responsibility for making charge decisions and trying cases is often left to inexperienced young assistants who receive little if any guidance from their superiors.[7]

New problems confronting the prosecutor become more and more evident as time goes on. Major decisions that have already been handed down from higher courts make necessary a new and different approach each time a question comes up about the application of that decision to the related subject. Old decisions plus new ones that come down from federal, state, and local courts, plus new laws from federal and state legislatures all have a profound effect on the prosecutor and his office in regard to prosecuting criminal as well as civil matters. Decisions on the rights of the accused, expansion of the rules of evidence, and so on influence prosecutory action and necessitate increased prosecutor time in pretrial and trial procedures and increased clerical work. Unfortunately, as mentioned, many prosecutors lack the necessary number of assistants to deal effectively with the vast volume of cases.

In addition to those already stated, a few more problems confront the prosecutor. He must deal with the tensions that arise from the fact that justice must be assured not only to the criminal but also to society; the fact that inexperienced prosecutors may neutralize the efforts of enforcement and the courts (much damage is done to the operation of the criminal justice system by inept trial attorneys); and greater scrutiny by higher courts of the conduct of prosecuting and defense attorneys. These and other problems must be tackled by the prosecutor so that he may operate satisfactorily and effectively. Because the responsibility of the prosecution covers the gamut from investigations through appeal, the prosecutor is exposed daily to the overall weaknesses and strengths of the judicial process.

Needless to say, the office of prosecuting attorney is entwined with political aspirations. In certain areas, real advantages can be realized from this fact. Practical politics operating on the prosecutor and his staff insure that the office will be responsive to the views of the majority. As mentioned in a report by the National Crime Commission, "political considerations make some prosecutors overly sensitive to what is safe, expedient and in conformity with law enforcement views that are popular, rather than carefully thought out."[8] In some places this has been bypassed by unusually able district attorneys who have developed highly efficient professional offices.

The training a prosecutor receives is limited to his legal education and whatever courtroom experience he has had. Whatever else this training does, it does not necessarily prepare him for his administrative and law enforcement abilities. Much harm is done by inept prosecutors who are not trained properly. One step toward helping prosecutors is the activities of the U.S. Department of Justice and the National District Attorneys Association, who jointly have started programs to train prosecutors. Since in-service training programs serve useful and extremely necessary purposes in police departments, why should not all trial lawyers as well as prosecutors have such programs? As recommended by the National Crime Commission, the federal government, states, and district attorneys' offices, with assistance from law schools and professional organizations, could develop curricula and programs for the preservice and in-service training of prosecutors and might well require the broadest possible participation in such programs by prosecutors.

Defense

The origin of the defense attorney is unknown. Legal defense for a person on trial was generally prohibited in early English law. However, as early as 1701, Pennsylvania law established the right of the accused to be represented by counsel.[9] As the need for prosecutions of individuals grew, so did the need for representation for those accused. But not until the formation of the Constitution and the Bill of Rights did formal representation for the accused become mandatory.

Whether accusation of an individual is civil or criminal in nature, the accused has a right to counsel. In serious criminal matters, representation by a lawyer is required and begins as soon as possible after the arrest. For those who do not have their own attorney, however, counsel is usually appointed at the time of arraignment in district court. It can be safely concluded that it is imperative that the criminally accused receive legal representation as soon as possible to insure that justice is dispensed equally.

The defense lawyer's active presence becomes most important once the trial stage is reached. He prepares his case in much the same way as the prosecutor. The defense attorney or an assistant questions parties, conducts interviews, does in-depth research regarding previous decisions that might help prepare a good defense, and plans trial tactics that might help his case. He has a hand in selecting the jury and holds the same discretionary power as the prosecutor in dismissing prospective jurors.

Two methods are used to provide defense counsel to persons who are unable to afford their own. The first is the assigned counsel approach, whereby attorneys are appointed by the court.

The second is the defender system, under which all defendants requiring counsel are represented either by a public defender or by an attorney from the Legal Aid Society. Founded in the latter part of the nineteenth century, the Legal Aid Society provides legal service to impoverished persons unable to hire a private attorney. Generally, the society is financed through private funds, although some public funds are provided.

Public defender systems appeared in ancient Rome, in fifteenth-century Spain, and in many European countries. However, not until 1913 in Los Angeles County did the public defender system come to this country. Like the Legal Aid Society, the public defender system provides legal counsel for the poor. Unlike the Legal Aid Society, the public defender system derives all its funding from state or local government.

The use of public defenders is increasing every day. As of January 1973, 280 public defender offices with some two thousand five hundred attorneys existed in the United States, and thousands of other attorneys served on a part-time basis. Their importance is underlined by the fact that 60 percent of all persons charged are too poor to hire their own attorneys.[10] Fourteen states have established systems whereby taxpayer-supported lawyers represent the poor. In this realm there exist three little-known agencies that also provide legal representation for the poor—the Neighborhood Law Offices, the Office of Economic Opportunity Legal Assistance Programs, and VISTA (Volunteers in Service to America) lawyers.

Needless to say, the best possible defense comes through a private attorney hired by the client. For this reason, almost every accused person would like to hire his own attorney and will do so if he can possibly afford it. Also, many big corporations and wealthy individuals keep a private attorney or a staff of attorneys on hand by paying a retainer fee. Should the individual or corporation ever be involved in court proceedings, counsel is readily available.

If an individual cannot afford a private attorney of his own choosing, one is usually assigned by the court to represent him. Assigned counsel may take the form of appointment from a list of attorneys that the presiding judge has before him, or assignment of counsel may be through appointment by the judge from among lawyers he happens to know or who happen to be in the courtroom. The National Crime Commission recommended that all jurisdictions that have not already done so should change from random assignment of defense counsel by judges to a coordinated assigned counsel system or a defender system, where there are full-time defenders available to indigents. The former assignment system leads to an unfair allocation of cases, and sometimes, when assigned lawyers receive compensation from the state, it is grossly abused.

Justice George Sutherland of the U.S. Supreme Court observed the following many years ago on the subject of legal representation for the accused:

> The right to be heard would be, in many cases, of little avail if it did not comprehend the right to be heard by counsel. Even the intelligent and educated layman has small and sometimes no skill in the science of law. If charged with crime, he is incapable, generally, of determining for himself whether the indictment is good or bad. He is unfamiliar with the rules of evidence. Left without the aid of counsel he may be put on trial without a proper charge, and convicted upon incompetent evidence, or evidence irrelevant to the issue or otherwise inadmissible. He lacks both the skill and knowledge adequate to prepare his defense, even though he have a perfect one. He requires the guiding hand of counsel at every step in the proceedings against him. Without it, though he be not guilty, he faces the danger of conviction because he does not know how to establish his innocence. (*Powell* v. *Alabama,* 287 U.S. 45, 69 (1932).[11]

Types of Courts

Two types of courts exist in the United States—civil courts and criminal courts. Cases arising from one act may be heard in a court of each type. This is not considered to be double jeopardy, because the courts deal with the defendant in different ways. An example of a case heard by both kinds of courts would be an assault. The person accused of the assault could be tried in criminal court for the crime of assault, while monetary damages could be sought by the victim in civil court.

A civil action may be initiated by anybody who feels that he has been aggrieved. The person initiating the suit is called the plaintiff. The person who is accused in the suit is called the defendant. Civil courts have been established to insure justice for the victim. The Constitution guarantees the rights of persons involved in civil suits through its Seventh Amendment, which states: "In suits at common law, where the value in controversy shall exceed twenty dollars, the right of trial by jury shall be preserved, and no fact tried by a jury, shall be otherwise re-examined in any Court of the United States, than according to the rules of common law."

Congress has also given the states jurisdiction in civil suits in which the value of damages is less than ten thousand dollars, even if the dispute is federal in nature. Federal courts have jurisdiction in all cases in which the value of damages is in excess of ten thousand dollars, even if issues of state law are involved. The caseload for the state courts is greater because a larger number of civil suits involve small sums of money

To win a civil action, the plaintiff must prove his case by a preponderance of evidence. This means that the quality of proof he offers must be greater than the quality of proof offered by the defendant. If the proof offered is less than, or equal to, that of the defendant, the plaintiff loses his case. The duty of proving his accusations rests on the plaintiff.

There are two types of authority for civil disputes, statutory law and common law. In criminal law, statutory law has all but displaced common law. In civil law, however, common law is still the basis for most decisions. When there is a dispute between the common and statutory law, the statutory law is the one which must be obeyed.

In a criminal case, the victim is the aggrieved party. However, the crime is considered to have been committed against society as well. A prosecutor acts on behalf of the people in criminal courts.

> A crime, or public wrong, is considered a social offense against the state. In criminal actions, the people prosecute, damages, by ways of fines, go to the state rather than to the victim (or are otherwise allocated for some specific purpose), and penalty is an essential part of the process. Very few criminal cases are settled out of court, and the public prosecutor may or may not appeal an adverse decision of the court. (Whether an appeal can be taken depends upon statutory provisions.)[12]

The person initiating the case in a criminal action is the prosecutor. He must prove his accusation beyond a reasonable doubt. If the prosecutor fails in this effort, the defendant is set free. The victim of the crime is considered to be only a witness in court proceedings.

The basis for criminal law exists in codified statutes or in the common law. Most states have adopted laws that have negated common law, so common law is rarely used in criminal matters.

The constitutional rights of persons involved in criminal proceedings are protected by the Fourth, Fifth, Sixth, and Eighth Amendments of the Constitution. These protections originally applied only to persons involved with federal processes. The citizens of states have also been given this protection by the Supreme Court in state proceedings, because the court has stated that the citizens of states should also receive this benefit by virtue of the Fourteenth Amendment.

The various state governments, and also the federal government, have created courts to hear cases involving criminal matters. Complicated procedures and safeguards have also been created.

State Courts

State courts have various names, but they usually come under three headings—inferior courts, trial courts, and appellate courts. The authority for establishing these courts is in the constitutions of the various states. Their jurisdictions cover all state laws of the state in which they were created. State courts may have concurrent jurisdiction with the federal courts in certain areas. Robbing a bank, for example, is both a state and a federal offense. A person committing this act could be tried in either court.

Inferior Courts. Several names used by the inferior courts are justice of the peace courts, police courts, traffic courts, magistrate courts, municipal courts, and district courts. These courts are not always courts of record; that is, they do not necessarily keep a written transcript of their proceedings. Inferior courts have jurisdiction in minor matters only. In Michigan, the office of justice of the peace has been phased out. Its inferior court, called district court, may hear cases involving misdemeanor and civil matters.

Bail may be set by the judges in inferior courts. Usually the preliminary hearing for a person accused of committing a felony is held in these courts to determine if the accused was arrested under the principle of probable cause. If so, he is bound over for trial in a higher court—that is, a circuit or superior court.

The inferior courtroom setting is often informal. In addition to the court official hearing the case, the defendant and his accuser may be the only persons present. Even defense attorney and prosecutor may be absent. If the defendant in the criminal case or either the defendant or plaintiff in a civil case wishes to have a jury trial, a jury will be selected for the misdemeanor or civil matter.

Trial Courts. Most of the cases heard by the trial courts are either high misdemeanors or felonies. Some of their caseload involves appeals from the inferior courts. These courts are courts of record; a written transcript is retained of all its proceedings. The trial is conducted by a judge, and a prosecutor and a defense attorney are present at the trial. If a defendant cannot afford an attorney, one will be appointed for him by the court.

The felony trial court may have several names. In Michigan it is known as the circuit court; in California it is known as the superior court.

Appellate Courts. An appellate court is a court of appeal. That is, if a person is able to claim errors by a lower court, he may ask the appellate court to review the case in hopes of getting a favorable ruling. Each state has at least one appellate court level. Some of the more populous states have two.

If the case on appeal was heard in a trial court, the court transcript will be examined to determine whether the verdict was just. If the case on appeal was heard by an inferior court, the case may be heard *de novo* (as new), and the whole trial would be repeated. Appellate courts may either uphold or reverse a conviction.

Federal Courts

A federal court system was established in the Constitution. According to the Constitution, a United States Supreme Court was to be created, and the power was vested in Congress to establish any inferior federal courts that would be required. The federal system consists of trial courts and appellate courts.

Trial Courts. The federal trial court is called the United States district court. U.S. district courts are trial courts and have original jurisdiction; that is, they may hear cases as new. Each state has at least one district court, and populous states have more. There are ninety-four U.S. district courts and 287 federal district court judges.

The district courts hear cases regarding offenses against federal laws. In the federal system the U.S. district courts hear and determine cases of criminal offenses that occur in the United States, in the territorial possessions of the United States, and on vessels of this nation.

Appellate Courts. There are two appellate court levels in the federal judicial system, the United States Court of Appeals and the United States Supreme Court.

The ninety-four district courts are grouped into ten circuits, each of which has a court of appeals. If a case is heard by that court, which contains from three to nine judges, at least three judges must hear the case, and the decision rendered depends on a majority vote. Decisions made by the court of appeals are based on the court transcript and motions rather than on a trial basis.

The U.S. Supreme Court is the court of last resort in America. Its decisions are binding on all lower courts. Constitutionally, the Supreme Court is given original jurisdiction in cases involving ambassadors, ministers, consuls, or state governments. As mentioned earlier, it also has appellate jurisdiction in all cases involving constitutional questions.

Congress may set the number of justices who sit on the Supreme Court. At the present time, there are nine Supreme Court Justices—one chief justice and eight associate justices. A quorum of six must be present to hear a case, and the majority opinion is the decision of the Court.

The Supreme Court chooses the cases it wishes to hear. Before a case is heard from the state courts, every effort possible must be made to have the case heard by the state appellate courts. After this is done, appeal may be sought on the federal level.

Most of the cases heard by the Supreme Court are brought up from the lower courts through the writ of certiorari. A writ of certiorari is simply an order for the lower court to produce the case for deliberation by the Supreme Court.

Criminal Court Processes

Criminal court processes begin well before the opening of the trial, and the influence of the courts is felt in every step of the process from arrest to appeal. Basically, the steps in the court process are as follows: arrest and booking, arraignment, preliminary hearing, accusation, trial court arraignment, pretrial motions (if any), trial, and appeal (if any).

Arrest and Booking

A person who comes in contact with the criminal courts must initially be arrested. Arresting a person is taking him into custody for the purpose of charging him with a specific offense. The arrest may take place with or without the use of a warrant. All arrested persons are then booked by the law enforcement agency that took them into custody. The booking card of the law enforcement agency contains information such as the date and time of arrest, the charge or crime for which the person was arrested, the name of the arrested person, the name of the arresting officer, and other information concerning the physical description of the defendant. This record or booking card is permanently stored in the files of the police department. It is removed only upon the death of the arrested person or upon a court order if the charges are dismissed.

The defendant in custody may gain his freedom in several ways. The charges against him may be waived or dismissed by the prosecution. (Often charges against military personnel are waived because it is a financial saving to have the government punish the offender under the Uniform Code of Military Justice.) The charges against a person may be dismissed if it is believed that he is innocent of the crime for which he was charged. A suspect may also gain his freedom through the use of bail. Bail guarantees that a person will not unnecessarily lose his freedom. The poor person, however, in contrast to the affluent citizen, does not have an equal chance to use this guarantee.

Arraignment

After a person is taken into custody, the law enforcement agency must take him, without delay, in front of the nearest committing magistrate or judge. This is his first contact with the court system and is called the arraignment. At the arraignment, the accused is advised of the charges he is facing; he is advised of his rights; and his plea is sometimes taken. If the accused is charged with a misdemeanor and pleads guilty, the magistrate or judge may pass sentence on him. If the accused is charged with a misdemeanor and pleads not guilty, he may be tried at this time if he waives his right to a jury trial. If the accused wishes to have a jury trial, one will be scheduled for him. When the person is charged with a high misdemeanor or a felony, this committing magistrate may not take a plea. He may merely set the date for preliminary hearing and set bond, thus allowing the defendant to go free while awaiting his hearing.

Preliminary Hearing

The purpose of the preliminary hearing in the lower court is to determine whether there is reasonable cause to believe that a felony was committed and also whether there is reasonable cause to believe that the accused committed the crime. If so, he is ordered to stand trial in a higher court. In a felony or high misdemeanor case, the lower court judge is usually empowered to conduct a preliminary hearing. This judge does not usually have the legal power to conduct trials in felony cases.

Upon the determination of the judge, there are two possible outcomes of the preliminary examination. The accused may be released because he was not arrested for probable cause, or he may be placed on bail or remanded back to jail until his case is tried by the higher court. It is said that he is "bound over" for trial. If the person has been released for lack of probable cause, he may be recharged with the same crime if new, or more, evidence is found. He is not being put in double jeopardy in this case because he has not yet been brought to trial

Habeas Corpus. If the law enforcement agency takes a person into custody and fails to take him before a magistrate or judge for arraignment, a writ of habeas corpus may be filed with the court by the accused or by someone else on his behalf. The writ demands that the arresting agency bring the prisoner before the judge or magistrate and name the specific charges and the reason for the delay in the arraignment or else release him.

> Upon the police showing adequate cause, a court may continue the hearing in order to give the police a little more time to conduct a further investigation before making the formal charge against the arrestee. Many times, however, the police are required to file their charges immediately or release the prisoner.[13]

This writ protects the suspect from prolonged detention and other illegal police practices.

Coroner's Inquest. In homicide cases the coroner must conduct an inquest to determine the cause of death. The finding of the coroner is not a proven fact; it is just a deduction. A person may be charged with a homicide even if the coroner found that a death was accidental or self-inflicted. The coroner is not usually a doctor and often is ill fitted for this task. Some states are changing to a system of medical examiners, who are doctors and are more qualified to determine cause of death.

The Accusation

After a crime has been committed, the police, a witness, or the victim must make a complaint to the prosecutor. An informal complaint may be sufficient for the trial in certain minor offenses, while a formal complaint is needed for offenses involving high misdemeanors or felonies.

A second type of accusation is the information. The information is signed by the prosecutor and filed with the court, in some states as an accusation in the higher trial court after a felony defendant has been bound over for trial. The information circumvents the use of the grand jury. It can usually be used in misdemeanor cases and in some states in felony cases as well. Some states, however, require a grand jury hearing in felony cases.

The grand jury, although used to a limited degree, is nonetheless a part of the criminal system. It is believed to have started in

England around the twelfth century. Initially, it was created as an accusatory body. Its main function was to identify local offenders and state the charges they should face before a traveling judge. As the accusatory function became the responsibility of the prosecutor, the grand jury began hearing witnesses in private and evolved into an intermediary between the people and the state.

No official policy existed in twelfth-century England to make trial before a grand jury mandatory. Today, however, the grand jury is preserved in the Fifth Amendment to the Constitution, which states in part that "no person shall be held to answer for a capital or otherwise infamous crime, unless on a presentment or indictment of a grand jury." With the presentment, the grand jury, through its own investigation, finds that a criminal act has been committed and brings the wrongdoer to justice. Grand juries rarely conduct their own inquiries. In the indictment, a motion is made by the government for a hearing before a grand jury. After hearing what the prosecutor has to say, the grand jury either finds that the charges are supported because the facts show probable cause to believe that the accused committed the crime (true bill), or that the charges are unsupported (no bill). If a true bill is returned, the accused is held for trial. If a no bill is returned, however, the case of the accused may still be reopened, since he has not been placed in jeopardy.

The grand jury system varies from state to state. In some areas, judges choose grand jurors from among persons known to them or recommended by previous jurors. Today, however, many grand jurors are picked from voter rolls. The grand jurors number from twelve to twenty-three and sit for three to eighteen months depending on the jurisdiction. Generally, they meet a few days each week. They make twenty dollars a day on federal panels.[14] When the grand jury is composed of twenty-three citizens, as it usually is, a quorum of sixteen jurors must be present to obtain an indictment, and twelve votes, which is barely a majority, must be obtained to get a true bill. The grand jury concerns itself only with the government evidence. The defense has no right at the grand jury to cross-examine witnesses or to present its side of the case. Usually, the defense is not even present at the hearings. A grand jury hearing is designed to safeguard the accused from arbitrary action of the prosecutor or the police. In actuality, however, the prosecutor usually appears before the grand jury, briefly outlines his case, and asks for an indictment. The grand jury generally approves whatever charge the prosecutor recommends. For this reason, grand juries are sometimes referred to as rubber stamps for the prosecution.

The accusation aids the defendant, the prosecution, and the courts by defining the issue that is to be tried.

Trial Court Arraignment

After the grand jury returns a true bill or after a lower court, through a preliminary hearing, determines that there is probable cause to believe that a crime was committed and probable cause to believe that the accused committed that crime, the accused is bound over to a higher court, a trial court. A defendant may go directly from his initial hearing to the trial court arraignment by waiving his preliminary hearing.

During the arraignment, prior to the actual trial, the accused is told what the charges are against him; he is advised of his constitutional rights and asked how he pleads to the charges. A permanent transcript is maintained of the proceedings, and a judge who may hear felony cases is in charge. The defendant has a choice of several pleas.

The accused person may plead guilty, either to the original charge or to a reduced charge if it is agreeable with the prosecutor. The judge does not have to accept the guilty plea, and if he does not, a plea of not guilty is entered on the court record. If the guilty plea is accepted, sentence may be set immediately. Most states, however, require a presentence investigation of the defendant by the probation department and sentencing is set for a later date.

Nolo contendere (no contest) is another of the possible pleas a defendant may make. By this plea, he states that he is not contesting the charges that were brought against him. This plea is often utilized when a person is facing both criminal and civil charges. It is much the same as a guilty plea, and the accused will be sentenced for his act. However, when the person goes to court on the civil action, he does not have a guilty plea on the court

firemen, police officers, and other public servants fall in this class. Most states have formalized in law the persons not to be called for jury duty on these grounds.

The size of the jury is arbitrary. When the desired number of jurors is chosen, the *voir dire* examination begins. *Voir dire* simply means to speak the truth. During this examination, the judge, the prosecutor, and the defense may ask questions of the prospective jurors. In criminal cases the prosecutor starts the examination; he is followed by the defense.

A member of the jury panel may be excused from sitting on the jury by a challenge from the prosecutor, the defense attorney, or the judge. There are three types of challenges—challenge to the array, challenge for cause, and peremptory challenge. When there is a challenge to the array, the entire jury panel may be excused because of a technical error in its selection. A challenge for cause is used when it is believed that a member of the panel would be a biased or prejudiced juror. Each side may dismiss as many jurors as necessary on challenges for cause. A peremptory challenge is an arbitrary challenge, and each lawyer has a set number. If an attorney does not like the looks of a prospective juror, he may excuse him by using a peremptory challenge.

The functions of the voir dire examination by the prosecution and the defense are as follows:

1. To select jurors most favorable to the position of the attorney asking the questions;
2. To create a favorable atmosphere for the presentation of evidence by the same party;
3. To prepare the jurors for some of the problems that opposing counsel feel may arise during the trial which could be detrimental to their case.[19]

When the prosecution and the defense believe that the members of the jury panel should stay seated as jurors, they proclaim so to the court. The jury is then sworn in and jeopardy to the defendant starts in the jury trial.

Opening Statements. Next in the trial process come the opening statements. The functions of the opening statement by the prosecution or defense are:

1. It acquaints the jury with the testimony to be presented;
2. It may help to create or sustain the type of atmosphere that will put the jurors in the frame of mind to convict or acquit;
3. It prepares the jurors for testimony which the prosecutor or defense attorney knows will occur during the trial which could be detrimental to their side of the case.[20]

The prosecutor is the first to give his opening statement. The defense attorney may follow the prosecutor in giving his opening statement, or he may waive it until the prosecutor rests his case. When giving his opening statement, the prosecutor outlines his case and emphasizes the seriousness of the offense, always talking in a matter-of-fact manner. He is careful not to inject humor into the trial at this point.

Usually the defense attorney gives his opening statement prior to presenting his case, because what he says at that time is more likely to be remembered by the jury. When it is beneficial to his case, however, he will give his opening statement after the prosecuting attorney:

1. If he does not intend to put any witnesses on the stand himself, this is the only chance he has to address the jury prior to closing argument.
2. If the defense counsel feels that the prosecutor's opening statement has been unusually effective, he may wish to provide an antidote to its effect at this early stage in the proceedings.
3. When alibi or temporary insanity is to be the defense, some defense attorneys feel it advisable to make the jury aware of this fact at the beginning of the trial.[21]

When giving his opening statement, the defense attorney will explain his defense sharply and concisely. He may attempt to understate the seriousness of the crime, create side issues, deny that his client committed the crime, or attempt to show that his client committed the act out of ignorance or that his client should be pitied, not punished. After the opening statement, the prosecutor begins his case.

The Prosecution's Case. While the prosecutor is presenting his case, he places his witnesses under direct examination. During his questioning, he may not phrase his questions in such a way as to suggest an answer. The defense attorney cross-examines the prosecutor's witnesses. In doing this, he *may* ask questions that suggest an answer. When the defense attorney presents his case, the roles of the attorneys are reversed; the defense attorney conducts direct examination and the prosecutor conducts cross-examinations.

The prosecutor must prove his case beyond a reasonable doubt. If the judge feels that he has failed to do so when he rests his case, the judge may dismiss the charges. The defendant is now in jeopardy so care is taken in this regard by the prosecutor to prevent the guilty from going free.

The order of witnesses is planned by the prosecutor for maximum effect on the jury. The first person he calls to the witness stand is usually a strong witness or one who can establish an element of the offense. All available witnesses must theoretically be called to the stand by the prosecutor, whether they are friendly or hostile to his case. He attempts to present his case chronologically from each person called to the stand. The prosecutor must appear impartial, not attempting to persecute the accused. The crime itself must remain the center of attention while he presents his side of the case. When he has completed the testimony of a witness to his satisfaction, the prosecution rests with his witness.

The defense attorney then begins his cross-examination. He may not ask questions covering material that was not discussed under direct examination. After asking questions to ascertain the truthfulness of the witness and his testimony, the defense rests.

The prosecutor may then conduct a redirect examination of the witness. He may ask only questions regarding new material that arose in the cross-examination.

The defense attorney may then recross-examine the witness on new material that came out of the redirect examination. When the prosecutor believes that he has retrieved all possible evidence from the prosecutor's witnesses, he concludes his examination of the witness.

When the prosecutor has presented all his witnesses in this manner and has extracted all the testimony he believes is necessary, he rests his case.

The Defense's Case. When the prosecutor rests his case, the defense attorney has the opportunity to present his witnesses. Prior to this, however, the defense attorney may make a motion for dismissal of the charges against his client because the prosecutor has failed to prove the charges beyond a reasonable doubt. If this attempt fails and the defense attorney has not given his opening statement prior to this time, he may do so.

If the defense attorney calls witnesses, he must call his first witness and place that witness under direct examination. The defense attorney may attempt to cloud the central issue and create side issues. He may attempt to place the blame for the crime or its actual commission on somebody else. He usually attempts to gain sympathy for his client.

The Fifth Amendment to the Constitution protects a person from self-incrimination. It states, "No person . . . shall be compelled in any criminal case to be a witness against himself." If the defendant does not testify, the prosecutor may make no comment about this fact to the jury. The judge often explains this right of the defendant to the jury when he gives the jury its instructions.

After the defense attorney extracts all pertinent information from a witness under direct examination, he concludes with this witness. The prosecutor then cross-examines the witness to check the testimony for truthfulness. As with witnesses called by the prosecution, the defense attorney may then conduct a redirect examination on new material brought out in the cross-examination, and the prosecutor may recross-examine the witness on new material brought out in the redirect examination. After the defense attorney believes that he has elicited all pertinent information from his witnesses, he rests his case.

Prosecutor's Rebuttal. If the prosecutor believes that his case has been weakened by the defense, he may wish to shore it up by recalling witnesses or calling new witnesses to strengthen his case. The defense attorney may cross-examine each witness; the prosecutor may redirect examine; and the defense attorney may recross-examine. After he obtains the information he wants, the prosecutor again rests his case.

The Defense Attorney's Surrebuttal. If any weaknesses have developed in the defense case due to the prosecutor's rebuttal, the defense may call new or additional witnesses in a surrebuttal. The same sequence of cross-examination, redirect examination, and recross-examination is followed. When the desired testimony is extracted, the defense again rests its case.

Closing Arguments. In their closing arguments, the defense attorney and the prosecutor each weave their cases from the testimony given and explain them to the jury. Each argues for a verdict favorable to his side. They may argue for two different verdicts on the basis of the same facts.

The prosecutor is the first to give his closing argument (also called a summation). He is followed by the defense attorney. Then the prosecutor gets another chance to talk to the jury. The defense attorney has one opportunity to give his argument to the jury; the prosecutor has two.

The prosecutor attempts to show that hc is impartial in his argument. He does not wish to have the guilty party go free,

> Therefore, as an undertone to his argument, he weaves into it the seriousness of the offense, the need to protect the public safety, the duty of the jury not to allow sympathy to enter into its deliberations, and the fact that once the jurors have performed their sworn duty of rendering a verdict, the sentencing is the sole responsibility of the judge.[22]

The defense attorney attempts to show the results of the testimony in a different light:

> He may do any of the following, singly or in combination: emphasize as more important those fragments of testimony or evidence that favor his case; interpret apparently unfavorable facts in a way favorable to the defendant; hammer at the weak link in the prosecution's case, and attack the credibility of a principal prosecution witness. In a murder case, if possible, he will try to discredit the deceased.[23]

Instructions to the Jury. After the closing arguments are completed, the judge sums up the case. He usually meets in private with the prosecutor and defense attorney. Together they agree on the instructions to be given the jury. The judge explains the law pertaining to the offense, including the element and amount of proof needed. The judge then charges the jury to give a true and just verdict.

Deliberation and Verdict. After instructions by the judge, the jurors are escorted out of the courtroom by the bailiff. They are taken to a jury room, where the bailiff shields them from public contact. The jury may request additional material on the case or additional instructions from the judge. The judge usually allows them to have this material. The jury also selects a foreman.

In criminal cases a unanimous verdict is needed for a conviction. Failure to reach a unanimous verdict results in a hung jury, and a new trial in front of a new judge and jury may be ordered. If a verdict of not guilty is rendered, the defendant is given his freedom and is immune from any future prosecution on the same charge. After the jury reaches the verdict, their foreman announces the verdict to the court. Each member of the jury may be polled to verify his or her individual verdict.

Motions for a New Trial. At this point the defense attorney may move for a new trial or a mistrial. His motion is usually based on some error that occurred during the trial or a new revelation regarding the case. It could be based on misconduct of the judge, jury, or bailiff that may have threatened or damaged the defendant's chances to obtain a not guilty verdict.

> Defense may move for a new trial or for a mistrial if any error or irregularity prevented justice from being served. He may point out errors of the judge in admitting or excluding evidence, in directing or charging the jury, for a finding contrary to law or evidence, or for being absent during the trial. He may point out misconduct of the jury in casting lots to decide the verdict, in receiving evidence out of court, or in communicating with outsiders. He may point out that the defendant was absent during part of the trial, or he may point out that newly discovered evidence would serve to clear the accused.[24]

If the motion for a new trial is sustained by the judge, the jury is dismissed and the verdict is set aside. A new trial is scheduled, and the defendant may be set free on bail or remanded back to custody in jail. If the motion is overruled, the judge proceeds by either passing sentence or setting the date for sentencing.

If a new trial is ordered, the case is returned to the court of original jurisdiction. If the earlier decision is upheld in a second trial, another appeal can be made to the state supreme court, where the same alternatives are present. The final step of appeal is to the U.S. Supreme Court, but that court will hear only cases in which a constitutional issue is in question. Only rarely is a case on appeal heard before the U.S. Supreme Court. The basis of appeal must be significant abuse or neglect of a constitutional right.

The Sentence. At the conclusion of the trial, the judge usually orders a presentence investigation by the probation department. The sentence is usually given after this investigation is completed. This short delay between the end of the trial and sentencing means that justice is not as swift as it could be, but the extra time gives the court a chance to determine the proper sentence for the individual defendant.

The judge usually determines the sentence. In some states the jury may determine the sentence in murder or rape cases, but this practice may soon be abolished because of the jury's unfamiliarity with the individual involved and with sentencing procedure. Passing of the sentence itself may be placed in the hands of the sentencing courts so that a more uniform system of sentencing may be established.

The sentence may consist of a fine, imprisonment, restitution for damages, probation, death, mandatory medical or mental hospital institutionalization, confiscation of property, and/or the forfeiture or disqualification from holding public office.

In a judgment that involves a fine, the defendant is required to pay a monetary sum. A fine is usually used when the person on trial is not a danger to society but nevertheless must be punished for his wrongdoing. Fines are usually considered a light form of punishment.

If the judge determines that the accused will be sent to a correctional institution, he may set the punishment between the minimum and maximum sentences established by law. For example, if breaking and entering calls for a minimum sentence of four years and a maximum of ten years, the judge's sentence may be six to ten years in prison. He has leeway between the minimum and maximum sentences.

The judge may break the rules of sentencing procedure or circumvent the intent of state laws pertaining to specific crimes. For example, a state law may require that a person using a gun during an armed robbery receive a mandatory two-year sentence in prison. The judge, however, may place the person on probation.

In giving an indeterminate sentence, the judge does not set a specific length for incarceration. This sentence is based on the assumption that reform takes place in the correctional system. The correctional officers are given the discretion to determine when the criminal has reformed. They may then set him free on the grounds that any further serving of a sentence would be useless.

When the punishment involves restitution for damages, the defendant is required to make good the injury or loss. If the criminal act was vandalism, the person may be forced to pay for any damages he caused. If the act was assault, the person may be forced to pay any hospital costs incurred by the victim. This is also a mild form of punishment, used when the criminal is not a danger to society. It is often used when sentencing white-collar criminals.

Another possible sentence, mentioned before, is probation. If the judge believes that the person will be more receptive to rehabilitation in society rather than in an institution, he may place that person on probation. Probation can be an effective tool in correcting offenders. The probationer may be placed under the supervision of a probation officer and must abide by certain rules made by the court (often on the recommendation of the probation officer). These rules may be lax or strict; they may govern who the probationer is allowed to associate with, where he may work, his mobility, and his behavior. Failure to abide by these rules can result in the probationer's being placed in a correctional institution for the remainder of the probationary period. If the probationer obeys the rules set up for him for the desired amount of time, he is set free again. If the offender is found guilty of a second crime, the punishment for the second crime will probably be more severe.

In the United States probation is not used as effectively as it could be. The staff and budget of probation departments are too meager. Taxpayers are not always persuaded that if they are to stem crime, they must place money in the correctional system to rehabilitate offenders. Probation departments could use such money to supervise and care for offenders and help them become functioning members of society.

In the mid-1970s, the death penalty was in effect banned in most states by the U.S. Supreme Court because the state statutes were not explicit enough. Some states have now rectified their statutes to reinstate this penalty. It is not a proven fact that this penalty has any deterrent effect. Criminals do not intend to get caught when they commit a crime, and the death penalty is strictly a punishment contrary to all rehabilitation logic.

In sentencing, the judge may also require the convicted person to be committed to a medical or mental institution. Drug addicts or alcoholics who commit crimes may be sentenced to drug abuse centers to overcome their addiction. Mentally disturbed criminals may be sent to mental institutions for treatment and for the protection of society. This treatment, in both cases, is designed to allow the criminal to be reformed and to return to society.

A convicted felon may be disqualified from holding public office or barred from certain professions, such as medicine or law. He may be refused government jobs. A problem has arisen from the tendency of employers not to hire persons who have ever been convicted of a felony. When one of these persons has completed his sentence and tries to reenter the job market, he cannot get a job. And unemployment can reinforce whatever antisocial tendencies he may have. Perhaps even more serious is the case of a person who is denied employment because he was once arrested, even if the charges were dismissed. This kind of situation could be avoided if it were mandatory that police departments return all information in their files pertaining to such persons. In this way a person seeking employment would not be persecuted for a crime he did not commit.

Civil Court Processes

When a person has suffered a civil wrong, he may take the wrongdoer to court for a redress of grievances. As mentioned earlier, the plaintiff has the burden of proving the wrongdoing of the second party. He does not have to prove his case beyond a reasonable doubt, but he must prove it with a preponderance of evidence.

Most civil actions are settled out of court, so the pretrial processes are very important. When the plaintiff first approaches an attorney, the attorney must gain as much information as possible about the incident and decide whether the plaintiff has grounds for pursuing the matter.

Settlement Tactics

Prior to taking the case to court, the plaintiff's attorney must weigh certain factors. He must consider what the possible prejudices of the jury may be in the matter at hand, and he must consider the best interests of the client. If the client could obtain a reasonable settlement out of court, the attorney probably will recommend that the client accept it, because if the client goes to trial he may get nothing.

Settlement negotiations must take into account how the jury may be expected to react to the particular facts of the case: the nature of the injury, the nature of the liability, who it is that is being sued and who it is that is suing.[25]

The Trial

If all attempts to gain a fair out-of-court settlement for the plaintiff have been exhausted, a trial will be scheduled.

Choosing the Jury. Jury selection in civil cases is conducted in much the same manner as it is in criminal matters. As in misdemeanor trials, seven persons are selected. Six of these persons serve as jurors and one serves as an alternate.

During the voir dire examination, as in criminal trials, the jurors may be challenged as an array, for cause, and on a peremptory challenge. Questioning of the jurors for the voir dire examination is started by the plaintiff's attorney. The defense then gets its turn to ask questions. When the defense and the plaintiff believe that they have reached the goal of a fair and impartial jury, they advise the court that they are satisfied. The jurors are then sworn in and the opening statements begin.

The Opening Statement. When the attorney for the plaintiff addresses the jury for the first time, he usually has their undivided attention. He must attract and retain this attention while presenting his case. The opening statement allows him to explain clearly to the jury the facts that he is attempting to prove.

Because the American people frequently support the underdog, he must show the jury that an injustice was committed against his client by the defendant. He may also attempt to show the jury how this situation can be corrected through a verdict with compensation.

The defense attorney in his turn must show that his client was not responsible for the bad luck of the plaintiff. He may attempt to shift the blame for the occurrence to a second person or even to the plaintiff himself. The defense attorney will advise the jury what he will attempt to prove while presenting his case so that the jury may follow the case closely with some sort of outline.

Both attorneys will attempt to explain to the jury that the information received from a witness is more important than the manner of its presentation, particularly when either side must call a witness who performs poorly under examination or who does not appear to be very intelligent. If either side presents scientific evidence, that attorney will also explain to the jury why this evidence is being used and what it is meant to prove.

The Direct Examination. During direct examination, the plaintiffs and defense attorneys attempt to question a number of witnesses called to the stand. They take care, out of court, to show the witnesses the type of questions that will be asked of them. The testimony should not be rehearsed, but the lawyers must find ways to extract the desired information from the witness. They caution scientific witnesses to explain their scientific findings in a language the jury can understand while still giving all the information required.

The first witness for the plaintiff is usually one who can place blame for the incident on the defendant. He is likely to be a good witness, because he will face the brunt of the cross-examination of the defense. The defense attorney attempts to prove that the defendant was not responsible for the act in question by showing evidence that runs counter to the evidence presented by the plaintiff.

Cross-Examination. During the cross-examination, the plaintiffs and defense attorneys attempt to cast doubt on the evidence given by the witnesses of the opposing side. Cross-examination serves two purposes: "Generally speaking, there are two things: to prove 'recollection' of events from 'reconstruction' and to test motivation and interest."[26] If a witness may benefit from the verdict, his testimony could possibly be attacked on this basis. Through cross-examination, both sides attack the weak points in the case of the opposite party and test the truthfulness of each witness.

The Final Argument. In the final arguments the defense attorney may try to show that the plaintiff was guilty of contributory negligence—that is, that he was partly responsible for the misfortune. The facts on the opposite side may be attacked on an individual basis or disregarded in their entirety. Each side may bring out different facts favoring its own case. This, in effect, confuses the issue and may be in the defendant's favor.

Charging and Deliberation of the Jury. The judge finally instructs the jury on the applicable laws and advises them about the amount of evidence needed to sustain a verdict. He may give the jury a formula to determine the amount of monetary damages awarded to the plaintiff if the jury rules in the plaintiff's favor.

Summary

The courts in the United States operate on an adversary system. A prosecutor represents the people or the state, and the defense represents the accused. The criminal court process begins with the arraignment of the accused after arrest and booking. The next step is a preliminary hearing, at which it is determined whether or not a felony was committed and whether there is reasonable cause to believe that the accused committed the offense. If there is reasonable cause, the person is bound over to a higher court for the actual trial. The adversary system then comes into effect with each side presenting its evidence and witnesses. Each side also cross-examines the opposing side's witnesses and questions admittance of various evidence. The court procedure ends with the verdict by the jury, and, depending on the verdict, the sentencing of the convicted person by the judge.

The civil court process is much the same as the criminal court process. Some pretrial tactics allow for settling out of court in much the same way as plea-bargaining tactics in the criminal process. If there is no settlement, the case goes to trial, and the same kinds of exchanges between attorneys occur as in the criminal court process—presenting evidence and witnesses and so on. There is no sentencing in the civil court. Normally, the jury decides whether the plaintiff will receive an award; the size and type are based on the judge's instruction to the jury.

CHAPTER **5**

The American Correctional System

Considering alternatives to prisons is like seeking a permanent end to war. A drastic reordering of American priorities would be necessary for significant, practical change to take place.

One could consider several theoretical alternatives in passing. Public shaming in stocks was an effective method used by the Puritans. Drug control of society's deviants has been offered as another alternative. Aldous Huxley, for example, developed this idea in his novels *Brave New World* and *Island*. In *Brave New World* eugenics and drugs controlled all but a few dissidents. For these few, exile was offered as an alternative to adjustment in the "perfect" society. Historically, exile has been a viable substitute for prison, as evidenced by the fact that Georgia and Australia were settled by England's felons.

Background and History

For most convicted criminals exile is not necessary. The professional literature on prisons is almost unanimous in its judgment that only dangerous offenders need be held in total isolation from society. This group makes up no more than 20 percent of all inmates. For the remainder, except for those who are mentally ill and should be treated as such, the idea of dealing with offenders within the community holds the most promise. The National Crime Commission recommended small facilities, located as close as possible to the areas from which they would draw their inmates—in or near the city rather than in a remote location. Rooms would have doors rather than bars. Inmates would eat at small tables in an informal atmosphere. They would have access to classrooms, recreation facilities, dayrooms, a shop, and a library. But education, vocational training, and other such activities would be carried on in the community at large, and parole officers would help arrange for participation by offenders in community activities and would guide and counsel them. Inmates could leave the facility by day for work or study and return at night. This model approximates that of the halfway house, where parolees live to ease their transition to community life. But while halfway houses are available to only a few parolees, these treatment centers would serve the majority of those convicted.

This approach to the problem of prisons hardly seems utopian, but it is doubtful that the American public is quite ready for a system that emphasizes adjustment instead of retribution and control. To many, such a program would seem to give special treatment to lawbreakers, while the "law-abiding" put up with poor services of all kinds. Society has so far been reluctant to spend on rehabilitation the money it now spends for punishment.

Study after study has shown that prisons fail to do the job we expect. They do not reform; at the most, they provide society with a means of retribution for crimes committed. Imprisonment of law-breakers is an easy way for society to identify its scapegoats.

The earliest behavioral norms were developed by groups of people as folkways and customs. They were simply the habitual ways of doing things. An expedient for adjustment of social ills among primitive people was the blood feud, in which one family avenged the wrongs to its members by assaulting or killing the offender or members of his family. Primitive man had no conception of "crime" or of "private property." He did know when his brother had been killed, but he did not rely on expert witnesses or rational proof. In case of doubt, he relied on oaths and ordeals. Primitive man was a slave to custom but recognized an obligation as binding only when he had received equivalence—one basis of the civil law of primitive society.

While deviation from these folkways and customs was not illegal, it did concern other persons in the group whose anticipation and prediction of expected behavior had been violated. As man became further civilized, he began to attach emotional values to some of these customs, and certain things became "right" and "wrong."

With the development of organized primitive religion, conceivably around 25,000 B.C., creeds emerged to control the interaction among people within the social formation. The creeds controlled social behavior and were more complex and refined than the early folkways and customs.[1]

When criminal law first emerged, the theory was that man was reasonable and behaved of his own free choice. This approach was known as the classical school of criminology, and the key to its practical application was "Let the punishment fit the crime." During the early part of the twentieth century, significant moves were made relating to the field of corrections. In 1908 England began the Borstal institutions, which were minimum security schools for delinquent youth. Belgium began classifying prisoners.

"Corrections is defined as the community's official reactions to the convicted offender, whether adult or juvenile."[2]

Corrections clearly has many purposes. It is important to recognize that correctional purposes can differ for various types of offenders. In sentencing a convicted murderer, society usually serves punitive and deterrent rather than rehabilitative purposes. The contrary is true with respect to a deprived, ill-educated, vocationally incompetent youth who is adjudged delinquent; with him, rehabilitation and reintegrative purposes predominate.

The American penal system had two principal models. The Pilgrims, who left England because of social injustices, brought with them criminal codes almost as severe as those they left behind. The only exception to those harsh colonial laws was the "Great Law" of William Penn, embodying the comparatively humane Quaker criminal code. The Quakers provide the keystone for penal reform in America. This New World reform was accompanied by parallel developments in England and on the continent. Following the revolutions that brought democracy to France and America, the Quakers developed strong allies in their drive for humane treatment of offenders and in the substitution of imprisonment for corporal and capital punishment.

In 1794 Pennsylvania adopted a new code that made first-degree murder the only capital crime and prescribed imprisonment for other offenses. The Quakers began the "penitentiary," and the word was taken from the Quaker concept of giving a man a Bible and putting him in a cell to repent.

Whether the productive labor of the prisoner was to be given priority over his moral regeneration became the basis of a long conflict between the Quaker model penitentiary constructed at Cherry Hill, Pennsylvania, in 1829 and the Puritan prison built at Auburn, New York, in 1823. The objective of the Quaker penitentiary system was to save the sinner through reflection and penitence. The objective of the Puritan system, on the other hand, was to produce obedient citizens. Prisoners at Auburn were confined to solitary cells at night and during the day worked together under a rule of silence. Since the "congregate" or Auburn system was copied in one form or another in many states, the Puritan model became the prevalent prison system in the United States until the Civil War, when industrialized prison labor for profit increased. Following the Civil War, however, the radical changes that shook the nation's economy had an adverse effect on prison industries, and prison overcrowding began to alter the Auburn single-cell theory.

At the turn of the twentieth century, reforms included construction of heating and toilet facilities, provision of health and medical services, and provision for athletic activities. Although many prisons remained industrialized, pressure against prison-made goods was mounting, and by the 1930s federal legislation virtually ended the sale of prison goods. World War II saw the introduction of the concept of "classification," which was used initially in relation to security. Classification is the correctional process of dividing offenders based on known characteristics for security and treatment purposes. During the 1940s, too, prisons began to open their gates to a limited number of teachers, social workers, and psychologists.

In the 1950s and 1960s little advancement in penal reform was made, although a small number of progressive institutions made headway in developing concepts aimed at rehabilitating the prisoner rather than maintaining a system directed toward the eighteenth and nineteenth centuries' focus on retribution, penitence, and punishment.

In the United States today the differences among offenders do not account for the differences among correctional facilities. Procedures can be traced to historical development, admininstrative fragmentation, and divergent and unreconciled purposes and theories.

The federal government, all fifty states, the District of Columbia, the Commonwealth of Puerto Rico, most of the country's 3,047 counties, and all except the smallest cities engage in correctional activities—if only maintaining a small jail in which to lock up overnight those who are "drunk and disorderly." Each level of government typically acts independently of the others. The federal government has no direct control over state corrections. The states usually have responsibility for prisons and parole programs, but probation is frequently tied to court admininstration as a county or municipal function. Counties do not have jurisdiction over the jails operated by cities and towns.

The responsibility for the administration of corrections is divided not only among levels of government, but also within single jurisdictions. There has been a strong tendency historically, for juvenile and adult corrections to follow separate paths. Public support for rehabilitative programs first developed in connection with juveniles.

In many instances it is difficult to determine the objective of the institutional administration and program. As far as the public is concerned, the objective appears to be protection as opposed to punishment or treatment. The public is favorably disposed to education and religion, but there is little consensus about anything else. Prison riots and escapes seem to produce apprehension for the safety of residents in the areas surrounding prisons.

The attitude of the public is related to the type of administration that prevails at any institution, since it influences the political leadership, which in turn appoints the prison administrator. The system of appointment, or influence, has resulted in three broad classifications of styles of prison administrations. First, many prison administrators want to exert complete control, "to be on top of any situation," and leave no doubt as to who is in charge. Their need for control results in rigidly regimented prisons with strict rules and harsh discipline. Such a prison is known as a "tough" prison in which tension and apprehension prevail.

Second, many correctional administrators are political appointees without much knowledge of correctional procedures. This type of administrator tends to simplify procedures so that prison life may be as nearly "normal" as possible. The result is an institution in which discipline is used sparingly and only when necessary, and where a significant treatment program is lacking. The prime objective is to run the institution as quietly as possible.

Third, the prison may be treatment-oriented, generally headed by admininstrators whose careers have been committed to the field of corrections. The type of "treatment" may vary widely from programs placing a heavy emphasis on education and training, such as those found in many reformatories and smaller correctional institutions for youthful offenders, to the sophisticated treatment programs based on group living and guided group interaction.

The effective supervisor is not born; he becomes effective through training and experience. There is no question that some prison supervisors have personal qualities that make them more effective than others. Generally, however, the use of certain techniques will result in an effective supervisory approach. The effective supervisor must know his job well, be self-confident and consistent in temperament, and be able to communicate with others and to recognize individual differences.

Jails, prisons, and almost all other agencies of the criminal justice system have had problems recruiting personnel for a number of reasons. In almost all cases low salary and unattractive working conditions make it difficult for jails to compete in the labor market with local industries. In the majority of jails surveyed by the National Crime Commission, starting salaries were found to be under $6,000 a year. Another significant factor is the low status of work in corrections. A public survey of attitudes toward correctional work found that people considered it an unattractive career, ranking it below military and police work. The same survey revealed that people have least confidence in prison guards when compared with other law enforcement personnel and consider their jobs the least rewarding in the field of corrections. Jail and workhouse personnel are poorly paid, enjoy little status, and are generally required to have little education; the same is true of prison guards, whose work is comparable and is carried on in similar circumstances.

Thus, the jail administrator in carrying out his responsibilities in personnel management must try to find answers to a number of vital questions. How can the work be made more attractive? How can the status of the work be improved? Will an increase in salaries improve the status of the work and facilitate recruiting? How can salaries be increased? How can the performance level of persons now on the job be upgraded? Obviously, the answers to these questions are interrelated. For example, the status of a position will not change as long as the salary and the personal and educational requirements remain low. Nor will the status of the work improve as long as the level of skill required to perform it remains low.

In order for a jail administrator to solve his personal problems, he should make use of personnel in local government. He should realize, however, that such persons are technicians and that their usefulness depends on his ability to define the problems and make his personal needs known. The administrator who is not interested in change will have little difficulty defining the needs, for he will use traditional methods to fill traditional jobs. He may or may not be successful, depending on local economic conditions and labor supply, but he will not be able to meet the increased need for capable people in changing times.[3]

Community-Based Correction

Probation is a judicial function in which the convicted offender is formally placed under the supervision of court personnel, usu ally a probation officer or probation agent. Probation is the most successful phase of the correctional process because it involves supervision of persons in the community who have not entered the criminal justice system very far. The presentence investigation report prepared by the probation officer can constructively influence all subsequent work with the offender whether on probation, in prison, or on parole. There is a trend toward state control of subsidization of probation because most probation services tend to be in large metropolitan areas. There is considerable need for more and better-trained personnel in the area of probation, for probation serves a larger number of people than prisons and parole combined.[4]

The use of probation as a sentencing alternative began in the United States in the 1840s. Current estimates indicate that slightly over half of all convicted offenders are placed on some kind of probation.

Although there are still problems associated with the use of probation, it appears that probation has an extremely high rate of success. The F.B.I. Uniform Crime Reports show a lower rate of recidivism, or repetition, for offenders who receive probation or a suspended sentence in conjunction with probation than for those who go to prison. In an exhaustive seven-year survey of probation in California, George F. Davis found that about 72 percent of 11,638 adult probationers granted probation in a two-year period completed their probation without having it revoked.

Offenders can be kept under probationary supervision in the community at a cost far below that required for incarceration. The average state, for instance, spends $4,000 to $8,000 a year to keep a youth in a state training school, while it costs only about one-tenth as much to keep him on probation. Similarly, the cost of keeping an adult prisoner in an institution runs from $3,000 to $6,000 a year, while less than $1,500 is needed to keep the offender on probation at an adequate supervision level.

The California Probation Subsidy Program is an example of how corrections can be made less costly and more effective by keeping the offender in the community. In the last five years approximately 15,000 California offenders who ordinarily would have spent time in prison were kept in their home communities. Instead of spending $6,500 a year to maintain each inmate in a state institution, the state spends $4,000 a year per inmate on intensive probation. The state has saved $196 million in new prison construction.[5]

Release from prison can be by parole, by discharge, by conditional or mandatory release, by pardon or general amnesty, by return on court order for a new trial, by death, or by escape. About 61 percent of the releases from prisons in this country are by parole.

Parole is the conditional release of a prisoner before his sentence has been completed. Its use in the United States dates back to the 1870s. Today, estimates indicate that 60 percent of all adult felons are released on parole prior to expiration of their sentences. Like probation, parole has proved to be successful as an alternative to incarceration, especially in relieving the chronic overcrowding in the nation's prisons. Unfortunately, parole services suffer from inordinately large caseloads. As a result of the lack of quantity and quality of supervision, too many parolees get in trouble while on parole, causing a recidivism rate which, with proper supervision, could be much lower.

More than half the states and the federal government have combined probation and parole services in the same agency. For example, a Federal probation officer prepares presentence reports and supervises probationers and parolees. These combined systems have generally started in sparsely settled areas where probation services varied so widely that they were incorporated in the state parole system to provide some uniformity. In many cases the combined system was a vehicle by which the state parole officers could be made available to prepare sentence investigations for local judges. Combined probation and parole services generally result in greater supervision of parolees, because this is where the greatest need is. The preparation of presentence reports became most important because it is a tangible service provided to local courts that can be counted, seen, used, and included in annual reports.

One duty of a parole officer is to provide liaison between the paroling authority and the institution, particularly when certain problems arise concerning release of parolees. Sometimes the institutional parole officers from the area hold pre-parole preparation school. On occasion, outside employers, law enforcement officers, Chamber of Commerce representatives, and other persons from the community lecture and discuss problems of reentry into society. Increasingly, employers or prospective employers are less concerned with what the inmates have done in the past than with what they can do now. Supportive peer associations, continuity between institutional and community vocational training programs and employers, and proposals to involve community leaders, influential employers, service agencies, and school officials are all important in improving the parole program.

When a parolee takes a job, it is general practice for only the personnel officer of the company, the parolee, and the parole officer to know that he is on parole. When he arrives on the job, however, he frequently encounters other former convicts whom he recognizes or who recognize him. The approach most employers take is that if anybody learns that he has served time or is an ex-convict, it is generally not the fault of the management but the fault of the parolee himself or other parolees who work in the company. Parolees are generally instructed not to conceal their parolee status from official records but not to advertise it to the general public. The parole officer generally points up the problems that previous parolees have had and, on the basis of experience, attempts to make prospective parolees aware of these problems.

Many prisoners are suspicious of authority and tend to consider all people unsupportive. It is essential to orient inmates as to official action and the reasons for it. After the parole board leaves, inmates talk in the cell block and in the prison yard about what was done and why. They want to know why some people received parole and others were "flopped." Many parole officers holding pre-parole preparation classes find it difficult to explain all the nuances and minor factors that enter into a parole decision and simply indicate that the parole board thought that everybody in the group of parolees had intended to make good in the free world. Further, it was the parole board's judgment that those chosen for parole had the ability to make good. Some of the inmates who were not parolled also intended to make good, but their capabilities of doing so were considered in doubt.

Supervision of Parolees

Parolees are more difficult to supervise than are probationers generally if the criterion is success in casework or treatment supervision. While probationers are often grateful that they have not been sent to prison, parolees have been sent to prison as poor risks for probation. In addition, they have been conditioned by an average of slightly more than two years of institutionalization in an adult prison or correctional institution. The parolee has learned to "play the odds" in prison, acquiescing to authority on a superficial basis while maintaining his basic behavioral pattern essentially unchanged. Many parolees have learned to manipulate their way through social situations and official contacts with authority in the form of prison personnel, parole boards, and parole officers. They have learned the poker-faced social veneer that makes diagnosis and evaluation difficult. They regard the parole officer as another prison official.

Successful parole supervision involves casework service with the parolee and his family, a good relationship with the police, and a thorough knowledge of all available employers in the area who will hire parolees. Consequently, the parole officer has an unusual mixture of roles.[6]

Prison Programs

The current emphasis on prison and community corrections programs is changing and will continue to change the role of prisons. The prison administrator bears the primary responsibility for creating change in the prison and thus has a central role in program development. This role is primarily an exercise in leadership—identifying program objectives, making them understood and accepted by prison personnel, and selecting program specialists and coordinating their activities. In order to introduce programs for the prisoners and to use program specialists effectively, the administrator must understand the objectives of program planning, the information requirements, and the development problems that can arise.

The task of corrections has been and still is to build bridges to the community to help the offender maintain, strengthen, or develop ties with the community. This trend has resulted from recognition of the fact that the institution is an unnatural environment that does not permit the offender to learn to solve problems, make decisions, or develop new behavior patterns. The limitations of the institution have required the development of new programs and administrative arrangements to implement them.

Work Release

Work release is a means of extending the limits of confinement into the community. The prisoner assigned to work release is evaluated as requiring some supervision during the working day and confinement after working hours. This program permits a great deal of flexibility in sentencing and lends itself to a number of variations. Prisoners may be released for educational or vocational training in the local school, for psychotherapy at a mental health clinic, or for employment counseling. Thus, economic use is made of community facilities and the burden of developing expensive programs in the jail is avoided.[7] When a jail does not have a bail program, pretrial prisoners can be confined during nonworking hours and weekends, permitting them to continue working or to prepare their defense.

Work release has the advantage of bringing the jail, the prisoner, and the community together into a comprehensive correctional effort. It places the burden for change on the prisoner and exposes him to the reality of day-to-day problems and responsibilities in the community and on the job. At the same time, the prisoner is serving a sentence under the amount of restraint felt necessary to achieve an acceptable level of law-abiding performance. The program has general application; it can be operated in almost all jails with few additional requirements in terms of staff, budgeting, or space.

Education and Literacy Programs

Education and literacy programs in the jail or prison can be implemented using either paid employees or volunteers. An educational program can be either specific or general; its objectives can be to begin an educational process that can be continued in the community when the offender is released or to assist the offender in securing a high school equivalency certificate while he is confined.

A general education program would be concerned with teaching certain skills. In one community program, volunteers taught courses in the jail, including needlecraft, typing, personal grooming, nursing, and arts and crafts. Although this program did not have a specific educational objective, it enriched the inmates' activities.

Treatment of Alcoholics

Many jails now have Alcoholics Anonymous programs, although a comprehensive program for treating alcoholics should not be limited to an AA chapter. It should include, in addition, medical care, group or individual therapy, a job placement service to help the prisoner when he is released, and procedures for introducing the offender into the local AA group when his sentence is completed. The jail and the community AA groups must have close ties to enable prisoners to make the transition from the jail program to the program in the community.

Counseling

A counseling program can be tailored to meet the specific needs of the jail population; it may be staffed by lay counselor volunteers, professionally trained volunteers, or paid professional personnel. The program can include group psychotherapy conducted by professionals, employment counseling, counseling to alcoholics, or supportive counseling for work release prisoners. Counseling can also be extended to the community to include the prisoners permitted to attend.

Types of Correctional Institutions

Most correctional institutions in the United States today are huge maximum security prisons symbolized by walls and guns or by a myriad of more subtle inhibitions of personal liberty that arise from the isolation and alienation of the institutional community and the inmate society from the outside world. There inhibitions include the strangeness of living apart from families with no choice about place of residence, selection of intimate associates, or type of occupation—all crucial values that are taken for granted in the outside world. The restraints have both advantages and disadvantages. On one hand they may serve the function of punishment and deterrence. They also prevent the dangerous offender from committing further crimes in the community during the term of his sentence. And they keep him apart from the conditions of community life and subject him to a special environment that can be controlled. On the other hand, an artificial environment that works against self-reliance and self-control often complicates and makes more difficult the reintegration of offenders into free society. Sometimes institutions foster conspicuously deleterious conditions—idleness, corruption, brutality, and moral deterioration.

There are may ways in which the advantages of institutionalization can be exploited and the disadvantages minimized. For many offenders, institutionalization can be an extremely valuable prelude to community treatment. For a few—those who must be incapacitated for society's protection if not their own—it may be the only possible alternative.

As mentioned earlier, a model institution would be relatively small and located as close as possible to the area from which it draws its inmates. While it might have a few high-security units for short-term detention under unusual circumstances, difficult and dangerous inmates would be sent to other institutions for longer confinement. Architecturally, the model institution would resemble as much as possible a normal residential setting, and classrooms and recreation facilities would be available, although most education and vocational training would take place in the community or would draw community-based resources into the institution.

Even in institutions committed to longer term custody, many steps can be taken short of this model to improve their capacity to contribute to the reintegration of offenders. The most fundamental of these changes may be summed up as the establishment of a collaborative regime in which the staff and inmates work together toward rehabilitative goals, and unnecessary conflict between the two groups is avoided.

Most offenders are severely handicapped by educational deficiencies and prevented from succeeding in a labor market that increasingly demands at least high school education. One of the most promising approaches to this problem is the use of programmed learning techniques. Special texts and machines present the material to be learned in small units. The student must master each part before he proceeds to the next. He goes at his own pace. It then becomes possible to use a variety of incentives and rewards for achievement.

Vocational training can best be carried out in conjunction with operating prison industries. In the absence of good industrial programs, maintenance and details are usually so heavily overmanned that offenders do not learn from them the habit of working independently and with dispatch.

Prison-made goods tend to be inferior in design and workmanship compared to those available from private enterprise. Delivery has been unreliable, and despite availability of cheap prison labor, the products frequently cost more than similar items that are privately produced. This is the result of many factors, including the small size of prison shops, the lack of strong administrative support for industrial programs, and the lack of imaginative and aggressive sales operations.

Possible solutions to these problems might include states' working with the federal government to institute modern correctional industry programs in prisons aimed at rehabilitation of offenders through instilling good work habits and methods as well as modification and repeal of state and federal laws restricting sale of prison-made products.

Even within the limitations of most existing institutions, the transition from institution to community can be made less abrupt and the resources of community institutions drawn upon to help in rehabilitation. Short-term furloughs from institutions have been used most extensively in Mississippi and Michigan, each of which has reported less than 1 percent failure to return. Juvenile institutions have used such procedures successfully, though parsimoniously, at family gathering times such as Christmas, Thanksgiving, weddings, and funerals. Furloughs are useful in helping prevent the deterioration of family ties and in allowing offenders to try new skills and test the insights they have developed in counseling experiences.[8]

The most striking increase in temporary release from institutions in recent years has been in work release programs. Introduced in Wisconsin institutions for misdemeanants over forty years ago, their use spread slowly until large-scale extension to adult felons began in North Carolina in 1959. Favorable experience there led to work-release provisions for federal prisoners under the Prisoner Rehabilitation Act of 1965.

No part of corrections is weaker than local facilities that handle persons awaiting trial and serving short sentences. Because their inmates do not seem to present a clear danger to society, the response to their needs has usually been one of indifference. Their crimes are considered petty, and the sentences they serve are relatively short. Many local jails and misdemeanant institutions are administered by the police or county sheriffs, authorities whose experience and main concern are in other fields. The facilities lack well-developed recreational and counseling programs, sometimes even medical services. The first offender, the innocent awaiting trial, sometimes juveniles and women are imprisoned with confirmed criminals, drunks, and the mentally disturbed or retarded.

Local jails and misdemeanant institutions should be integrated into state correctional systems and not be operated by law enforcement agencies. Rehabilitative programs and other reforms need to be instituted. Other needed reforms include providing separate detention facilities for juveniles and facilities outside the correctional system for abandoned, neglected, or runaway children. Whenever possible, persons awaiting trial should be housed and handled separately from offenders.[9]

A core responsibility in all phases of the correctional process is gathering and analyzing the information about the offender that will provide an adequate basis on which to predicate the series of correctional decisions concerning him.

Whether the decision be to invoke the judicial process, to choose between probation and imprisonment, to select the appropriate degree of security in a correctional institution, to determine the timing for release from incarceration or the necessity for revocation of parole, the judicial and administrative decision-makers are concerned with the following issues:

1. The extent or degree of threat to the public posed by the individual. Clues will be provided by the nature of the present offense and the length of any prior record.
2. The extent of an individual's commitment to criminal values and the nature of his response to any earlier correctional programs.
3. The kind of personal stability and responsibility evidenced in his employment record, residential patterns, and family support history.
4. The kind of personal deficiencies apparent, including educational and vocational training needs.
5. The personal psychological characteristics of the offender that determine how he perceives the world and his relationship to it.

A few correctional research programs are seeking to test the way in which these personal dimensions can be subjected to objective analysis and used as the basis for predicting the probable response to alternative correctional programs. Some progress is evident in both statistical and psychological research experiments.

Central to such evaluation is the necessity for identifying dangerous or habitual offenders who pose a serious threat to the community's safety. These include those individuals whose personal instability is so gross as to erupt periodically in violent and assaultive behavior and those individuals whose long-term exposure to criminal influences has produced a thorough commitment to criminal values that resists superficial efforts to effect change.

Federal support is needed at every significant decision point to strengthen existing screening and diagnostic resources. Classification and assignment of offenders can be made according to their needs and problems, giving separate treatment to all special offender groups when this is desirable. Joining together to operate joint regional facilities and making use of neighboring facilities on a contract basis are necessary to achieve these ends.

The National Advisory Commission on Criminal Justice Standards and Goals suggested the following standards regarding the rights of prisoners: A prisoner should have access to courts, access to legal services, protection against personal abuse, healthful surroundings, medical care, nondiscriminatory treatment, rehabilitation, retention and restoration of rights, reasonable rules of conduct and disciplinary procedures, procedures for nondisciplinary change of status, grievance procedure, free expression and association, exercise of religious beliefs and practices, access to the public, mail, and remedies for violation of an offender's rights. Correctional agencies, said the NACCJSG, should develop explicit standards and administrative procedures to enable those under correctional control to test the fairness of key decisions.

A large share of responsibility for providing impetus and direction to needed changes belongs with the federal government. It should take increasing responsibility for helping to upgrade the correctional programs of state and local government. Ultimately, federal authorities might provide only those direct services that cannot be operated effectively and economically by state and local government. A sizable number of nongovernmental organizations operate nationally to improve correctional practices. They can conduct surveys in states and localities, provide consulting services, and help with the exchange of research and information. Above all, they can inform the public about needs and problems and mobilize the grassroots support required for major change. Ideally, public funds should be made available to help private agencies perform these functions, but it is imperative that they maintain a perspective from outside the system in order to be incisive critics and monitors of its operations.

At present, university curricula generally ignore the field of corrections. Correctional concerns tend to be invisible to students and faculty at both the undergraduate and graduate levels, despite the fact that many disciplines and professions—psychology, sociology, public administration, law, and social work, among others—have legitimate responsibilities in this area. Universities have an indispensable role to play in filling the knowledge gap that exists throughout corrections. Two hazards exist, however: (1) heavily vocational programs that purport to answer questions about how to perform correctional functions without addressing the complexities of what and why and thus further isolate corrections from the university community, and (2) the reluctance of scholars to address the specific problems faced by those charged with the perplexing task of controlling and rehabilitating offenders.

The costs of action are substantial, but the costs of inaction are immensely greater. Inaction would mean, in effect, that the nation would continue to avoid, rather than confront, one of its most critical social problems, that it would accept for the next generation a huge, if not immeasurable, burden of wasted and destructive lives. Decisive action, on the other hand, could make concrete differences in the foreseeable future.

Some of the toughest roots of crime lie buried in the social conditions, especially poverty and racial discrimination, that prevail in the nation's inner cities. These conditions not only make it difficult for millions of Americans to share in America's wealth but make them doubt society's good faith toward them, leaving them disposed to flout the conventional social order. How successfully America reduces and controls crime depends in the end on what it does about employment and education, housing and health, areas far outside the day-to-day job or the ability of the police officer. This is not to say that improvements in the correctional system are beside the point. The point is that improvements in the correctional system can lead to no more than small and short-term successes unless they are executed as part of an overall plan to improve all the nation's systems and institutions.

CHAPTER 6

State and Federal Agencies

Police agents and agencies are authorized to maintain public order and to enforce the law. The terms most frequently apply to local police forces, but other types of police exist as well. Most countries have at least one agency to handle investigative or police work that is national in nature and that concerns national security. Some nations have regional police forces, such as the county and state police in the United States. Military police are a part of the armed forces of many countries. National borders are guarded by special police forces, such as the U.S. Immigration Border Patrol and a branch of the Royal Canadian Mounted Police. In addition, the International Criminal Police Organization (Interpol) encourages cooperation among police of all nations.

State Agencies

Each state has several agencies with policing functions.

State Police and Highway Patrol

All states have either state police or state highway patrol forces. State police have full police powers throughout the state. State highway patrols may have full police powers, or they may have authority to enforce only traffic laws. A commissioner or superintendent appointed by the governor heads each state law enforcement agency.[1] State police are often called troopers because in earlier days they were organized along military lines.

The oldest state police force in the United States is the Texas Rangers, who were organized in 1835 to patrol the borders of Texas. They were a mounted military police force that played an important part in the history of Texas. The Texas Rangers originally numbered about one hundred men in three companies, and their enlistment was for twelve months.

In 1935 the Texas Rangers became part of the state highway police under the Department of Public Safety. Although they now use advanced methods of crime detection, the Rangers' job is still essentially the same as it always has been, to help control emergency situations wherever they occur in the state.

The Pennsylvania State Police were adopted in 1905 when the state legislature passed a law that "created a mounted State constabulary for the purpose of preserving peace and order in the rural districts of that state."[2] Pennsylvania had a peculiar police problem in that the terrain was mountainous and covered a very large area. Also, because of labor problems with the iron and coal industries, some type of law enforcement was needed. The legislature appropriated $425,000 and approximately 230 men were hired.

In 1916 the New York Legislature proposed a system of mounted state police modeled after the Pennsylvania State Constabulary "to prevent crime, to detect and punish criminals and to preserve the peace of the people throughout the country districts."[3] Two hundred and forty-three horses were bought from the Canadian Royal Northwestern Mounted Police and posts were established in different areas. Troopers were to control the roads, watch traffic regulations, enforce quarantine laws at the Indian reservations, raid gambling resorts, and find stolen horses and lost children. The men were to work in pairs, much like the Canadian Mounties.[4]

In 1919 the Michigan Legislature passed an act that authorized the formation of the Michigan State Police, "an organization semi-military in character, but the members of which had the powers of deputy sheriffs and whose duties were those of police officers."[5] Two years later, the State Department of Public Safety was created and the Michigan State Police became part of this department.

Because of the rising crime rate in rural and suburban areas, many states came to believe that there was a need for a state police, an entirely separate body of men working with crime outside the city limits.[6] "The development of state police agencies has not resulted in a state central law enforcement unit which supplants the police of the counties, towns, and villages."[7]

By 1936 twelve states had established separate state agencies exclusively or primarily concerned with state policing. The evolution of the motor car and the extension of good highways made it possible for criminals to travel long distances rapidly. State law enforcement officers, not handicapped by minor jurisdictional limits imposed upon them by law, were able to cope more successfully with the modern criminal.[8]

Each state police unit has developed in its own way, but there does exist an Organization of State and Provincial Police, whose objectives "are carried out by regional and annual meetings, workshops, and other programs for the exchange and dissemination of information to improve management, technical, and operational practices, including public information and support."[9] Each year, this organization publishes a report that represents the cooperative effort of all state police and highway patrol agencies.

State-level police organizations are changing, tending toward expansion of police authority where highway patrols exist. The result could be that all states will, in time, have forces that operate as state police rather than highway patrols. Such a change would reduce cost, improve the quality of service, and eliminate duplication. In order to improve the efficiency of state police agencies and provide more services to local police, many state police and highway patrols have redesigned their entire structure to provide closer supervision of personnel, projects, and duties and to eliminate delays in action. Because of the increase in crime, there is now, more than ever, a demand for improved police services.[10]

Criminalistics Units

The crime laboratory, organized at the state level but available to local law enforcement, is now common in law enforcement.

> Criminalistics—a term which has come to mean the work of the police laboratory—is no longer viewed with an insidious suspicion or subjected to the specious criticisms of those with little knowledge of its nature and even less understanding of its proper applications.[11]

Criminalistics serves an essential function in crime detection and can provide expert testimony for the prosecution in a major case. The National Science Foundation has awarded a number of grants and contracts for research projects that examine the criminal justice system as a whole. Just recently this foundation funded a research project to examine the cost and benefits of the application of scientific technology to the field of law enforcement. The study is being carried out through a $150,000 grant to the Stanford Research Institute.[12] Some state criminalistic units are mobile and can travel throughout the state upon request.

Liquor Control Boards and Commissions

Every state has some form of board or commission charged with licensing and regulating the manufacturing, importing, and sale of alcoholic beverages and assessing and collecting various revenues from their sale. The work of the liquor control board involves the investigation of persons who apply for licenses and enforcement of the state laws that prohibit or regulate the sale, use, possession, dilution, and branding or labeling of alcoholic beverages. These units work closely with local law enforcement agencies and with the Alcohol and Tobacco Tax Division of the Internal Revenue Service.[13]

Department of Motor Vehicles

The department of motor vehicles has several functions. It registers motor vehicles, collects registration fees, and maintains registration records. It also licenses drivers, collects license fees, and maintains files on registered drivers. In some states it also administers the financial responsibility laws. It has the authority to revoke or suspend a license if a person has a bad driving record, and it administratively enforces the implied consent laws where applicable. The department of motor vehicles has the authority to investigate altered or forged documents pertaining to motor vehicles, or alterations on license plates.

Conservation Agencies

Every state has some unit of law enforcement to protect and conserve natural resources. Although most of these organizations operate as state forestry departments, some are divisions of larger organizations, such as conservation or natural resources departments. Each organization varies according to historical background and the development of each state. State foresters are used to protect the timber and watershed areas of the state, to prevent and suppress fires, and to protect the forests from insects and diseases. State fish and game wardens conserve and protect birds, animals, and fish, license fishermen and hunters, and enforce the fish and game laws of the state. State park systems often have their own law enforcement units to protect parks, historical landmarks, beaches, hiking and riding trails, and recreational areas.[14]

> More than 15,000 permanent personnel are employed by the state forestry agencies and, of these, over 3,000 are graduate foresters. Operating budgets of these 50 agencies total over $200 million for all programs. The size of the various forestry departments varies from that of California, which is the largest with 2,500 permanent positions, to that of smaller state organizations which may employ less than 10 full-time people. Generally speaking, the larger forestry departments are found in the Southern States, although California, Washington, New York, Michigan, and Pennsylvania are exceptions.[15]

Bureau of Narcotics

The state bureau of narcotics investigates and enforces the state narcotics laws. Its agents investigate unlawful possessors of drugs, who may unlawfully or negligently dispense them. They also enforce laws pertaining to legitimate dispensation of drugs and the records of their sale. When possible, they seek out illegal drug operations and prosecute the offenders.

Fire Marshal

The health and safety codes of most states provide for a state fire marshal. The fire marshal is often a peace officer. His primary duty is to prevent fires, and he performs the following functions:

1. Study and elimination of fire hazards
2. Investigation of questionable fires
3. Enforcement of fire and panic safety regulations in all public or commercial buildings
4. Development of fire prevention programs
5. Development of educational programs
6. Establishment and enforcement of minimum safety requirements for clothing and fuel industries

Gaming Commission

The state gaming commission has the authority to grant licenses for wagering, lotteries, or any other means of gambling. It also has the duty of granting licenses to establishments to hold bingo games, horse races, or rabbit races. Its goal should be to keep dishonest persons from cheating the public so that every person has the same opportunity to win on a wager.

National Guard Units

In 1802 Congress formed the District of Columbia Militia, from which the present National Guard evolved. The National Guard exists for two purposes: to provide additional military manpower in time of war or national crisis, and to act in emergency situations on order of the president or another federal authority.[16]

Each state has a National Guard Unit. The Second Amendment to the Constitution provides that, "a well-regulated militia being necessary to the security of a free State, the right of the people to keep and bear arms shall not be infringed."

If, in time or war, rebellion, invasion, riot, public calamity, or major catastrophe, the emergency cannot be handled by the ordinary governmental law enforcement or military units, then the militia may be called. The National Guard has the authority to protect the state against disaster when all else fails.[17]

Federal Agencies

Like the states, the federal government has various departments and bureaus with law enforcement powers.

Department of the Treasury

Four major enforcement agencies are administered by the Department of the Treasury: the Bureau of Customs, the Internal Revenue Service, the Secret Service, and the Bureau of Alcohol, Tobacco and Firearms.

Bureau of Customs. The Bureau of Customs, created in 1927, engages in activities for the collection and protection of the revenue; the prevention of fraud and smuggling; and the processing and regulation of people, carriers, cargo, and mail into and out of the United States. It also performs a variety of functions for other government agencies in safeguarding agriculture, business, health, security, and related consumer interests.

Customs is active in suppressing the traffic in illegal narcotics (in conjunction with the Drug Enforcement Administration and in cooperation with foreign governments); in enforcing munitions control in cargo theft prevention; in enforcing regulations affecting articles in international trade where parallel regulations control domestic articles; and in providing for special marking for wool, fur, and textile products (controlled domestically by the Federal Trade Commission).

The Bureau of Customs enforces certain environmental protection programs for other agencies, such as enforcing the prohibition of discharge of refuse and oil into or upon U.S. coastal and navigable water as outlined in the Oil Pollution Act; enforcing laws and regulations regarding wild animals and birds of endangered species and those that might be harmful to community health; enforcing other agriculture and plant quarantine regulations concerning animal, poultry, and animal byproducts; and insuring that imported vehicles and equipment conform to safety and emission standards required under the National Traffic and Motor Vehicle Act of 1966 and the Clean Air Act.

The Bureau of Customs is under the supervision of the Commissioner of Customs, appointed by the Secretary of the Treasury. Although its headquarters is in Washington, D.C., the Bureau is decentralized and most of its personnel are stationed throughout the country and overseas, where its operational functions are performed. The fifty states, plus the Virgin Islands and Puerto Rico, are divided into nine customs regions. Within these regions are forty-three subordinate district offices that oversee approximately three hundred ports of entry.

International activities often related to organized crime—narcotics trafficking, unlawful importation of firearms, and illegal activities at ports and international airports—all come under the investigative responsibility of the Bureau of Customs.

> All aircraft, cargo, vessels, vehicles, mail, and persons entering the United States are being more closely inspected than ever before by the Bureau's customs officials. The use of X-ray machines for package inspection; detector dogs at docks and borders, narcotics test kits for quick analysis of possible illegal drugs have greatly increased the Bureau of Customs' capabilities in this particular area.[18]
>
> In 1970, there was an intensified enforcement program geared toward increased antidrug and narcotic law enforcement. This program utilized "blitz" tactics by mobile forces and 100 percent examinations and detailed searches by agents of everything and anything arriving from abroad. The enforcement effort, lasting about 3 months, resulted in 1,316 narcotic and dangerous drug seizures.[19]

Internal Revenue Service. The Internal Revenue Service, created in 1862, administers and enforces the internal revenue laws except those relating to alcohol, tobacco, firearms, and explosives, which are the responsibility of another bureau. The scope of activities includes tax information and assistance to taxpayers in the preparation of their returns; the determination, assessment, and collection of all internal revenue and other miscellaneous taxes; and the administration of the service and compliance aspects of the president's program for achieving stabilization of the economy. Most of the revenues are derived from individual income tax and social insurance and retirement taxes. Other major sources are corporation income tax, excise taxes, and estate and gift taxes.

The IRS is decentralized, and the function of the headquarters organization or national office is to develop nationwide policies and programs for the administration of the internal revenue laws and to provide overall direction to the field organization. Most IRS personnel are located, and most of the work is performed, in the field.

The Intelligence Division of the Internal Revenue Service is a major unit that is responsible for overseeing enforcement of federal tax laws. This division is concerned with audit and investigation; it has the responsibility for investigating suspected violations of tax law; for recommending prosecution when warranted; and for collecting information concerning the extent of criminal violations of federal tax laws. Nineteen hundred special agents assigned to fifty-nine Internal Revenue districts throughout the United States help accomplish this mission.

In general, the efforts of the Intelligence Division in combating organized crime are related to two methods of attacking the problem—the conviction of organized crime figures for income tax evasion, and the lessening of profits from organized crime activities through taxation.[20]

Secret Service

The United States Secret Service, created in 1860,

> is authorized to protect the person of the President of the United States, the members of his immediate family, the President-elect, the Vice President or other officers next in the order of succession to the Office of President, the Vice President-elect, major Presidential and

> Vice Presidential candidates, former Presidents and their wives during his lifetime, widows of former Presidents until their death or remarriage, and minor children of a former President until they reach age 16, and visiting heads of a foreign state or foreign government.[21]

The Secret Service is also authorized to detect and arrest any person committing any offense against the laws of the United States relating to coins, currency, and other obligations and securities of the United States and of foreign governments; to execute warrants issued under the authority of the United States; to carry firearms; and to perform such other functions and duties as are authorized by law.[22]

The director of the Secret Service also is charged with the supervision of the Executive Protective Service and the Treasury Security Force.

Bureau of Alcohol, Tobacco and Firearms. The history of the Bureau of Alcohol, Tobacco and Firearms dates back to the Civil War, when the first commissioner of internal revenue was appointed and three "detectives" were hired "to investigate the illicit manufacture of distilled spirits."[23] This investigative function continued through the years and became predominant during Prohibition, when gansters took over the manufacture and distribution of illicit liquor. With the repeal of Prohibition in 1933, the investigative force became known as the Alcohol Tax Unit. Responsibilities for tobacco and firearms were added later. In 1972 the Department of the Treasury transferred ATF out of the Internal Revenue Service and gave it bureau status.

The headquarters of the bureau is in Washington, D.C., but most of its personnel are stationed throughout the country where many of its operational functions are performed. The director supervises the entire bureau from Washington. He is appointed by the secretary of the treasury and is under the supervision of the assistant secretary.

> This Bureau is responsible for enforcing and administering firearms and explosives laws, as well as those covering alcoholic beverages and tobacco products. Basically, this work has two main goals—revenue protection and consumer protection. The objective of this Bureau is to eliminate illegal possession and use of firearms, destructive devices, and explosives; assure full collection of revenue due from legal indus-

tries; cooperate with State and local law enforcement agencies to reduce crime and violence; and work in areas of industrial development, ecology, and consumer protection.[24]

Department of Transportation (Coast Guard)

The United States Coast Guard, a military service and a branch of the Armed Forces of the United States, was established in January 1915 by the Department of the Treasury. In 1967 it was transferred to the Department of Transportation. In time of war or when the president directs it, the Coast Guard operates as a part of the Navy.

The Coast Guard evolved from the Revenue Marine, which was established in 1790 as a federal maritime law enforcement agency. Many other major responsibilities have since been added:

1. Coast Guard vessels assist in searching for persons lost at sea in State jurisdictional areas.
2. Coast Guard firefighting vessels assist local municipalities in quelling waterfront fires.
3. Coast Guard helicopters fly officials of States and the Federal Government to view flood and disaster areas, major pollution cases, and hurricane or tornado areas.
4. The Coast Guard works with State governments in protecting wildlife and fish by assisting in enforcing State conservation laws.
5. The Coast Guard assists State agencies by providing law enforcement training to boating safety personnel at the National Boating Safety School.[25]

The Coast Guard also offers other services to law enforcement agencies when needed.

Department of Defense

The Department of Defense coordinates the operations of the army, navy, and air force to provide protection for the nation. This department advises the president on matters of national defense and international security. Its main function is to provide the manpower and equipment for all military operations and to direct the job of protecting the United States and its interests at sea and abroad.

The Department of Defense includes criminal investigation units and intelligence units within each branch of service. Criminal investigation related to offenses within or against the armed forces are conducted similarly to civilian detective functions but under military law.

Department of Justice

Three major enforcement agencies are administered by the Department of Justice: The Federal Bureau of Investigation, the Immigration and Naturalization Service, and the Drug Enforcement Administration.

Federal Bureau of Investigation. The FBI provides many services to law enforcement agencies at all levels of government free of cost. These include the services of the FBI Laboratory, the Identification Division, and the National Crime Information Center, as well as a broad range of training and other forms of assistance.

The Federal Bureau of Investigation was established in 1908. It has responsibility for investigating all violations of Federal law that are not already the responsibility of another agency.[26] The FBI investigates such federal crimes as kidnapping, bank robbery, transportation of stolen property out of a state, and crossing a state line to escape prosecution. In order to maintain the internal security of the country, the bureau investigates acts of treason, espionage, and sabotage. The jurisdiction of the FBI does not include counterfeiting, customs offenses, misuse of mails, or violations of local laws. However, investigative assistance is given in local investigations upon the request of any chief of police or in the investigation of police killings.[27]

The FBI Laboratory has facilities to handle a wide range of scientific investigations, some of which are useful in organized crime cases. These facilities are also available to other federal, state, and local law enforcement agencies. The FBI Identification Division has the largest collection of fingerprint cards in the world—over 171 million. The prints of noncriminals are filed separately from those of criminals and are used for identifying missing persons or victims of disasters.

The purpose of the bureau is to collect and analyze facts that can be used to help solve crime and convict criminals.

Immigration and Naturalization Service. The Immigration and Naturalization Service is responsible for administering the laws relating to the admission, exclusion, deportation, and naturalization of aliens. Through offices in the United States and in other areas around the world, the service provides information and counsel to those seeking U.S. citizenship. It also works in cooperation with other federal, state, and local law enforcement agencies to stop the inflow of illegal drugs. It apprehends those who have entered the United States illegally and determines whether to deport or prosecute such individuals.

Personnel are located at border crossing points for inspection purposes. However, INS Border Patrol officers keep watch over large areas of the Mexican and Canadian borders.

Drug Enforcement Administration. The Drug Enforcement Administration, formerly called the Bureau of Narcotics and Dangerous Drugs, is the primary federal law enforcement agency concerned with control of drug traffic and prevention of drug abuse.

> The Bureau investigates major domestic and international drug traffickers, including organized crime figures, who are increasingly involved in the illicit drug trade. To carry out these duties, the Bureau has 1,334 agents located in 61 cities in 40 states in the United States and in 44 cities in 31 foreign countries.[28]

The bureau also assists state and local agencies in their enforcement of drug laws. Functions include intelligence activities, undercover "buy programs," surveillance, and apprehension of offenders.

U.S. Postal Service (Postal Inspection Service)

Postal inspectors safeguard and improve postal services. They investigate post office personnel and routines and suggest ways of improving services. Other inspectors deal with crimes involving the mail—the mailing of explosives, pornography, firearms, poisons, and illegal drugs and mail fraud violations. These investigations are often conducted in cooperation with the Drug Enforcement Administration, the Bureau of Customs, and local law enforcement agencies.[29]

Department of Agriculture

The Department of Agriculture has two major units that perform some law enforcement duties: the National Forest Service and the Commodity Exchange Program.

National Forest Service. The National Forest Service manages the country's national forests and national grasslands. Their law enforcement responsibilities include timber theft, trespassing, and other forest-related problems. The amount of time these employees devote to law enforcement activities varies, but the Forest Service estimates that their enforcement activities cost $1.1 million.[30]

Commodity Exchange Authority. The Commodity Exchange Authority administers the regulation of trading and pricing on designated commodity exchanges. The main function of this authority is to maintain fair and honest trading practices and competitive pricing designated on contract markets. Other responsibilities are to protect market users against cheating, fraud, and abusive practices in transactions and to provide information, statistics, and reports to the public on trading and marketing.[31]

Department of Commerce

The law enforcement and criminal justice assistance programs carried out by the Department of Commerce are funded by the Law Enforcement Assistance Administration to utilize the resources of the National Bureau of Standards and the Bureau of the Census in LEAA's programs of aiding state and local law enforcement efforts.

National Bureau of Standards. The National Bureau of Standards aids law enforcement agencies in all levels of government in the selection, evaluation, and procurement of equipment. The eight categories of equipment for which standards are made are protective equipment and clothing, communications equipment and supplies, security equipment, weapons, emergency equipment, concealed object detectors, vehicles, and correctional institution building systems.[32]

Bureau of the Census. The Bureau of the Census has initiated planning on an LEAA-sponsored survey on expenditure and employment data for the criminal justice system, including federal, state, and local governments. One of the purposes of this survey is to implement and make available to local governments funds to spend on criminal justice activities. (An example is the Safe Streets Act.)[33]

Department of Labor

The Department of Labor is primarily charged with administering and enforcing statues designed to advance the public interest by promoting the welfare of wage earners, improving their working conditions, and advancing their opportunities for profitable employment. It provides criminal justice assistance in the form of programs aimed at rehabilitating, training, and employing persons returning to society from correctional institutions. These rehabilitation programs come under the Manpower Development and Training Act and are administered by the Office of Employment Development Programs.

Penetration of labor unions by organized crime is a continuing problem in the United States and one that the Department of Labor addresses through its Labor-Management Services Administration. Department of Labor investigators probe into labor racketeering activities to uncover involvement by organized crime in extortion, embezzlement, fraud, and other illegal acts pertaining to labor unions.

Department of Health, Education, and Welfare

The Department of Health, Education, and Welfare conducts several programs of criminal justice assistance to states and municipalities. Most of these programs are in the areas of training and research and of planning and action programs to combat juvenile delinquency.

The National Institutes of Mental Health conducts programs in drug treatment, rehabilitation, research, training, and education through the Division of Narcotic Addiction and Drug Abuse. The National Clearinghouse for Drug Abuse Information in the Office of Communications collects and distributes drug information, and the National Institute on Alcohol Abuse and Alcoholism administers all HEW alcoholism programs. HEW administers many programs in varied areas.

Department of the Interior

United States Fish and Wildlife Service. The United States Fish and Wildlife Service was established in the Department of the Interior on August 1, 1956. It has two main bureaus: the Bureau of Sport Fisheries and Wildlife, which was established in 1956, and the National Park Service.

The main objective of the bureaus of the Fish and Wildlife Service is to assure maximum opportunity for the American people to benefit from fish and wildlife resources as part of their natural environment.

> The Bureau assists in the development of an environmental stewardship ethic for our society based on ecological principles, scientific knowledge of wildlife, and a sense of moral responsibility.[34]

National Park Service. The National Park Service was established in 1916 in the Department of the Interior. It administers for the American people an extensive system of national parks, monuments, historical sites, and recreational areas. The objectives of the National Park Service are to watch over the properties under its jurisdiction for the enjoyment and education of the citizens, and to protect the natural environment in those areas. The protection program consists not only of the prevention of fires, stream pollution, and injury to natural historic or prehistoric features, but also of the restriction of uses that are incompatible with the basic purposes of the parks.[35]

Conclusion

Law enforcement in the United States is carried out by many diversified agencies. On the state level, one usually finds a state police body or highway patrol unit, some type of investigative unit, control boards, and National Guard units. On the federal level, almost every major department of the government has one or more units that engage in law enforcement duties of some kind. The best known are the Federal Bureau of Investigation and the Drug Enforcement Administration, both units of the Department of Justice. Also widely known are units of the Department of the Treasury: the Bureau of Customs, the Secret Service, the Bureau of Alcohol, Tobacco and Firearms, and the Internal Revenue Service. Whether well known or little known, they all perform the same basic function: enforcing the law.

CHAPTER **7**

Police Operations

"Police operations" encompasses many functions—the organizational structure of the department, the administrative leadership, and the organization and deployment of patrol and other operations. A well-run police department has good leadership and is structured to operate efficiently and effectively on all levels. The effective patrol operation is organized so that it is responsive to the changing needs of the community.

Police Organization

A police force, like any agency, is organized in order to facilitate the attainment of its objectives. Organization is the arrangement of persons with a common purpose in such a way as to make possible the performance by specified individuals of related tasks grouped for the purpose of assignment, and the establishment of areas of responsibility with clear-cut channels of communications and authority.[1]

Principles of Organization

It is difficult to generalize about organization and to isolate principles that are applicable to all organizations at all times. Organizations are made up of persons, not things, and no realistic approach to organizational problems can ignore this fact. It does not follow, however, that each police department is confronted by such unusual problems as to make impossible the application of certain principles that have been found applicable in other organizations. Out of the experiences of hundreds of administrators in many areas of endeavor, there appear to be at least six principles that are generally applicable:

1. The work should be apportioned among the various individuals and units according to some logical plan.
2. Lines of authority and responsibility should be made as definite and direct as possible.
3. There is a limit to the number of subordinates who can be effectively supervised by one officer, and this limit seldom should be exceeded.
4. There should be "unity of command" throughout the organization, i.e., no person should answer to more than one immediate supervisor.
5. Responsibility cannot be placed without delegating commensurate authority, and authority should not be delegated without holding the user to account for the use he makes of it.
6. The efforts of the organizational units and of their component members must be coordinated so that all will be directed harmoniously toward the accomplishment of the police purpose, the components thus coordinated enabling the organization to function as a well-integrated unit.[2]

According to O. W. Wilson, these sound administrative principles are intended to facilitate the operation of the force, not to hamper it. If they do hinder performance, it is not because the principles are invalid; it is because the organization is applying them improperly. For example, a too rigid adherence to lines of control might inhibit the chief or other commanding officer from entering a district station or other police facility at a late hour of the night in the absence of all officers in the chain of command between himself and the watch commander. Yet it is important that all commanding officers be free to circulate and observe operations anywhere within their pyramid of authority in the absence of the subordinate commanders and supervisors. In fact, they have an obligation to do so. The supervisor in command, however, has a responsibility to report to his immediate superior that the higher commander has been present on such a tour.

The organizational structure by itself, because it is simply a static, mechanical concept, will not help the force deal effectively with real and constantly changing situations. In order to meet the daily problems that arise, the organization must be readily adaptable to any situation that confronts it.

Flexibility in an organization is obtained by creating procedures that make it unnecessary to adhere to formal channels for supervision and control in routing operations. Staff command, supervision, and inspection provide the desirable flexibility. Adaptability to meet emergency needs is provided by defining situations that automatically cause a shift in command. Deviations from rigid lines of control are thus possible without violation of the administrative principles.[3]

Specialization in Police Service

Specialization results from the division of the force into separate units to perform police tasks. The degree of specialization, in turn, is determined by the number of special units created and by the extent to which each has exclusive responsibility for the performance of each group of distinctive tasks. Even in a force with specialized departments, however, most of the duties in several fields may be performed by the patrol division. For example, in spite of the creation of a traffic division, most street traffic duties will be performed by the motorized beat patrolman. Similarly, even though a detective division is established, much of the work of investigating crimes may be performed by beat officers.

Decisions relating to specialization are extremely important to police administration and will greatly affect the operation of the department. Specialization has a direct bearing on the relationships of members in their performance of police duties; it also complicates direction, coordination, and control.[4]

Because of these complications, specialization should be held to the minimum consistent with effective operations. In order to comprehend more readily the need for specialization, it is necessary to understand four fundamental processes that occur in an organization. It will then be apparent that the extent of specialization may be sharply restricted to avoid the disadvantages without interfering with effective operation.

Four processes of operation at work in the organization are planning, doing, controlling, and evaluating. They must operate to accomplish any one of the primary police tasks. For example, traffic control must be planned; the plans must be put in operation; controls must operate to assure their satisfactory accomplishment; and then the accomplishments must be evaluated.[5]

The Organizational Structure

Once the administrator has made a preliminary study of policies, functions, duties, and practices and has made some determination of the need for specialization, he must plan his organizational structure. A police force is organized for the purpose of enabling its members to attain their police objectives more readily and effectively. This fact must not be ignored in planning the organizational structure. To the extent that the structure impedes the work of the members, it fails to accomplish its purpose. When the force operates effectively as a unit, it is well organized.[6]

A police department is formed to provide services to the public; therefore, in planning its structure, three facts must be kept in mind. First, one segment—which we will call a "line section"—of the organization actually performs each of these services—through patrol, crime investigation, vice control, traffic control, and so on. Second, services cannot be readily provided unless the line sections of the organization are aided through the provision of supplies, the maintenance of equipment, the keeping of records—in other words, there must be auxiliary services constantly supporting the line divisions. And finally, there must be planning, direction, and control; and the organization must be staffed and provided with buildings, equipment, and supplies. These are the administrative services.[7]

Organization by Function, Time, Place, and Level. Efforts of the department are most easily coordinated and most effectively directed when the force is organized to facilitate the assignment and performance of tasks on the basis of type of duties and time and place of performance.

The force is organized primarily according to function. That is, it is divided into groups that are assigned similar and related duties. For example, most members will be assigned to patrol duties, but some may be assigned to traffic control, others to criminal investigation, and so on as shown in Figure 1. Figure 1 is an example of an organizational chart—a graphic means of depicting, by an arrangement of symbols, the relationships that exist between individuals, groups, and functions within an organization. Lines of authority and responsibility and functional relationships among groups and individuals are shown as lines on the chart.

It may be pointed out here that the divisions on this chart do not encompass all the services to the public that must be provided by the police department. They do not include the units designed to perform auxiliary and administrative tasks.

The functional units are divided into shifts or watches according to the time of day when the members are to work as a platoon, as shown by the solid lines in Figure 2.

A territorial distribution of the platoon, accomplished by assigning patrolmen to beats, is necessary to facilitate the direction and control of the officers and to ensure suitable patrol service at every point within the jurisdiction. The area distribution of a platoon is shown by broken lines in Figure 2. Patrolmen on street duty are usually under the supervision of a patrol sergeant. When the number of patrolmen is great, it may be desirable to divide them into squads assigned to specific sectors of the jurisdiction, with a sergeant in charge of each squad.

Figure 1. Organization of Police Force by Functions

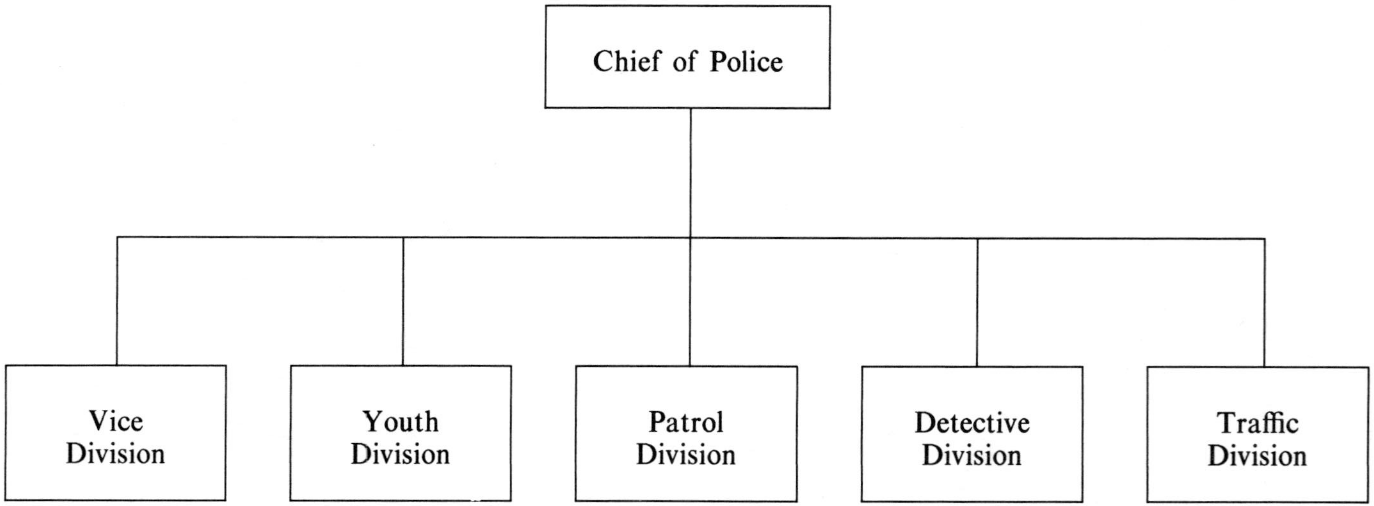

Figure 2. Distribution of Patrol Force Among the Three Shifts

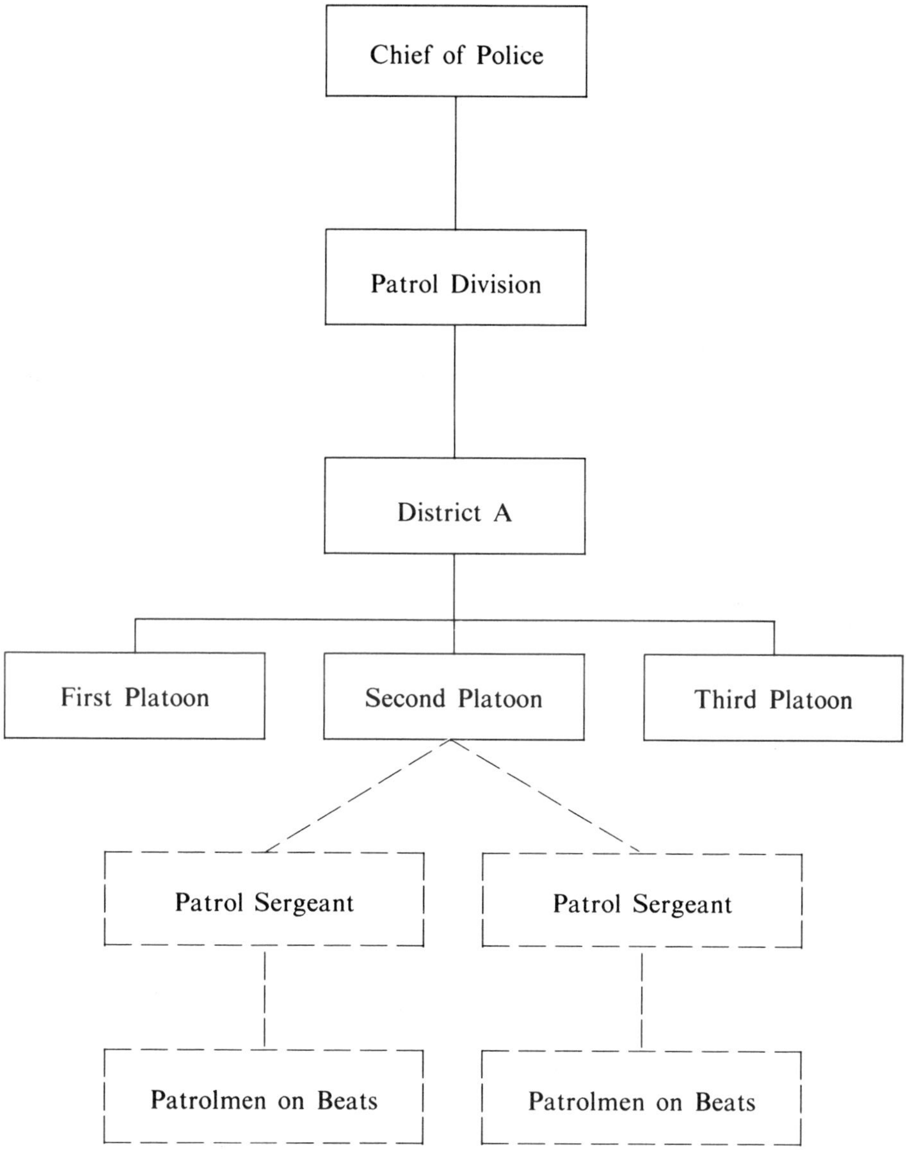

A large city is divided into geographical districts and the patrol force apportioned among them; the organization of the force then reflects the organization of the territory, as shown in Figure 3. In some departments, personnel engaged in one or more specialized tasks are apportioned among the several districts, with their control vested in the district commanders; in others the head of each functional unit retains direct control over all personnel performing tasks in his field, even though they may be physically decentralized in district stations.

The force is also divided according to the level of authority; that is, the force will consist of patrolmen, sergeants, lieutenants, and so on, as illustrated in Figure 4. Vertical combinations of superior officers, with each rank at a different level from any other, form channels through which operations may be directed and controlled. These chains of command, or lines of direct control, facilitate the delegation of authority and the placing of responsibility; supervision is thus ensured and coordination effected.[8]

The Supervisor's Function in Organization. The existence of an organization presupposes an orderly arrangement between individuals and groups, but structure alone will not assure the effective accomplishment of organizational objectives. Direction and control must be provided by a directing authority or supervisor so that the necessary coordination of effort can be achieved. Without direction, each individual will do what he wants, when he wants, and any integrated effort and achievement will be impossible. Direction is the essence of supervisory function.

The major portion of the supervisor's job may be categorized into three broad areas—leading, directing, and controlling individuals and groups formally or informally arranged. Formally structured and recognized relationships within the organization will have superimposed upon them informal groups with their own indigenous leader or leaders unrecognized on the charts. Through these natural leaders—often without bars or stripes—the wise supervisor will accomplish many of his objectives.

While the supervisor's job deals primarily with directing his subordinates, he must concern himself also with practical matters such as environmental working conditions and the provision of equipment and those more abstract factors such as morale and esprit de corps. These concerns cannot be separated from his typical administrative functions.[9]

The Exception Principle. The exception principle specifies that the head of an organization should not have to act personally on each matter coming under his general jurisdiction. Rather, he should have to act only on those exceptional matters that require his personal attention.

This principle prevails at all levels of the hierarchy and involves the delegation of functions, which, if done effectively, will free the superior from a mass of routing detail that might better be disposed of by others below him. Training is the key to the effective application of the principle. Superior officers should pass on to subordinates all work possible except that which is appropriate to the particular level that the superior occupies. He should reserve for himself only those decisions that his subordinates are not equipped to make. He should avoid becoming "bogged down" with detail so that he can be free to integrate the work being performed within his sphere of operation into that of the entire organization. It is only by consciously stripping the higher jobs of all minor tasks that artistry, ingenuity, and creative thinking are invoked or even made possible.[10]

Types of Organizational Structures

Three examples of types of organizational structures are the line organization, the functional organization, and the line and staff organization.

The Line Organization. The straight line organization, often called the individual, military, or departmental type of organization, is the simplest and perhaps the oldest type. It is seldom encountered in its true form, however, in any but the smallest of establishments. The channels of authority and responsibility extend in a direct line from the top to the bottom of the structure. Authority is definite and absolute, as seen in Figure 5.

While the line type of organization has many advantages, it also has some inherent weaknesses, which make its use impracti-

Figure 3. Territorial Organization of a Large Patrol Force

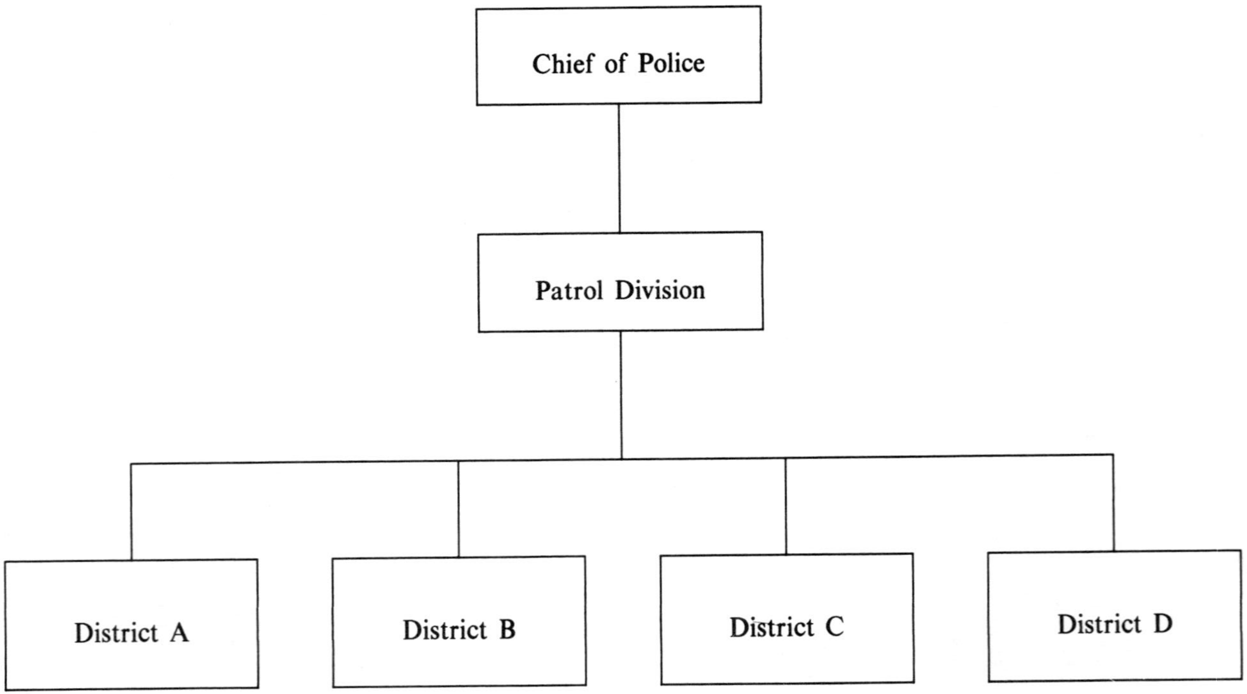

Figure 4. Division of Force According to Level of Authority

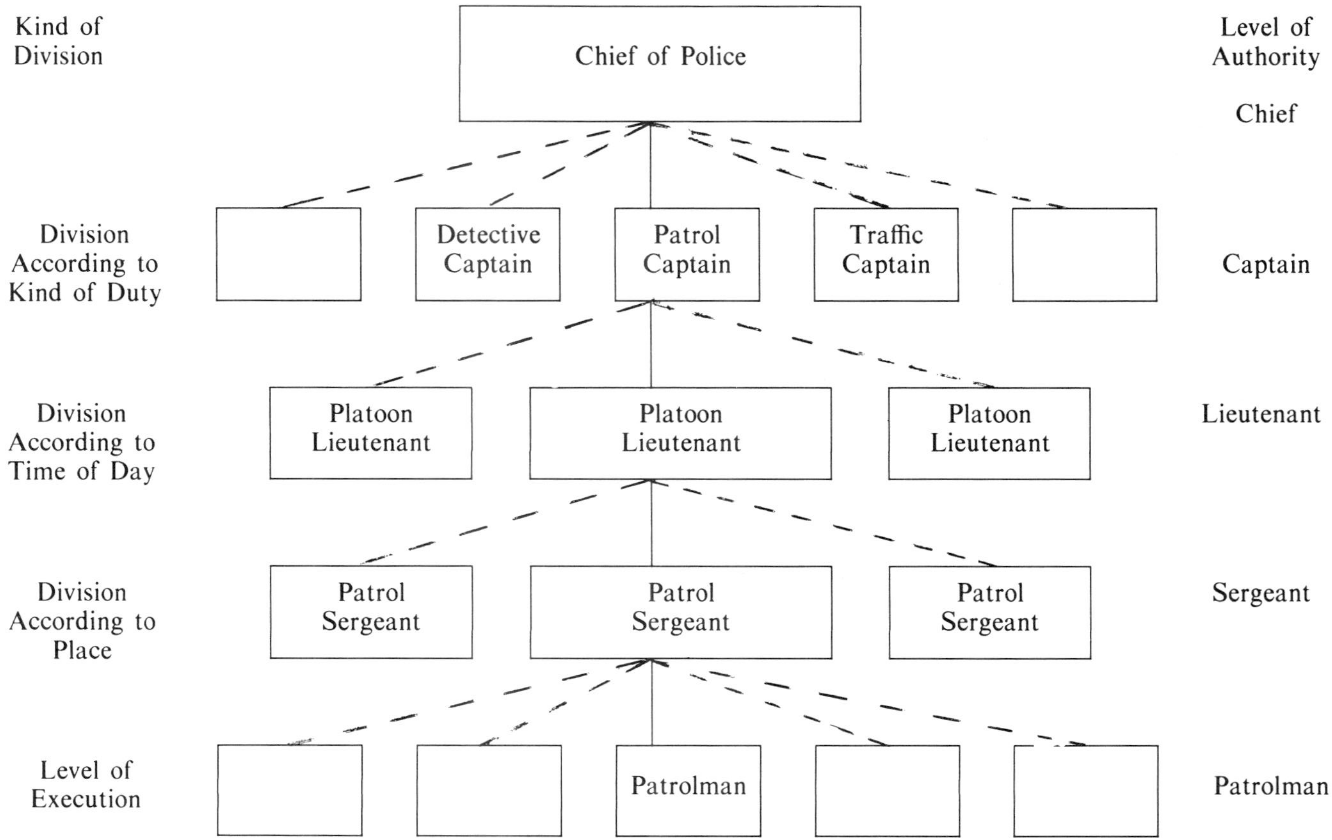

Figure 5. Line or Military Type of Organization

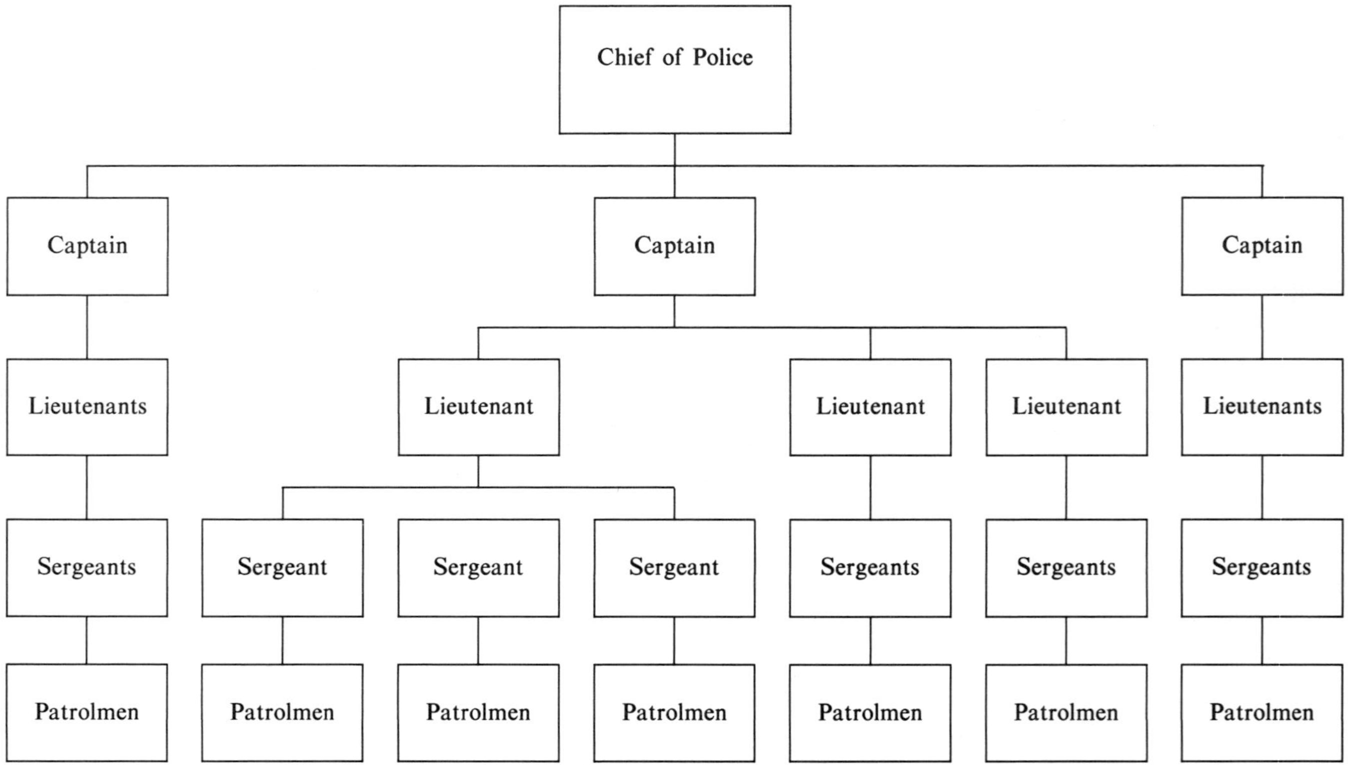

Figure 6. *Functional Type of Organization*

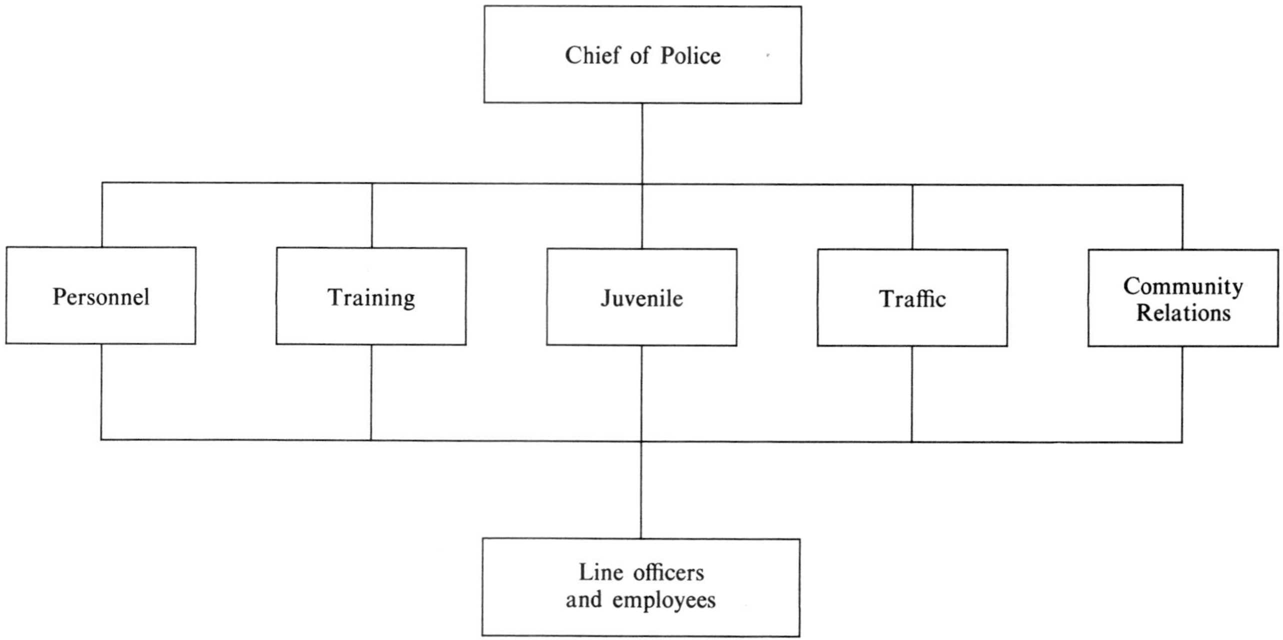

Figure 7. Line and Staff Type of Organization

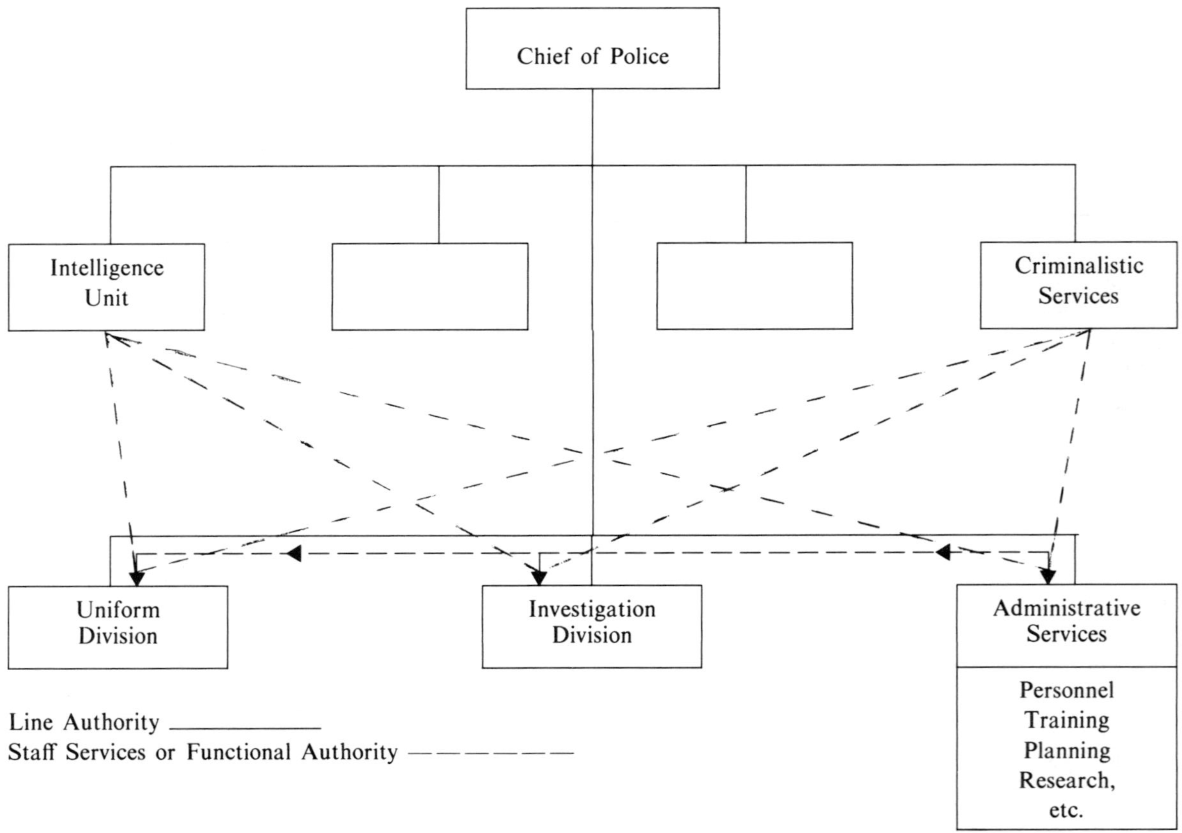

cal for many organizations. Perhaps its greatest advantage is that it is utterly simple. It involves a division of the work into units with a person in charge who has complete control and can be held directly accountable for results or lack of them.

Quick decisions can be made in the line organization because of the direct lines of authority and, because of these direct lines, each member in the chain of command knows to whom he is accountable and who is accountable to him. Because responsibility is clearly fixed, discipline is easily administered in this type of organization and responsibility for making decisions is well identified. Coordination of effort and singleness of purpose are relatively easy to achieve because functional overlapping between units, a prime cause of friction in any organization, can be minimized.

Some of the disadvantages inherent in the line type of organization are that supervisory personnel are often required to perform the duties of specialists, since little use is made of the latter for giving advice and counsel to line units. It is also often difficult to establish functional definition at the outset, but once it has been achieved, duplication of effort can be reduced. If jealousies exist between managers of the various units, each unit will tend to become "departmentalized," fostering disharmony of operation and internal frictions.[11]

The Functional Organization. The functional organization in its pure form is rarely found in present-day organizations except at or near the top of the very largest. Unlike the line type of structure, establishments organized on a functional basis violate the prime rule that men perform best when they have but one supervisor. The functional organization divides responsibility according to function. For example, all training might be done by one officer; all community relations activities of the department might be handled by another; one officer might have line authority over any employee in the department handling a case involving a juvenile, and so on. The responsibility of each "functional manager" is limited to the particular activity over which he has control, regardless of who performs the function, as illustrated in Figure 6.

Coordination of effort in this type of organization is difficult, since the employees who are responsible for results may be subject to the functional direction of several persons. Discipline is difficult to administer because of this multiple leadership. Ambiguity of responsibility may cause considerable conflict among the functional administrators and result in much confusion among line personnel. Line of authority and responsibility are fragmented into many functional channels, making each supervisor responsible to several superiors depending upon the function he happens to be performing.[12]

The Line and Staff Organization. The line and staff type of organization is a combination of the line and functional types and is found in almost all but the very smallest police agencies today. It combines staff specialists or units with line organization so that the service of knowledge can be provided to line personnel by specialists such as the criminalistics expert, the training officer, and the intelligence specialist. Channels of the specialist's responsibility and authority are thus left intact, since the specialist's responsibility is to think and provide expertise for the line units, which are responsible for carrying out the actual activities. The line supervisor must remember that he obtains advice, not commands, from the staff specialist. Figure 7 shows this relationship.

In normal operations, the staff supervisor has line command only of those subordinates in his particular unit. If he and the line supervisor recognize this limitation, coordination between line and staff personnel can be achieved without undue friction. Failure to recognize these line and staff relationships is the greatest and most frequent cause of friction in an organization and one of the greatest barriers to effective coordination.[13]

Organizational Behavior

Organizational behavior stems from the organizational climate, communication within the organization, the type of leadership and supervision, and the means of planning for and adapting to change by the organization as a whole.

The Organizational Climate for Work. The release of human potential through motivation depends largely on the existence of the proper conditions or climate within the organization. Every organization has a climate or personality of its own that distinguishes it from other organizations and that influences the behavior of its members. Management, therefore, should strive to create the type of climate that will permit the goals of the organization to be attained and will at the same time satisfy the psychological and social needs of its personnel. The achievement of this goal requires more than merely constructing organizational charts and detailing job responsibilities; it requires that the human dimension of the total work environment be considered. Organization development is based on the assumption that human resources demand equal if not greater attention than physical resources if the organization is to function effectively. The criteria for organizational effectiveness will vary from one type of organization to another. Generally, however, these criteria may include such factors as productivity; operating efficiency; satisfaction of individual needs and wants; employee health, safety, and emotional adjustment; and the development of favorable group relationships.

According to Herbert J. Chruden and Arthur W. Sherman, many characteristics distinguish one organization from another and give it a particular personality. One of them is its goals. The fact that governmental, charitable, educational, and profit-oriented organizations differ in their goals produces different climates in these organizations. The structure of an organization—for example whether it is "tall" or "flat," whether it is line or line-and-staff—also influences the organizational climate. Such intangibles as the methods that managers and supervisors use to direct and control the activities of their subordinates, the nature of the relationships among individuals and groups and the interactions between persons in different levels of authority within the hierarchy are some of the other major determinants of organizational climate.[14]

Communication. Good communication is essential to the effective operation of any organization. Because of its pervasive nature, communication is often referred to as the network that binds together all the members and activities within an organization. Through the transmission of information, ideas, attitudes, and feelings, the personnel and their activities may be coordinated in the pursuit of organizational goals and individual satisfaction. Within the organization, the communication process is in action continuously among individuals and groups, up and down and laterally.

In the past, management has measured the effectiveness of its communication primarily in terms of how well it explained itself to employees. Currently, however, there is an increasing recognition of the importance and value of obtaining feedback from employees. This form of communication, commonly called two-way communication, is the only approach to the development of mutual understanding between management and employees. Without understanding, there is no communication. The achievement of mutual understanding requires that managerial and supervisory personnel be aware of the dynamic nature of the communication process and that they establish a climate that encourages the continuous exchange of information and feelings among the members of the organization. Through their efforts to establish effective formal communication and to keep communication channels open to all members, the formal organization will be strengthened, and at the same time individual needs, especially for affiliation and esteem, will be satisfied.

Although their main concern will be with establishing and keeping formal communication operating effectively, managerial and supervisory personnel will find that the informal communication that develops among the members of the organization requires their attention and understanding if they are to be effective leaders. Through an awareness of the nature of the communication among employees outside formal channels, managers and supervisors will have a better understanding of employee attitudes toward their jobs and relationships among employees, and they will be in a better position to lower the barriers to communication. Managers should recognize, however, that an employee's effectiveness, regardless of his job, is determined in some degree by his ability to communicate with his supervisor, fellow officers, and others. Basically, then, effective communication is a responsibility of every person in the organization.[15]

Leadership and Supervision. The talents and enthusiasm of the members of an organization are of little value unless they are carefully directed toward the objectives of the organization. Providing the type of leadership that will result in the most effective utilization of personnel is a primary responsibility of managers and supervisors. However, because of his position in the organization, the first-line supervisor has one of the most important leadership roles. He has many responsibilities, but of primary importance is the part he plays in developing efficient employees, in motivating and controlling their performance, and in facilitating their adjustment. The manner in which he does this may vary from one individual to another, but the effective supervisor is one who is aware of the important factors in the leadership role and is flexible in his relationships with individuals and with the work group. The ability to provide for group participation in decision-making is a leadership skill that contributes greatly to personal as well as organizational success.

The supervisor's ability to relate to individuals, particularly those with backgrounds different from his own, can go a long way toward making him an effective leader. The supervisor's effectiveness, however, is determined not only by his own personal characteristics, but also by his status, primarily a result of management's attitudes toward supervisory personnel. The personnel department also has an important role in helping preserve the supervisor's status, and personnel workers need to recognize the value of the supervisor's contribution to the entire organization and especially to the personnel department.[16]

Administering Change. A major source of problems faced by organizations is the rapid rate of change in modern society. Discoveries in the sciences, improvements in technology, and changes in social behavior create conditions that can have a profound effect on organizations. If they are to continue to function effectively, it is essential that organizations and the personnel who comprise them be capable not only of adapting to change, but also of planning for it. While functions of management traditionally have included forecasting and anticipating future problems and requirements, the modern concept of organizational development connotes a more scientific and professional approach to their functions. Organizational development, among other things, emphasizes the need to improve the capabilities of an organization by placing particular emphasis on the training of managerial and supervisory personnel. Such training should provide them with skills and attitudes that enable them to help subordinates cope with the ever-changing conditions occurring within their organizations in a manner that will permit a high level of performance and personal adjustment.

Within an organization, changes take place continually with respect to the structure, functions, and workload of the organization and the numbers and types of jobs that are to be staffed within the organization. Changes also occur in terms of the qualifications, capacities, attitudes, and behavior of the personnel who are available to staff these positions. Many of these changes in the placement of employees take place by means of transfers, promotions, demotions, or even lay-offs. Regardless of their nature, however, placement changes ideally should place the employee in the job for which he is best suited and most needed, thus contributing to his adjustment and to effective performance of the organization.[17]

Organization in police department operations should be as simple as the size and functions of the department permit. The chief should maintain direct contact with his division heads and should permit only as many levels of supervision as are required to obtain effective operation and to maintain a workable span of control. When the detail in his office becomes more than he can handle alone, he should appoint one or more aides or assistants rather than establish an extra level of authority. Aides may function in planning, inspection, or personnel in the name of the chief, but with no command authority of their own.[18]

Organization of police operations varies from city to city and depends upon available personnel, quality of supervision, and the nature of community problems.

Administrative Leadership

In police work, as in any other area of endeavor, when the planning and organizing are over, it is time to administer or carry out the plans based on the total organization of the project. In order to assure that jobs are performed effectively, that orders and policies are carried out, and that the organization works toward accomplishing its goals, a police force, like any other organization, needs top quality leaders or administrators.

In police work the requirements of the job at hand often dictate the kinds of leadership qualities needed for that specific task.

However, leadership qualities and standards should be uniformly of the highest caliber available. The effective leader must have and display to subordinates, as well as superiors, a strong working knowledge of his duties, and he must also demonstrate that he can meet any challenges that are inherent in his particular job. A good leader does not resort to dramatics in performing his duties, but merely calmly and competently completes each duty. In order to inspire his men to follow his example, the competent administrator must have a personality that enables him to reach out and maintain the enthusiasm and loyalty, as well as the trust, of his men. A good leader must instill qualities of honesty, integrity, and responsibility, which are basic necessities for all public servants who have the responsibility to protect life, property, and the personal liberty of all people within their jurisdiction.

Levels of Leadership

As an administrator moves from one level of leadership to another, the duties and requirements change. Police work encompasses three general levels of leadership, all with varying responsibility.

The Chief. The department head, or chief, is the top man in the chain of command. It is the chief's duty to provide for the completion of the department's goals, to supervise the execution of the department policies, plans, and other administrative functions. The chief should set an example of competent leadership, and those under the chief should follow his example in carrying out his delegated policies and authority. When it comes to decision-making, the chief must be highly intelligent and flexible enough to consider all possibilities before arriving at a suitable answer to the major problems concerning the police department. Since he is the one who submits and prepares the annual budget, he must be competent in his analysis of the strengths and weaknesses of the department and in considering proposed improvements for the next fiscal year. If he also has a flair for salesmanship in the actual presentation of the budget to the governing body, he will increase the chances of attaining his requested funds and manpower.

Those of lesser rank are directly responsible to the chief and answer to him through the chain of command. In order to fulfill his duties and responsibilities adequately, the chief must be thoroughly familiar with all phases of management and personnel relations. It is his duty, alone or with his top assistants, to analyze and evaluate the problems of law enforcement within his jurisdiction and to establish working policies and guidelines to overcome them. When a problem area is identified, the chief might institute a change in manpower placement to ease the situation, or possibly establish an investigative unit for a serious specific problem.

The Commanding Officer. Once the policy has been determined by the chief, it is the responsibility of the command officers—captains and lieutenants—to see that the matter is properly executed at the line level. The command officers provide direction for the accomplishment of organizational goals by "meshing personnel with methods and procedures, by maintaining operational control, and by setting standards and reviewing accomplishments."[19] Command officers should be competent and skillful in devising ways to attain the department's goals in a manner that will require the least amount of expenditure and manpower, yet will complete the task satisfactorily. This does not mean that cost alone is the deciding factor, but rather that duplication and waste should be kept at a minimum.

The Field Supervisors. Once the command officer has formulated a plan, it is the responsibility of the field supervisors, or sergeants, to make sure that the task is properly carried out. This is accomplished by informing the officers of the problem to be corrected, presenting the proposed plan, and then discussing the plan with the officers to make sure that everyone fully understands what is expected of him. The best way to get any order carried out is to make sure that it is fully understood and to align the officers behind the plan so that they actually feel a part of it. To carry out his duties properly, the field officer must observe the people he supervises and must be observed by them. In order for the field supervisor to be most effective, he must have a thorough understanding of his duties and the duties of each and every officer under his supervision. A strong sense of loyalty and confidence should flow from superior officers to subordinates, and vice versa.

Leadership Qualities

The effectiveness of a leader can be measured by one simple question: "Do your men perform well and willingly for you, the leader?"[20] The words "perform well and willingly" are very significant, because they connote good rapport and morale. A true leader has the qualities given in the following definition of leadership: "The art of imposing one's will upon others in such a manner as to command their respect, their confidence, and their whole-hearted cooperation."[21] Any leader who knows that art will have no problems accomplishing any objective while supervising his employees or followers.

The competent leader will not only lead his men formally through the use of orders and other directives, but will also provide informal leadership through accessibility, praise, correction or instruction, and a strong sense of loyalty and responsibility toward his men. A leader without the ability to make decisions, based on his evaluation of the problem at hand and the various methods of overcoming the problem, will be totally lost. Not only will the decisions that the leader makes be wrong, but more important, a leader without the ability to make correct decisions will very soon lose all trust and confidence of his subordinates and his superiors. Under situations of extreme stress, poor leaders can, and do, lose officers' lives needlessly due to poor decisions. "The power of decision is no more than vision to see that which needs to be done, and how and when to do it."[22] Once a proper decision has been made, the leader must have the courage to execute it. The courage to act can be as important and decisive as the ability to make a decision.

Administrative Principles

In day-to-day police operations, administrators use a series of techniques to provide for more complete and efficient control of the men under their command. These techniques, or administrative principles, include the following: unity of command, span of control, chain of command, delegation of authority, organization for administration, direction and coordination, and maintenance of control.[23]

Unity of command. Unity of command, simply stated, requires that "only one man be in complete command of each situation and that only one man be in direct command or supervision of each officer."[24] The principle is not as simple as it sounds, however, for in the organization of a department, there is sometimes an overlap of authority that causes friction and morale problems until detected and corrected. No man can accomplish a job to the satisfaction of two bosses when they may be asking for different performance. The commander uses his authority to accomplish efficiently what he has determined should be done, by the people he feels should do it, and also by the means he has decided should be used. The commander has authority only within his pyramid of authority or area of control and selects men with the proper qualifications and abilities to perform the duties to which they will be assigned. When working outside his normal pyramid of authority, as when two equal commanders are sharing the supervision of a joint project, one commander should be selected as being "in charge" until the assignment is completed in order to reduce discussion and argument over the best way to do the job. No officer should try to assume control over officers or projects outside his unit of command.

Span of Control and Chain of Command. Span of control and chain of command are important principles of administration, for they allow the commander to exercise direct or indirect control over all subordinates and also insure that personnel at each level in the organization are aware of what is taking place. Chain of command means simply that each man is responsible to a given individual with rank or authority in the unit of command and that all orders must come through that same individual for the smooth, efficient completion of all assigned tasks. The chain should allow a two-way flow of information and ideas if the morale and efficiency of the organization are to be at their highest. All orders flow down through the chain of command so that each supervisor and officer knows what is expected of him.

The span of control is "the ability of one man to direct, coordinate, and control immediate subordinates."[25] The supervisor should control only the number of personnel that he is able to supervise effectively. The complexity of the particular assignment can often determine how many men can be controlled. The more uniform and simple the task, the greater the number of officers that can be controlled. On a project that requires a wide divergence of technical skills or activities, the commander will be able to supervise fewer officers, depending on his own technical knowledge and ability.

Delegation of Authority. Delegation of authority is the assignment of authority to a commander so that he can insure that those tasks assigned to him are properly accomplished by the officers charged with the job. O. W. Wilson stated: "A person cannot be held responsible for the accomplishment of an order unless he has delegated to him the authority necessary for its accomplishment."[26] Under this principle the commander of each unit has authority over each person below him in rank. This authority is limited to those under his command and to the accomplishment of the particular task he has been assigned.

Organization for Administration. When a department becomes very large, or very complex in its operational requirements, the administrative function of the chief increases to the point where adequate supervision cannot be provided by the chief alone. At this time it becomes necessary to organize the department for more efficient supervision, using a principle called organization for administration.[27] This organization can be accomplished in two ways. Either the chief can select a top assistant or aide who is not a direct link in the chain of command to assist in the administration of the department, or he can create positions for line or field supervisors. Persons in intermediate positions have the primary function of carrying out the chief's policies and orders through meaningful, responsible, and productive leadership. The purpose of their assignment is to make the whole department run more smoothly and efficiently.

Direction and Coordination. For any organization to be successful, there must be complete coordination among departments and among employees. Such coordination increases productivity and reduces duplication of effort. With responsible leadership to dictate policies and goals, the organization can have meaningful direction. The direction is the responsibility of those within the chain of command, but coordination is the responsibility of all members of the police department. Many investigations are not completed at the end of a shift, and in order to handle the investigation effectively, the succeeding shift will have to take over the workload until the investigation is completed or until the process repeats itself. If there is no coordination among shifts, or among the road patrol, traffic divisions, and the criminal investigation (detective) division, much information will be gathered during each shift that will never be passed on and coordinated. There have been cases when personnel in a department possessed partial bits and pieces of information that, put together, would have nearly solved a crime or a series of crimes. A well-organized, coordinated plan should exist in the event of emergencies. For example, only a planned and coordinated roadblock plan will have any measure of success.

Maintenance of Control. While performing his duties, any administrator will face incidents that require some sort of discipline. In order to maintain control over his subordinates, the supervisor will have to give orders to direct them in the accomplishment of each mission. Inspections help detect officers who are not properly dressed, equipped, or physically able to perform their duties. If corrections cannot be made immediately, the officer must be judged unfit to work at that time and relieved of duty. A periodic evaluation of the officer as he performs his duties in the field, coupled with an evaluation of his work (attention to detail, quality and quantity of work, and consideration of constitutional issues) should be made of all officers under the command of a supervisor.

Many citizens complain to police departments that they have been unjustly treated by officers with whom they have been in contact on the street or in some incident. The formation of an internal affairs investigation unit within a department, whether staffed by one officer in a small department or by many officers in a large one, should be considered to investigate such charges in an unbiased manner. Many times the incident was a matter of misunderstanding or the citizen's complaint was unfounded, but sometimes the officer did act without authority (if not illegally), and it is the responsibility of the department head to detect and rectify any such occurrences. When officers are found to be in violation of department policies and regulations, disciplinary measures are called for. These measures can range from an oral reprimand for minor mistakes, to a written warning for more serious mistakes, to forfeitures of pay and temporary suspensions, to dismissal from the police force. The gravity of each offense and the officer's record should be the deciding factors.

Administrative Planning and Evaluation

From the business profession police departments have learned the value of planning. Before planning can be truly productive, the administrator must recognize and consider many basics. The primary step is to understand the task or mission to be accomplished. The officer in charge of planning should know exactly what is to be done and how. Often, the objective can be reached with personnel, materials, and training that are on hand at the time. Once the goal is fully understood and an impartial assessment of the present strengths and weaknesses of the department is made, the planning can begin. If the objective is fairly simple, then a short-range plan may be instituted. Short-range plans can be started immediately and are usually quickly completed. Long-range objectives, however, will require long-range plans and will take a much longer time to complete, often more than a year. Generally they will require more in the way of manpower, materials, training, and funds. Before embarking on any mission, the administrator should have a detailed plan stating what must be done, who should do it, and how it must be done. Each person in the chain of command responsible for seeing that the plan is carried out should be thoroughly familiar with the total plan, including the ultimate objective, so that they can provide meaningful direction to the officers below them.

From time to time the whole planned project should be evaluated to see whether it is still on the original course and whether it is accomplishing what it was supposed to accomplish. If the plan has any weakness, the administrator can make any corrections needed. If changing external conditions have altered or eliminated the need for the project being executed, the plan should be changed or canceled. It is a waste of time, money, and manpower to continue any project for which there is no longer a definite need.

Policy-making is much like planning. The administrator should know precisely his own as well as the department's strengths and weaknesses. As stated by V. A. Leonard and Harry W. More:

> The evaluation of a police system is a task for the expert. Therefore, the proposed . . . appraisal will prove of limited value in the hands of anyone unfamiliar with the police techniques and procedures now accepted as standard by the profession. Properly employed, however, it should serve the public interest by pointing the way for both executive and layman toward the development of police organization and administration upon a rational and professional level. It should expose those deficiencies which must be remedied before the community can expect to receive a reasonable return on annual expenditures for police service.[28]

When the administrator realizes exactly what the situation is and what he wants to achieve, then he must set standards, which, coupled with his planning policies, move toward the accomplishment of the department mission. The administrator should be alert for and be aware of any special situations or regional problems that may confront him. A thorough knowledge of the mission and his officers (native ability, training, skills, and any other pertinent background information) are invaluable to the chief or commander. In order to insure that a project is being carried out according to his wishes, it will be necessary for the administrator to issue orders periodically. These orders will be of three types: general, special, and personnel. General orders are permanent orders that are general in nature. When given by the chief, they affect the entire department. Special orders concern an unusual event such as a parade or a demonstration, so they are temporary. Personnel orders are directed toward individuals and cover such circumstances as promotions, awards, and disciplinary measures.

Budget planning can be complex and always requires careful consideration. The process of preparing the police budget should be a cooperative one, with all division heads meeting to discuss problems encountered with the previous budget and projections for future needs. Many expenses can be eliminated since they are no longer needed, and new problems constantly arise and require new funds. The first step in budgeting is to outline the expenses incurred in the operation of the department—salaries, vehicles, transportation and maintenance costs, weapons, training materials and costs, heating and installation costs, the expense of providing the material for records, such as reports, citations, filing cabinets, typewriters, and other office machines (including repairs). The list is nearly endless, and old budgets and all lists of expenditures should receive careful scrutiny before a final decision is made. The budget planners can list such categories as transportation, salaries, operational costs, and so on and specify the amount of money that they will need for the particular expense. After careful examination and discussion, the figures are totaled. The budget should be examined on a monthly basis during the next year to compare expenditures with estimated costs, and adjustments, if any, should be made for the budget for the succeeding year.

In order to be an effective administrator of a police department, an individual must be well versed in police techniques and in the functions of effective leadership. The judicial use of the principles of administration will make the task easier and more productive. If the supervisor progresses to the point where he will be concerned with such phases of police administration as planning and budgeting, he will soon realize that in order to function effectively, he will have to widen his intellectual horizons in order to meet the challenge.

Police Patrol Operations

Patrol has been called the backbone of the police department, and with good reason. Almost any service rendered by a police department has its start with a patrol officer. A police department may operate without many of the divisions that a large department has, but a department can never operate without a patrol division.

The word *patrol* comes from the French *patrouille* and is from the Latin noun *pes, pedis,* which means paw or foot.[29]

At the present time over forty thousand law enforcement agencies are functioning in the United States at four levels of government: federal, state, county, and local (municipal).

The concept and objectives of patrol have remained basically the same since its inception. Patrol continues to operate on a twenty-four hour basis, 365 days a year. Its main function, as in the past, is the protection of life and property. This continuity, however, does not mean that performance and effectiveness will not be continually updated.

History of Patrol

Man has always felt the need to protect himself and his family. In prehistoric times, he found shelter in caves and stood guard at the entrance. As people became civilized and started to live together in communities, the need for special groups for protection increased. In the Middle Ages soldiers stationed in every town took on the job of protection. Many towns were walled or fortified in some way and had gates that were guarded at all times.

One of the earliest laws passed to provide patrol protection was the Watch and Ward Act in 1285, but it did not work very well.[30] A major reason for the failure was that the watchmen were drafted for duty and had no enthusiasm. Also, a man of financial means could hire someone to do his service for him. Most persons hired this way turned out to be crooks. Various other kinds of patrols followed, including constables and private protection organizations, but none were satisfactory.

Sir Robert Peel's Metropolitan Police of London were not well received, as its recruits were mostly Irishmen who had served in the British army. The people were not accustomed to the strict law enforcement imposed by the police, and they resented officers who were both foreigners and Catholic.

Theories and Objectives of Police Patrol

The basic theory of patrol is to cause the potential offender to believe that there is no reasonable opportunity to commit a violation of the law and successfully get away.[31] There are two ways to achieve this goal. The first is to maintain a low profile in patrol in order to attract as little attention as possible. Unmarked or semimarked cars are used to attract a minimum of attention to police vehicles. Uniformed foot patrolmen walk close to buildings, use alleys, and in general try to stay out of sight as much as possible. The goal of this technique is to apprehend the offender in the act of committing a crime.

The second is to use vehicles with police emblems, emergency lights, and distinct colors. They patrol with the intention of attracting as much attention as possible. The purpose here is to let the offender know that no matter where he turns, the police are nearby. In terms of public relations, the citizens of the community also see the police and feel safer on the street.

A variation of the second type of patrol is aggressive patrol, which carries visible patrol even further. The two basic methods of aggressive patrol are checking the physical security of business premises frequently to prevent burglary and robbery and also checking citizens frequently—stopping suspicious-looking persons, questioning identity and activities, and staying alert for persons intent on committing crimes.[32] On aggressive patrol, then, the officer does more than just patrol his beat; he looks for conditions that can breed crime. To the aggressive officer, radio calls are only a small part of the job of patrol. He checks out all information he receives, whether it be as a result of a radio call or information given to him by a citizen. His goal is to serve and protect the citizens of the community.

The objective of good patrol is to stop crime before it happens, not merely to catch the offender after he commits the act.[33] Today the officer who makes a good catch, rather than the officer who keeps crime to a minimum, is usually the one rewarded with the "hero badge."

Determining Manpower Needs

Once a department establishes its method of patrol, its administrator must determine the number of officers required in the uniform patrol force. To do this, the number of patrol beats required for each shift must be determined, and the number will vary from shift to shift. Distribution of the patrol force in proportion to relative need for service is known as the principle of proportionate need.[34]

Demands for police service have proven to occur in fairly systematic and predictable patterns over an extended period of time. Because of this, rather accurate predictions of future requirements can be made on the basis of historical data represented by calls for police service. The objective is to determine the number of beats required and to develop the individual beat structure so that each will have a proportionate share of the total workload.

There are five objectives of good patrol distribution. The first is to equalize the workload so that all officers, on the average, will be handling the same amount of work. The second is to establish area responsibility fairly. Each officer will feel responsible for his patrol area and know that he is being judged on his performance. The third is to minimize response time so that officers can arrive at the scene as soon as possible with little time between getting the call and arriving on the scene. The fourth objective is to plan beat configurations so as to minimize geographical problems by the use of natural barriers as beat boundaries. The fifth and last objective is to gather crime data to help in the possible revision of areas of responsibility or increased manpower allocation.[35]

The determination of proportionate need is affected by community factors.[36] While one community may have a high traffic accident rate and consider accidents an important factor, another may have only very few minor accidents and not consider them a factor at all. After the administrator determines what factors are going to be used to determine proportionate need, he must decide their relative importance. Each factor must be weighed against the rest, and some will be given emphasis or weight.[37]

By giving certain factors extra weight, the administrator can determine the percentage of need for any given hour or day, as well as any area of the city, for he knows when and where each kind of police problem is most likely to arise. Then he can compute the size of an area to be patrolled, manpower needs for shifts, shift starting times, and days off for patrol personnel.

When figuring beat assignments and manpower distribution, the administrator must consider that while a police department is at work 365 days a year, the patrol officers are assigned work only five days a week and have vacation time. A rule of thumb is to reduce the total complement assigned to a shift by one-third.[38]

What this means is that if the total manpower assigned to the third shift is thirty, then twenty men would be available on any given day.

In manpower distribution, then, the emphasis is on the concept of proportionate need in terms of time. In manpower deployment, on the other hand, the emphasis is on the concept of proportionate need in terms of geography. Geographical barriers, whether natural or man-made, must be considered in deploying the patrol force.[39] If due consideration is not given to natural barriers, reponse time can be affected to the point of isolating some areas from police protection. Determining what constitutes a geographical barrier is at times a matter of judgment. Railroad tracks with all streets crossing them would not be much of a barrier unless the crossing were blocked at intervals by heavy railroad traffic.

For each shift the weighted workload total should be divided by the number of beats to obtain the average workload per beat for that shift. The beats should then be structured so that the workload of each beat approximates the average workload. Patrol areas should be kept as compact as possible, with as few elongated or unusual shapes as possible.

In addition to adjusting for geographical barriers, the administrator should consider the rate of called-for services in each area and the character of each neighborhood in his jurisdiction. Large outlying residential districts should be combined into beats with somewhat smaller than average workloads to compensate for the greater area to be patrolled and the increased response time from extreme parts of the area. Areas with greater than average workloads should be combined into smaller beats to compensate for the increased workload.

Another condition to be considered in deployment is the "police hazard." A police hazard is a person, place, property, or situation that creates a potential need for police services.[40]

Deployment is also affected by the type of patrol to be used.

Types of Patrol

Patrol has evolved from the foot and mounted patrol that were used exclusively a hundred years ago to the motorized and air patrol available today. But even with modern means, foot and mounted patrol are still useful.

One-Man Patrol Cars. Ever since one-man patrol cars were instituted in the early 1950s in many large cities, their advantages and disadvantages have been argued. Use of one-man vehicles, as opposed to those occupied by two men, doubles the motorized patrol potential of the force. With more cars on the street, response time is less because of smaller beat area. Although more vehicles are needed, one-man cars can produce savings in the fact that more police services can be provided to the community with no manpower increase.[41] If two patrol cars cover the same beat area, the community can derive twice the patrol protection, yet on a hazardous call, the officers can work as a team.

Two-Man Patrol Cars. Two-man patrol cars were first used due to poor communications. The theory was that two men could help each other in an emergency even if they couldn't call on any additional forces. Police communications have improved over the years, reducing the need to have two men in all patrol cars. The need is still present in some areas, however. In high crime areas or in areas with geographical barriers that might cut off assistance, police need to have immediate back-up.

Advantages to two-man cars include the fact that offenders are less likely to assault the officers physically when they will have to contend with two opponents.

In addition, while one officer drives, the second can be checking; halfway through the shift they can change so that neither gets tired. Also, the second may catch something the first one missed.

Foot Patrol. Foot patrol was the first type of patrol used by police departments when the night constable shook doors in a downtown area. Today foot patrol is used in business areas as a form of public relations by some departments. Foot patrolmen are put out for the public to see and talk to. Foot patrols should be used in areas where inspectional services take up the greatest amount of patrol time. The beat of a foot patrolman should be as compact as possible.[42]

Mounted Patrol. Mounted patrol, like foot patrol, began early, but cities like New York and Detroit with large park areas still use mounted patrol. Riding a horse affords the officer mobility to go where motorized vehicles cannot, and, because of his height, he has a better field of vision. Sheriff's departments use mounted patrol in wooded or mountainous areas because of the need for mobility in that terrain.

Mounted patrol has also been used as a means of crowd control. The size and height of a horse can have a strong psychological effect on the crowd.[43]

Motorcycle Patrol. Some cities still use motorcycles as a form of patrol, usually in their traffic enforcement sections. The California Highway Patrol makes extensive use of motorcycles.

The motorcycle is more maneuverable than a patrol vehicle in crowded traffic conditions, but its disadvantages are great. Officers are likely to be off on injury time more, because an accident involving a motorcycle is more likely to involve an injury than one involving a car. Motorcycles can be used only in good weather, yet the need for traffic assistance is greater during inclement weather.[44]

Many cities are combining foot and cycle patrol and forming scooter patrols, which give the foot patrolman greater mobility.

Air Patrol. Police agencies use two types of air patrol today. Many cities and counties employ helicopter patrol, and many state police agencies have been using fixed-wing aircraft for years.

Helicopters are not hampered by geographical barriers, nor must they follow roadways and be delayed by traffic. With high-power lighting, they can arrive over the scene of a crime or emergency and keep it under surveillance until beat units arrive.

Fixed-wing aircraft are used in conjunction with ground units in traffic control and enforcement. They are also used to fly needed supplies to hospitals in cases of immediate need.

Marine Patrol. Cities built on or near bodies of water need a marine or harbor patrol, and cities or counties with water recreational areas need a marine patrol to insure safety for the people who use the waterfront facilities.

Canine Patrol. While dogs have been used for years for self-protection, the use of canine units in police work has only recently become widespread. Dogs are used at crime scenes to track suspects and at airports and borders to sniff out narcotics. Some dogs have been trained to find explosives and are used by airport security details to follow up on bomb threats. Dogs can also be used to check out industrial areas that could take five to ten officers to check on their own.

Use of Equipment

Before going into the field, the patrol officer should check his uniform and equipment to make sure it is clean and in good condition. The officer's appearance is important in gaining respect from people with whom he will come in contact.

Many cities have roll call inspections. In cities that have no inspection, it is the duty of the individual officer to make sure that all is ready before departing from the station. The officer's revolver should be clean, well oiled, and checked to make sure it is loaded before the officer goes on duty.

Because of the chance of high-speed pursuit driving, an officer should make sure his vehicle has had proper maintenance and is ready for the road. An inspection of the vehicle should identify any visible defect or apparent mechanical malfunction.

Any additional equipment that might be used on the shift should also be checked—radios, shotgun, flashlight, first aid kit, blanket, flares, spare tire, tear gas, notebooks, citation books, crime reports, and other forms.

Primary Investigation

Any criminal investigation starts with a patrol car being sent to the scene and a uniformed officer initiating a report. In some cases the officer will handle the entire incident. In others a secondary investigation will be handled by detectives, but it will still be the patrol officer who is the first on the scene.

An investigation is the gathering and evaluating of information, including evidence regarding the crime. Some information must be put together in a way that can be presented in court. Much of the information received cannot be used in court but must still be evaluated. As an example, information resulting from tips must be checked out for its probative value.

The patrol officer, in taking the original report, will talk with the victim to find out what happened. He must determine whether, in fact, a crime was committed. He will talk with witnesses to get their descriptions of what took place. The more information the patrol officer is able to obtain and pass on to the detective, the more time the detective will have to work on the detailed follow-up phases of the investigation. The original report should record fully and accurately the results of the primary investigation and all other vital information.

In interviews with victim and witnesses, the officer should obtain as much information as he can as quickly as possible in order to identify the perpetrator and broadcast what he learns to all available units.[45]

At the scene of a crime the officer must take care to protect and preserve the scene as it was at the time of the crime. All physical evidence must be protected for crime scene technicians or else important evidence may be destroyed. If need be, all witnesses may be removed from the building and sufficient personnel detailed to protect the scene while the officer conducts the primary investigation. When protecting a crime scene, the officer must remember that *nothing* is to be touched or moved.

Principles of Arrest

Arrest may be defined as "seize and hold by legal authority." A police officer is a legal authority and has been granted that authority by a governmental body.

Some officers see a difference between an arrest for a misdemeanor and an arrest for a felony. In reality, both should be treated the same. An officer stopping a person for a minor infraction of the law has no way of knowing whether the person is wanted for a felony in another city or state, is an escaped violent mental patient, or has a grudge against all police.

Any person arrested should be placed against the patrol car and searched for weapons. Hands should be handcuffed behind the back. The suspect should be placed in the right rear of the car. An additional officer should, when possible, accompany the arresting officer and sit next to the prisoner. At the time of the arrest, the subject should be informed of charges against him. If a suspect resists during the arrest, the officer may use only the force necessary to complete the arrest.

When stopping a vehicle believed to contain a known felon, the officer should try to pick a spot advantageous to him and away from the public and should try to have back-up units available. The officer should stop his car behind the suspect's vehicle, at such an angle that the driver's door is protected. A second officer should cover the passenger side of the suspect's auto. All persons inside should be ordered to place their hands in view of the officers. The driver should be ordered to turn off the ignition and should be the first one to come out of the vehicle. The officers should then follow standard arrest procedures.

Traffic and Accident Investigation

Traffic control is one of the most serious problems confronting police today. More people are killed or injured in accidents than in murders and assaults. Many police officers still feel that it is beneath their dignity to make a traffic arrest, yet they complain about the number of bad drivers on the streets.

Police officers should be familiar with the licensing laws for drivers and vehicles in their state. Some police officers feel that enforcement of licensing restrictions is not real police work, yet it is through this type of enforcement that bad drivers can be removed from the road.

At an accident the officer must take care of the injured, interview witnesses, find physical evidence and examine drivers for necessary licenses and registration, all to find out the cause of the accident.[46] Officers involved in traffic accident investigation do more than just write accident reports. They can make suggestions for placement of traffic control devices, road improvement, and other traffic-related changes.

Good accident investigation serves three general purposes. First, it obtains facts for accident prevention programs to be developed by police, traffic engineers, driver education directors, and others with an interest in traffic safety. Second, it determines whether a violation of the law has occurred and serves to support prosecution of the violator. Last, it obtains facts for any civil action that may occur.[47]

Conclusion

Good organization is essential to efficient police operations, and good leadership is a major influence in bringing it about. Organizational needs include a good organizational climate for work, established lines of communication among levels, and susceptibility of the organization as a whole to change.

Effective police patrol operations are the product of an efficient police organization. Patrol operations are the backbone of the police, their main function being protection of life and property. Patrol operations are ever-changing because the needs of the public change. An efficient police organization is responsive to the changing needs of the community.

CHAPTER **8**

Constitutional Considerations

There is a real tension in our society between those who advocate more effective police work to combat crime and those who point out this country's constitutional aversion to a police state. The tension cannot be avoided by calling for "law and order" and more aggressive police tactics. A balance must be found between security and liberty.

The first ten amendments to the Constitution—the Bill of Rights—provide that balance. Its authors realized the tendency, even by well-meaning officials, to use whatever shortcut seemed most effective in the pursuit, capture, and conviction of suspected criminals. Accordingly, the framers built into the Constitution certain principles to protect the liberties of U.S. citizens. They were designed as restraints on official action, not as a set of rigid rules to make the policeman's task more difficult. They were meant to protect the fundamentals of American liberty while at the same time protecting public order and citizens' security. Accordingly, the Bill of Rights limits the power of the policeman to stop a person from speaking or picketing, to arrest his freedom of movement, to search his person or home, or to subject him to questioning.

The purpose of the Constitution and the Bill of Rights is clear: Government must be restrained or it becomes tyrannical. In general, the U.S. Constitution stands for:

1. Government by the people. This means a republic with popular sovereignty rather than a dictatorship or a government solely by the state.
2. A limited government. The government has only the power given to it by the people; the rest remains with the states or with the people.
3. A federal government. Both state and national governments have powers.
4. A separation of powers. The legislative, executive, and judicial branches have separate functions.
5. Supremacy of federal over state governments. This means that states cannot prevent the federal government from exercising powers given to it by the Constitution.[1]

Living in a state as well as in the United States grants each person a kind of dual citizenship. The Fourteenth Amendment clarifies the issue:

> All persons born or naturalized in the United States, and subject to the jurisdiction thereof, are citizens of the United States and of the State wherein they reside. No State shall make or enforce any law which shall abridge the privileges or immunities of citizens of the United States; nor shall any State deprive any person of life, liberty, or property, without due process of law; nor deny to any person within its jurisdiction the equal protection of the laws.

So it is evident that the national government has an obligation to protect the personal liberties of its citizens from state action that unreasonably interferes with their rights as citizens of the United States. This amendment is generally cited as the authority for restraining unreasonable action by a state or local law enforcement officer.

But what is meant by "due process"? According to Supreme Court Justice Felix Frankfurter,

> . . . "due process" cannot be imprisoned within the treacherous limits of any formula. Representing a profound attitude of fairness between man and man, and more particularly, between the individual and the government, "due process" is compounded of history, reason, the past course of decisions, and stout confidence in the strength of the democratic faith which we profess. Due process is not a mechanical instrument. It is not a yardstick. It is a process. It is a delicate process of adjustment inescapably involving the exercise of judgment by those whom the Constitution entrusted with the unfolding of the process.[2]

It is often assumed that the most important task of any law enforcement agency in America is to protect the people. But law enforcement people must also bear in mind their constitutional obligations. Although only a small number of Americans are aware of their constitutional rights and fewer still know why they are so important, this should definitely not be the case with law enforcement personnel. Officers cannot be satisfied with reading the words contained in the first ten amendments. They must be prepared so that their day-to-day conduct will conform to constitutional standards, limitations, and duties.

Legally, the Bill of Rights is not a document to be molded according to personal, political, social, economic, or religious preferences. If it were, no person's rights would be safe.[3]

Some policemen and citizens argue that "good" or supereffective law enforcement policies or procedures are hampered by constitutional guarantees. Some police administrators believe that only "liberal" judges interpret safeguards too leniently or allow vicious criminals to return to the streets because of highly technical rulings. But little justification can be found for law enforcement that endangers the basic liberties of the individual. This is a chief danger that law enforcement must avoid. A partial answer may lie in placing more emphasis on adequate instruction for those entering the field. They should be charged not only with enforcing the law, but also with knowing it and its constitutional applications.

Law enforcement is a function of the executive branch of government, whether federal, state, county, or local. Law enforcement agencies carry out the legal mandates of the chief executive, whether he be president, governor, county supervisor, or mayor. It is generally recognized that the legislator makes the law, the executive enforces it, and the judiciary evaluates its practice.

The way laws are enforced determines to a great extent whether or not there is indeed "equal justice under the law." One of the most prominent distinctions between law enforcement in a democratic society and that in a totalitarian society is the sharp demarcation between the police role and the role of the courts. Here, the police only enforce the law; the job of interpreting the law and determining punishment is left to the courts.

Law enforcement officers would do well to remember that "the Constitution of the United States is a law for rulers and people, equally in war and in peace, and covers within the shield of its protection all classes of men at all times, and under all circumstances."[4]

The Limits of Police Discretion

Because it is impossible for legislatures to enact laws to interdict all antisocial behavior, they tend to pass broad legislative measures. This tendency can violate the first principle of a lawful, ordered society—the principle of legality itself. There is an inherent danger in vague and open-ended laws that allow police to define criminal conduct. These laws permit assertion of a broad range of power by policemen over everyday lives. It follows that we should have a government of clearly defined laws, not one influenced by daily opinions, values, and prejudices of a policeman on his beat.

A well-known scholar in criminology said in 1968:

> The patrolman's role is defined more by his responsibility for maintaining order than by his responsibility for enforcing the law. . . . Disorder . . . involves a dispute, over what is "right" or "seemly" conduct, over who is to blame for conduct that is agreed to be wrong or unseemly. A noisy drunk, a rowdy teenager shouting or racing his car in the middle of the night, a loud radio in the apartment next

door, a panhandler soliciting money from passersby, persons wearing eccentric clothes and unusual hair styles, loitering in public places—all these are examples of behaviour which "the public" (an onlooker, a neighbor, the community) may disapprove of and ask the patrolman to "put a stop to." Needless to say, the drunk, the teenager, the persons next door, the panhandler, and the hippies are likely to take a different view, to suggest that people "mind their own business," and to be irritated with the "cop" that intervenes.[5]

Vagrancy laws are a good example of constitutionally vague and open-ended laws that can cause errors in discretion. They typically state:

> Any and all tramps, vagrants, persons under suspicion who shall be found with no visible means of support, either male or female, shall not be allowed on the streets or other public place.

Another example is loitering laws, which define a loiterer thus:

> Any person, without visible means of support or unable to give a satisfactory account of himself, found loitering or strolling in, about, or upon any street, or other public way or place. . . .

Disorderly conduct laws are also highly discretionary:

> It shall be unlawful for any person to act in a violent, turbulent, quarrelsome, boisterous, indecent or disorderly manner, or to use profane, vulgar, or obscene language, or to do anything to disturb the good order, morals, peace or dignity of the city.

Granting the police such broad discretion is not without its social costs. They were discussed in the 1967 National Crime Commission in a task force report:

> One of the consequences is to communicate to the people who tend to be the objects of these laws the idea that law enforcement is not a regularized authoritative procedure, but largely a matter of arbitrary behavior by the authorities. The application of these laws often tends to discriminate against the poor and subcultural groups in the population. It is unjust to structure law enforcement in such a way that poverty itself becomes a crime. And it is costly for society when the law arouses feelings associated with those laws in the ghetto, a sense of persecution and helplessness, before official power and hostility to police and other authority that may tend to generate the very conditions of criminality society is seeking to extirpate.[6]

Because of the low visibility of the enforcement of these laws, they are rarely challenged in court. Occasionally, however, one of these questionably enforced laws reaches federal court and is declared invalid. Police must be cautious not to become a community tool for unconstitutional actions on behalf of those in the community who see law enforcement as a mechanism for making all citizens conform to *their* particular value system.

Key Enforcement Problems and the Bill of Rights

The Bill of Rights requires intelligent law enforcement if it is to function as a balance between law and order and the welfare of the individual. Only trained specialists can maintain order and at the same time preserve democratic values. Just being informed on certain rules of law is not enough. A devotion to impartial, competent enforcement under law as well as a dedication to the security of the community is required.

Some provisions in the Bill of Rights cause more serious enforcement problems than others. The average officer confronts many difficult tasks each day in such areas because there is some doubt as to the law in many situations. One reason this uncertainty exists is because the Supreme Court often fails to specify standards regarding rights and obligations of law enforcement personnel. The Court has an obligation to make the Constitution a living and applicable document, for it was written not only to create this government, but also to regulate it.

Following is an analysis of law enforcement functions in relation to key provisions in the Bill of Rights, showing the interrelation between security and liberty.

First Amendment Rights

Congress shall make no law respecting an establishment of religion, or prohibiting the free exercise thereof; or abridging the freedom of speech or of the press; or the right of the people peaceably to assemble, and to petition the government for a redress of grievances.

The right to speak freely and to practice and promote a variety of behavior is a basic one in the United States. Free speech almost encourages dispute, but it is not an inalienable right. Limits must sometimes be placed on speakers, but law enforcement officers must exercise extreme caution when imposing such limits. The burden of responsibility lies not only with officers, but also with police administrators, who to a large extent determine policy that influences the individual officers' discretion in free speech matters.

Law enforcement officers must understand the difficulties involved in controlling public meetings. The enforcement problems concerning freedom of speech are few compared with those in everyday police work. But this issue is fundamental, and officers must be able to handle these problems effectively when they arise, without the aid of their manuals and textbooks. And in performing these duties, they must do them in such a way that their actions will stand up in court if necessary.

The First Amendment's protection of free speech is aimed at insulating certain kinds of behavior from police interference. Restrictions may be imposed on First Amendment rights in three kinds of circumstances; the individual's interest must be adjusted when the government (1) seeks to protect the rights of others not to listen if they so choose, (2) seeks to protect others from injurious consequences of the communication, or (3) seeks to protect some governmental function.[7]

An example of the first case would be if a speaker physically restrained his audience in order to make them listen. An example of the second is Justice Holmes's famous statement that the Frist Amendment does not protect the one who falsely shouts "fire" in a crowded theater. Nor does it protect speech that incites others to riot, furthers a conspiracy to commit crimes, invades the privacy of others, or maliciously libels another. Examples of the third circumstance—prohibiting acts of communication to protect some governmental function—would be suppression of speech that was meant to plot a revolution, arrange a political assassination, or communicate information to the enemy.

Police regulatory action in relation to demonstrations requires a high degree of sensitivity on the part of the law enforcement officer toward the rights of the participants. Police need guidelines to help them perform their duties effectively and intelligently. Ideally, legislators would initiate laws that met constitutional mandates, and local governing officials would institute better policies in order to insure that all people are treated equally and fairly under due process of law.

Perhaps the constitutional limitations on First Amendment rights were best summarized by the Supreme Court in 1965:

> From these decisions certain clear principles emerge. The rights of free speech and assembly, while fundamental in our democratic society, still do not mean that everyone with opinions and beliefs may address a group at any public place and at any time. The constitutional guarantee of liberty implies the existence of an organized society maintaining public order, without which, liberty itself would be lost in the excesses of anarchy. The control of travel on the streets is a clear example of governmental responsibility to insure this necessary order. . . . One would not be justified in ignoring the familiar red light because this was thought to be a means of social protest. Nor could one, contrary to traffic regulations, insist upon a street meeting in the middle of Times Square at the rush hour as a form of freedom of speech or assembly. Governmental authorities have the duty and responsibility to keep their streets open and available for movement. A group of demonstrators could not insist upon the right to cordon off a street, or entrance to a public or private building, and allow no one to pass who did not agree to listen to their exhortations.[8]

Fourth Amendment Rights

The right of the people to be secure in their persons, houses, papers, and effects, against unreasonable searches and seizures, shall not be violated, and no warrants shall issue but upon probable cause, supported by oath or affirmation, and particularly describing the place to be searched, and the person or things to be seized.

The right of every person to enjoy personal freedom from unlawful restraint is firmly imbedded in the history of Anglo-American law.[9] The right of personal liberty is still a strong differentiating factor between our systems and others. In our system illegal arrest practices are a contradiction of personal liberty. An illegal arrest will usually render inadmissible any evidence obtained by search and seizure incident to such an arrest.

The provisions in the Fourth Amendment cover some of the most critical areas of criminal investigation—arrest, search, seizure, and in some cases, interrogation and lineup identification. These issues serve to sharpen the focus on the question of order versus personal liberty.[10]

The Fourth Amendment protects citizens against unreasonable searches and seizures, establishes the conditions under which a warrant may be issued and what the warrant must contain, and further establishes that the only reasonable searches and seizures are those conducted under a valid warrant. It is sometimes thought that only physical objects, and not persons, are protected from unreasonable searches and seizures, but this is a misconception.

Whether or not an action is "reasonable" depends on whether or not there is probable cause to believe the suspect is guilty. If there is, then a valid warrant may be issued and the arrest will be legal.

But what if a warrant cannot be obtained immediately and an officer believes a crime is being or has recently been committed? He may then arrest the suspected felon. The only really safe statements that can be made in regard to arrest without a warrant are: (1) anyone, law enforcement officer or private citizen, in all states, may make an arrest to stop the commission of a felony or to apprehend a felon; (2) anyone, law enforcement officer or private citizen, may in most states make an arrest when the offense is a breach of the peace actually being attempted or committed in the presence or view of the person making the arrest.[11]

Many pitfalls await an officer who deprives a person of his liberty through arrest. To perform his duty properly, the officer needs not only a knowledge of the law, but also good judgment in interpreting it. Since a search is almost always conducted and property seized when a person is arrested, the search and seizure must conform to the guidelines set by the courts in order to be used as evidence in a criminal trial.[12]

Audio-surveillance by mechanical devices has always been related to search and seizure issues. Electronic eavesdropping usually constitutes an invasion of privacy, and that is why it is not openly commended. The meaning of the "right to privacy" has been debated, but judicially it has meant the "right to be left alone."[13]

Stop and frisk, or "detention and questioning," as it was known under English common law, is nothing new. Yet it has become a topic for national concern and debate in recent years. Statutes and judicial sanctions of stop and frisk are based on the Fourth Amendment admonition against unreasonable searches and seizures. The question, therefore, centers on whether police conduct is reasonable or not when an officer detains and questions a suspect. Again, "probable cause" is a deciding factor. Law enforcement administrators are faced with the problems of formulating policy on stop and frisk practices that is constitutional as well as effective, and implementing it with adequate supervision.

Fifth Amendment Rights

> No person shall be . . . compelled in any criminal case to be a witness against himself, nor be deprived of life, liberty, or property, without due process of law. . . .

Another area in the criminal justice process that comes under close constitutional scrutiny is the taking of statements from suspects and using the information against the accused in a criminal trial. The use of confessions comes under the Fifth Amendment protection against incriminating oneself.[14]

Statements are significant, since about 85 percent of all police investigative time is spent talking to people to obtain information that often becomes part of a written record. Therefore, law enforcement officers must be well informed on the law of confessions, as well as problems related to lineup identification, if they are to discharge their duties legally and effectively.

The Fifth Amendment contains a number of rights, only one of which is protection against self-incrimination. Applications of the rights give rise to many problems; admissibility of confessions as well as the use of exculpatory and inculpatory statements now rests on whether or not the statement was obtained in accordance with a number of complex and somewhat ambiguous rules the Supreme Court has initiated in recent years. (An inculpatory statement is an oral or written statement from which guilt can be inferred. It is not a confession of guilt. An exculpatory statement is an oral or written statement that tends to show nonguilt. One incriminates and the other exonerates.)

Sixth Amendment Rights

> In all criminal prosecutions, the accused shall enjoy the right . . . to have the assistance of counsel for his defense.

The most revolutionary application of the Sixth Amendment right to the assistance of counsel brings the critical issue to the pretrial stage. The *Miranda* decision by the U.S. Supreme Court calls for the presence of counsel when the suspect is taken into custody. In addition, the Supreme Court has said that "in a capital case, where the defendant is unable to employ counsel, and is incapable of adequately making his own defense because of ignorance, feeblemindedness, illiteracy, or the like, it is the duty of the court, whether requested or not, to assign counsel for him as a necessary requisite to due process of law."[15]

The major law enforcement problems relating to the Bill of Rights are just some of the problems faced by law enforcement personnel daily. They are complex issues, but they must be solved within the framework of the Constitution. Some policemen see the Constitution and its amendments as a burden, an obstruction, a technical barrier to be avoided, evaded, or in some cases ignored. Although these policemen are pledged to preserve, protect, and defend the Constitution, sometimes through ignorance or inappropriate zeal, they defile and debase it.

The law enforcement dilemma resulting from judicial restrictions is based on a conflict between two responsibilities. On one hand, the officer must protect the individual's exercise of freedom. The basic purpose of the Bill of Rights and the Constitution is to protect the personal rights of each citizen, whether he is guilty or innocent. For the laws to be respected, the courts must be sympathetic to this purpose. On the other hand, the law enforcement officer must protect the community from crime. The recognition of this balance is a major police responsibility which should be emphasized in all police training.

Constitutional Limitations and the Police

Policemen should be aware of the constitutional limitations that apply to them in the areas of obtaining confessions, allowing suspects access to counsel and informing them of their rights, conducting searches, obtaining admissible evidence, obtaining valid identifications, and handling arrest and conviction records.

From the earliest times, confessions, evidence, and records have been used against wrongdoers. It is only in the past three hundred years, that anyone has expressed concern as to how evidence was obtained, whether confessions were voluntary, and whether proper rules were followed involving the use of records.

During ancient Roman days, if a suspect refused to confess after verbal questioning, his slaves were then tortured. If necessary, the suspect was tortured last. During the twelfth and thirteenth centuries the Catholic church favored obtaining religious evidence and confessions by the use of torture. In both France and Germany trial by ordeal and combat were used to secure evidence. The Star Chamber proceeding in England also used torture to obtain evidence, but in seventeenth-century England such practices came under sharp attack. The English Bill of Rights enacted in 1689 prohibited cruel and unusual punishment. Many English common law traditions were put into effect as the first written laws of this country, particularly the Fifth, Sixth, Eighth, and Fourteenth Amendments to the Constitution.

The Fifth Amendment, among other things, provides that no person shall be compelled to be a witness against himself. This generally has been construed by the United States Supreme Court to refer to words uttered from the mouth of the accused and not to substances removed from the body, such as blood, even when the substance is obtained without the consent of the accused.[16] This is provided, of course, that the force used does not shock the human conscience.[17]

The Sixth Amendment gives a person the right to be represented by counsel; this right exists at every critical stage during which the accused is in jeopardy,[18] including interrogation in a police-dominated atmosphere.[19]

The Eighth Amendment provides that people be secure from cruel and unusual punishment, and the Fourteenth Amendment makes all these concepts binding on the states through the due process of law clause contained therein.

Confessions

John H. Wigmore, one of the outstanding authorities on evidence in American jurisprudence, has said, "The general principle established in the 1700s was this: 'A confession forced from the mind by the flattery of hope or the torture of fear is inadmissible.' " This principle is as true today as when he wrote it nearly forty years ago. He went on to state the underlying test as to the trustworthiness and admissibility of confession: "Was the situation one likely to lead, in experience, to an untrue confession?"

The type of promises under the test that have resulted in confessions being ruled inadmissible have been promises of a lighter sentence, release from arrest, or a reward of money, and an offer to have the complaint withdrawn. One judge even ruled that the statement by police, "The judge may look kindly upon you if you tell the truth," constituted a promise.

Many of the stringent rules that we work under today are the result of a small number of abusive practices by police that we today find hard to believe could have taken place. For example, the sweat box, which was a small cell where a reticent prisoner was incarcerated with the heat turned up and the windows shut, was used in Michigan. The old term "sweating a confession" was to be taken literally.[20]

Other methods such as striking or whipping the suspected person,[21] hanging the accused,[22] giving the accused the water cure,[23] stripping the accused of his clothes and making him touch the corpse,[24] and making the defendant lie in some brush that was then set on fire[25] have all resulted quite appropriately in court rulings that the confessions did not meet the standards of admissibility.

Less drastic police methods have been employed more recently. As an example of trickery, a police officer was placed in a cell with a prisoner under the guise that he was a prisoner also. His job was to befriend the prisoner and try to obtain information on the suspect's criminal activities. Other examples of trickery were interrogating several suspects involved in the same incident in succession, then permitting one of the suspects to smoke and giving him a cup of coffee or a bottle of pop. This person was taken away from the remainder of the group, and the group was told that the person had confessed when in fact he had not. This was intended to "break" the other suspects.

In some cases suspects were told that non-existing informants had given the police information. In one case the suspect demanded legal counsel, and an obliging police officer played the part of an attorney and listened to his confession. The court ultimately decided that a confession made under those circumstances violated the attorney-client relationship.[26]

One of the leading United States cases in which trickery was employed was the Spano case. A close friend was used to trick the defendant into a confession. The court ruled that if a confession resulted from official pressure, fatigue, and sympathy falsely aroused, the confession was inadmissible even though no physical brutality was used. The court said that "it did not doubt the trustworthiness of the confession but felt the police had exercised impropriety in obtaining it."[27] This case, decided in 1959, is regarded by some jurists as one of the most important cases dealing with extrajudicial confessions in the past decade.

The Mallory, Escobedo, *and* Miranda *Decisions*

Mallory, Escobedo, and *Miranda* were three fairly recent cases that dramatically changed police practices. In 1957 the U.S. Supreme Court handed down a decision in the *Mallory* case, which indicated, in substance, that a suspect cannot be interrogated for long periods of time for the main purpose of securing a confession prior to his arraignment. The Court ruled that the arrested person should be taken without unnecessary delay before a magistrate.[28] To put teeth into the *Mallory* rule, the Michigan legislature passed an act in 1964 that provided:

> A peace officer who has arrested a person for a felony offense without a warrant must, without unnecessary delay, take the arrested person

> before the most convenient magistrate of the county in which the offense was committed and must make before the magistrate a complaint, stating the offense for which the person was arrested.[29]

The Michigan Supreme Court had already adopted the *Mallory* rule in an earlier case based on the due process clause in the Michigan Constitution.

In 1964 the U.S. Supreme Court handed down a decision that caused great consternation in police circles. Police in Chicago had arrested a suspect named Danny Escobedo for investigation of a murder. The evidence was fragmentary, but the finger of suspicion did point toward Escobedo. His attorney came to the police station and demanded to see his client, but was refused. While the attorney waited outside, Escobedo confessed to the murder. On the basis of this confession and little else, he was convicted. The confession contained information of which only the murderer would be cognizant.

Escobedo's attorney appealed to the Supreme Court. The majority of the court held, in substance, that when Escobedo was denied the right to talk to his attorney, it violated his Sixth Amendment right to counsel. At that time the court indicated that whenever an investigation shifts to the accusatory stage, the defendant must be told he has a right to remain silent, that anything he says may be used against him, and that he has the right to legal counsel.[30]

The decision was unclear on many points. Police, lawyers, and judges were all reading different things into the case, things that were not there, resulting in a great deal of inconsistency in its application.

In order to clear up this confusion, the Supreme Court in 1966 agreed to hear *Miranda* v. *Arizona.*[31] The guidelines set forth in *Miranda* are the main ones by which the judicial system operates today when it is concerned with extrajudicial confessions. This case built on *Escobedo,* and its requirements were fairly well defined. Under this rule the high court shifted its focus completely away from the concept of whether the police were involved in the accusatory stage or the investigatory stage, and centered on whether the questioning was a custodial interrogation occurring in a police-dominated atmosphere. If it was, said the Court, then the new rights set forth had to be given:

1. You have the absolute right to remain silent.
2. Anything you say can and will be used against you in a court of law.
3. You have the right to have an attorney present before you answer any questions.
4. If you cannot afford an attorney, one will be provided for you free of charge by the court.

The officer should then inquire whether the suspect understands these rights, and if, with his rights in mind, he wishes to discuss the case. Only if these conditions exist is there a legal custodial interrogation. This decision, like others previously mentioned, was aimed at correcting police abuses while officers were engaged in questioning criminal suspects.

In light of the foregoing, a police officer arriving at the scene of a homicide is not remiss in asking a person at the scene whether he knows who committed the crime. In such cases, even though no warnings were given, the confession has been held admissible. The phrase "police-dominated atmosphere" is an important one to remember. In another recent case, officers surrounded a suspect in his bed. They had full intentions of arresting him and were armed with heavy weapons. The court in that case held that even though the suspect was in his home, the circumstances made it a police-dominated atmosphere, and the warnings should have been given.

If the accused lacked the mental capacity to sufficiently understand his rights and make an intelligent waiver, the confession that followed would be inadmissible. It is a burden upon the people, represented by the prosecutor, to show that the waiver was knowingly and intelligently made. The court has gone on to say, "Moreover any evidence that the accused was threatened, tricked, or cajoled into a waiver will, of course, show that the defendant did not voluntarily waive his privilege."[32]

An example of the value of the *Miranda* decision is the case of George Whitmore, who was arrested in Brooklyn in April 1964. During an interrogation of some twenty hours, Whitmore confessed to a rape, an unsolved homicide, and a double murder. The confession to the double murder was sixty-one typewritten pages of specific details. Whitmore, however, had been subject to a great amount of fatigue and fear, which, combined with the limitations of his own intelligence, resulted in his answering questions as requested by the detectives. If it had not been for an informer who told the detectives that someone else had committed the murders, George Whitmore might well have remained in custody.[33]

The *Miranda* decision, as refined by the *Gault* decision, also protects the juvenile. The waiver of rights by a juvenile can be a problem when following the rationale as set forth in the *Miranda* case. In the *Gault* decision the court indicated that both the parent and the juvenile must be given the warnings as prescribed in *Miranda*. Both must indicate that they understand them, and both must waive them, but the rights cannot be waived solely by the parent because they belong to the juvenile.

Search and Seizure

A search is an examination of a person, place, motor vehicle, or any other thing with a view toward discovery of evidence (contraband, weapons, items used in committing a crime, stolen property, and so on). The examples in this section are grouped according to the common situations in which search opportunities arise: (1) when evidence is found in plain view or open view, and (2) when an arrest is made, either noncustodial, as in minor traffic cases, or, more typically, as in full-custody arrest, when the suspect is taken to a detention facility.

Plain View. Evidence is considered to be in plain view when an officer is lawfully in the place where he sees the evidence. He may then, without obtaining a search warrant, seize from that location any item that he observes in plain view or open view (including items observed with the aid of a flashlight), if he has probable cause to believe that the item is contraband, a weapon, anything used in committing a crime, stolen property, or other evidence of crime. This definition is derived from a series of Supreme Court decisions, with *Harris* v. *United States* as the key case.[34] Because the officer conducts no search, such discoveries are not within the purview of the Fourth Amendment.

The plain view doctrine applies only when a police officer has a prior justification for an intrusion in the course of which he inadvertently comes across an item incriminating the accused. *Katz* v. *United States* establishes the general principle that the Fourth Amendment protects a citizen's "legitimate expectations of privacy."[35]

Arrest Cases. Whenever an officer makes a full-custody arrest of a person, he may conduct a full warrantless search of the arrested person's garments and the surface of his body in a manner designed to reveal the presence of seizable items. If in a vehicle, an officer may conduct a warrantless search of those areas of the vehicle within which the arrested person might readily reach for a weapon or other seizable items at the time of arrest. The search must be conducted at the time and place of arrest in the immediate presence of the arrested person.

> The critical factor . . . is not the greater likelihood that a person taken into custody is armed, but rather the increased likelihood of danger to the officer *if* in fact the person is armed. When it becomes necessary that an officer confine a traffic law violator within his police vehicle, the officer risks the danger that the violator may be armed with and draw a weapon.[36]

On December 11, 1973, the Supreme Court reached a decision on two cases that involved searches of traffic offenders. The press reported this decision in a manner that resulted in misinterpretation and improper application by police officers. The cases were *U.S.* v. *Robinson* (No. 72–936) and *Gustafson* v. *Florida* (No. 71–1669).

The following is a brief digest of the *Robinson* decision:

> The 4th Amendment does not bar the admission in evidence of heroin discovered by a police officer during a thorough search of a traffic offender whom he was taking into custody for a serious traffic offense that carried a mandatory jail term, a mandatory fine, or both, since a police officer's authority to make a full search incident to a lawful custodial arrest requires no justification beyond the fact of the arrest itself. It is the fact of the lawful arrest which establishes the authority to search, and the court holds that in the case of a lawful custodial arrest, a full search is not only an exception to the warrant require-

> ment of the 4th Amendment, but is also a "reasonable" search under the amendment.[37]

The defendant in this case was arrested for driving while his operator's license was revoked. The officer searched the arrestee before transporting him to the station for booking. During this search, he discovered a crumpled cigarette package that contained heroin. The defendant was convicted of possession of heroin and the Supreme Court upheld that conviction.

The Gustafson case resulted in the following decision:

> The full search of the person of the arrestee made incident to a lawful custodial arrest did not violate the 4th and 14th Amendments, and it is of no constitutional significance that, contrary to the situation in the Robinson case, police regulations did not require that the petitioner be taken into custody or establish the conditions under which a full scale body search should be conducted nor, as in Robinson, is it relevant that the arresting officer had no subjective fear of the petitioner or suspect that he was armed, since it is the fact of custodial arrest which gives rise to the authority to search.[38]

In this case the defendant was observed driving a vehicle bearing New York plates in Eau Gallie, Florida, at 2:00 A.M. The vehicle was weaving across the centerline and the officer followed it into a parking lot where he confronted the defendant. Gustafson could not produce an operator's license, and he was placed under arrest and searched prior to being transported to the station for booking. This search produced marijuana, and Gustafson was convicted for possession of marijuana. The Supreme Court upheld that conviction.

In both the cases the Supreme Court placed much emphasis on the term "custodial arrest." When an officer stops a traffic offender for a violation resulting in physical arrest, the suspect may be searched, and what is discovered will be admissible.

In performing his responsibilities, a law enforcement officer must often approach individuals who appear to be engaged in some activity calling for investigation. Such activities may cover a wide range of situations. In some, the officer will be preventing or detecting crime; in others, he will be providing assistance to persons in need. Depending on the nature of the situation, the police response may vary from a mere "contact," to a formal "stop" or "frisk," or, under certain specified conditions, to a full "search" of the person. In handling these varied situations, the officer must promote public safety while keeping himself from harm, but should also hold invasions of personal rights and privacy to a minimum.

The court has stated that stopping a person for questioning must meet these legal prerequisites: 1) "belief by the officer involved that a crime might have been committed; 2) reasonable grounds for such a belief; and 3) absolute necessity for immediate investigatory activity."[39] There are several reasons why a policeman may stop and frisk a suspect. Do the clothes of the suspect bulge in a manner suggesting the presence of any object capable of inflicting injury? Did the suspect move as if to hide a weapon, or was he unusually nervous upon being contacted by the officer? Does the officer's suspicion of the suspect involve a serious and violent threat? Every officer who conducts a frisk must be prepared to cite the specific factors that led him to conclude that "reasonable suspicion" existed before the frisk began. A frisk is a limited search, for the purpose of protection only.

Limits exist on what an officer can lawfully do. The constitutional periphery of these limits has been set out by the Supreme Court in the cases of *Terry* v. *Ohio,* 392 U.S. 1 (1968); *Sibron* v. *New York,* 392 U.S. 40 (1968); and *Adams* v. *Williams,* 407 U.S. 143 (1972). All the cases try to help the officer on the street, for, according to the *Terry* v. *Ohio* decision, "the police are in need of an escalating set of flexible responses, graduated in relation to the amount of information they possess."

In *Harris* v. *United States* the Court stated:

> A community's attitude toward the police is influenced most by the actions of individual officers on the streets. No community-relations or recruiting or training program will avail if courteous and cool-headed conduct by policemen in their contacts with citizens is not enforced.[40]

As the quote suggests, a community's attitude toward the police is shaped largely by the encounters between officers and citizens on the streets. An officer may initiate a contact with a person as indicated in the "stop and frisk" limitations. He may make that contact in any place where the officer has the right to be. The officer should always identify himself as a law enforcement officer as soon as reasonably possible after the contact is made. The officer may make contact, and if the person refuses to cooperate, he must be permitted to go on his way unless certain additional circumstances exist that would justify physical detention. However, if it seems appropriate under the circumstances, the citizen may only be kept under surveillance if the officer lacks "reasonable suspicion."

If a stop and frisk is based in whole or in part on an informant's tip, the officer making the stop and frisk should make every reasonable effort to obtain the identity of the informant. Further, the officer should record the facts concerning such a tip, how it was received, the basis of the informant's reliability, and the origin of his information.[41]

Evidence

Evidence includes all the means by which any alleged matter of fact, the truth of which is submitted to investigation, is established or disproved.[42] There are three types of evidence. *Direct evidence* is facts that a witness gained through one of his own five senses, such as an eyewitness account of a homicide. *Circumstantial evidence* is the inference of the principal fact from one or more circumstances that have been established directly. *Real evidence* is evidence that can be seen or felt and speaks for itself and does not require explanation.

Evidence must meet requirements for admissibility. It must be relevant—that is, it must relate to or bear directly upon a fact in issue and prove or have a tendency to prove the truth or untruth of such fact. It must be material—that is, it must affect a fact or issue in the case somewhat significantly. It must be of some importance. If it is insignificant or unimportant, then it is generally not admissible even though it may be relevant. And the evidence must be competent, which makes it legally adequate and sufficient. All these requirements must be met before the evidence is admissible.

One of the most important rules of evidence with which an officer should be familiar is the "exclusionary rule." It came into existence with the *Mapp* case in 1961. The rule is very simple. It merely provides that evidence that has been illegally obtained will be excluded from use in court. The Mapp decision made the Fourth Amendment applicable to the states through the due process clause of the Fourteenth Amendment. The court stated: "We hold all evidence obtained by searches and seizures in violation of the Constitution is, by that same authority, inadmissible in a state court."[43] Until this case, there was no requirement on the states regarding how evidence was obtained, as it was usable in court so long as it aided in proving the guilt of the accused. As as result of the exclusionary rule and its historical background, other doctrines were developed. As an example, the rule first pertained only to federal officers. They circumvented the rule by getting from local officers evidence obtained illegally by the latter. This was known as the "silver-platter rule." As a result of this practice, other restrictions were placed on federal officers.[44] In the Silverthorne case the court decided that not only was illegally obtained evidence not admissible, but any information gained as a result of an illegal search was also inadmissible.[45] This is the "poisonous-fruit doctrine"—if the search itself is illegal, it is considered analogous to a poisonous tree, and any information gained as a result of it is also illegal and is considered the "poisonous fruit" of the "poisonous tree."

Through court decisions and the enactment of laws, three methods have been developed whereby a search may be made that is generally accepted as being reasonable, and property seized as a result of these searches may be admitted in evidence against an accused person. These methods are: (1) a search made after a valid consent is given, (2) a search made incidental to a lawful arrest, and (3) a search made pursuant to a search warrant.

In dealing with property and evidence, an officer cannot avoid the question of search warrants. An officer needs a search warrant unless:

1. The search is made incidental to a lawful arrest and confined to an area under the immediate control of the person taken into custody;
2. The officer searches a mobile vehicle with probable cause to believe it contains contraband;

3. The officer has probable cause to believe contraband will be destroyed;
4. An emergency exists such as a fire or blockade;
5. The officer is in hot pursuit of a felon;
6. The officer is acting under the stop and frisk provisions;
7. The person consents.

Two further questions regarding searches deserve attention. Can a visitor on the premises ever be searched? And may items not named in a search warrant ever be seized? The following two decisions attempted to provide answers regarding these issues.

The first case deals with a narcotics conviction. Washington police obtained a search warrant for narcotics in an apartment of a man named Steward, based on information that he was selling narcotics there. When they went to serve their warrant in the early morning hours, they knocked and announced their identity and purpose. Shortly thereafter, they heard a noise inside followed by the sound of a window breaking, whereupon they forced the door open. Steward was trying to get out the bedroom window and was arrested. The defendant in the case was sitting on a couch, and a purse was on the coffee table in front of her. Before entering the apartment, the police knew that she was a visitor on the premises. The officers seized her purse, searched it, found narcotics, and arrested her. This was claimed to be an illegal search because it preceded her arrest. The court held otherwise and said that under the facts, "the police could reasonably have believed that items sought and described in the warrant had been concealed in the purse in pursuit of items for which the warrant was issued." They then turned to a case they had previously decided and said that in that case, "this court permitted the search of a wallet and bag held by one who shared occupancy of the residence searched under authority of a warrant, holding that contrary result would be to suggest that a warrant to search premises may be frustrated by the device of simply picking up the guilty object and holding it in one's hand. Similarly here, frustration of the warrant's purpose would not be permitted where the facts reveal that to be the likely result were the purse not searched."[46]

The second example involves a conviction for burglary of the Troff Corral. The owner of the corral called the sheriff when he saw that his place had been entered and a number of saddles and other items taken. In the riding arena, the sheriff and the owner noticed boot marks that had not been there the previous day, and the sheriff took a cast of one of them. Another officer and the sheriff of a nearby county went to the home of the defendant and arrested him and his wife for a different offense. While making this arrest, they noticed some items of personal property that they believed to have been stolen in several other burglaries that they were presently investigating. They therefore got a search warrant to check for certain described articles that had been taken in two other burglaries. In the course of executing this warrant the officer found some of the articles they were searching for and also saw articles that were identified as having come from still other burglaries. Also, the local sheriff and the owner of the corral, who had accompanied the officers on this occasion, saw one of the saddles and several other articles taken in the burglary of the corral. So the next day another search warrant for these articles was obtained, and the articles were seized along with a pair of overshoes and pair of rubbers that were not described in the warrant. These items later linked the defendant with the burglary of the corral. He claimed that they were seized illegally and should not have been admitted as evidence.

The court affirmed the conviction. It pointed out that it is the general rule that where a search is pursuant to a warrant, the officer making the search cannot seize property other than that which is specifically described in the warrant, but it went on to point out that there are exceptions to this rule and that one of these was that, "where a police officer while in the course of a lawful search pursuant to a valid search warrant inadvertently uncovers evidence of another crime" it may be seized although it is not described in the warrant. "In order that he may do so, the original search must be directed in good faith toward finding articles described in the warrant, and he must have probable cause to believe the inadvertently discovered evidence is in fact seizable, that is, connected with criminal behavior." The court went on to hold that the officers had probable cause to believe that the overshoes and rubbers were related to the burglary of the corral because the officers were aware of the footprints found there. The defendant also complained that the overshoes and rubbers were not listed on the inventory filed with the return to the search warrant, but as to this the court said, "In any event the return of a search warrant is a ministerial act and any failure therein does not void the warrant."[47]

The importance of the matter contained in the foregoing recent cases should not be underestimated, for today's rules promise to have wide application well beyond the facts of the case. The cases suggest that if a police officer acts with discretion and common sense, keeping in mind his constitutional limitations and his proper police goal, his actions have a good chance of being upheld by the courts.

Eyewitness Identification

The purposes of decisions dealing with eyewitness identification are to establish uniform procedures for identification of suspects by eyewitnesses to a crime and to promote practices that will safeguard innocent persons while insuring that those who are guilty are prosecuted. Specific rules are provided for confrontations, use of photographs, and lineups.

Confrontations. One type of confrontation is presenting a suspect singly to a witness. This is permissible when the suspect is arrested or temporarily detained within two hours of the offense, and when the witness is cooperative and states that he might recognize the person who committed the offense. This is known as "one-on-one," "street I.D.," "bring-back," "field identification," "curbstone lineup," "show-up," or "on-the-scene identification." There are two elements to take into consideration. First, there is a two-hour time limit, which is an attempt "to balance the freshness of a confrontation against its inherent suggestiveness."[48] The suspect must be shown to the witness within this time limit. Second, the suspect does not have a right to a lawyer. The absence of a Sixth Amendment right to counsel for street confrontations is made clear in *Kirby* v. *Illinois.* It is hard to conceive a street confrontation within the time limit and with an attorney present.

Photographs. Another method of identification is through the use of photographs. Although most agree that a fair lineup remains the most accurate means of pretrial identification, it is not always possible to conduct a lineup. The perpetrator of the crime may be at large or unknown, or the police may not be able to locate him. Pictorial procedures are then the only means of identification available.

A prearrest display of photographs of known suspects was the procedure specifically and unanimously approved by the United States Supreme Court in *Simmons* v. *United States*.

> Despite the hazards of initial identification by photograph, this procedure has been used widely and effectively in criminal law enforcement, from the standpoint both of apprehending offenders and of sparing innocent suspects the ignominy of arrest by allowing eyewitnesses to exonerate them through scrutiny of photographs.[49]

Many departments use a "mug book." A properly conducted "mug book" or "rogues' gallery" procedure is in itself nonsuggestive. Since the investigator does not have a suspect in mind, he cannot suggest anyone to the viewer.[50] To avoid inadvertent misidentification, a reasonable number of photos must be shown and quick identification must not affect the viewing of the "reasonable number." The use of sketches and composites to recreate the image of the perpetrator also is proper.[51]

Lineups. Even the most neutral lineup imparts some suggestion. The witness may believe that he would not be asked to view a lineup unless the police believed they had the criminal. The witness may feel obligated to "reward" police efforts by selecting someone in the lineup. Because of these inherent influences, anything that focuses attention on the suspect in the lineup can affect its validity. Therefore, it is imperative that each lineup be conducted with the greatest care and diligence to assure fundamental fairness and preserve due process. As a result of the study of court decisions relating to lineups, the following checklist was made to assure the rules of lineup established by the Supreme Court in *United States* v. *Wade*.[52]

1. Are there four or five people in the lineup in addition to the accused?
2. Did the suspect pick his own spot?
3. Do all lineup members have resemblance?
4. Is each person in the lineup standing the same way?
5. Are their arms all hanging by the side?

6. Is each person looking straight ahead?
7. Are all persons dressed the same?
8. If not, is each person dressed differently?
9. Is the lineup basically fair?
10. Has a photograph been taken?
11. Was the defense attorney asked for objection?
12. Was the defense attorney told when the witness was being brought in?
13. Was the lineup set before the witness was brought in?
14. Was only one witness at a time permitted to view the lineup?
15. Have the officers avoided doing or saying anything to call special attention to the suspect?
16. Have the witnesses been separated before, during, and until the lineup was concluded?
17. Has putting two suspects in the same lineup been avoided?
18. Were witnesses instructed that they do not have to answer defense counsel's questions?

All the questions should be answered yes. Departure from the rules given above has resulted in decisions that improper procedures were used regarding the very important identification of a suspect. Compelling a suspect to appear in a lineup without the aid of counsel will not violate his right against self-incrimination, but it will violate his Sixth Amendment right to counsel.

Arrest and Conviction Records

It is important to be familiar with decisions that may have a lasting effect on the purpose for which records may be released, the procedures by which release is to be made, and the persons to whom records may be released. The decisions safeguard the privacy of the individual citizens and, at the same time, provide for essential law enforcement informational needs.

An arrest record (commonly known as a "rap sheet") is a compilation of information, centrally maintained in law enforcement custody, of any arrest or temporary detention. It includes the identity of the person arrested or detained, the nature of the police contact, the charge, and the disposition or present status of the case. A conviction record is an arrest record in which the disposition includes details of the conviction and the sentence.

Detention is a term often used to indicate restraint on liberty but not resulting in full-custody arrest.

Unless otherwise provided by law, arrest and conviction records may be released only to the following persons under the following circumstances: (1) to law enforcement agencies of any jurisdiction for law enforcement purposes; (2) to criminal justice personnel for purposes of executing the responsibilities of their position in a matter relating to the individual whose record is requested; and (3) to defense counsel or his agents for purposes of providing representation in a criminal or juvenile proceeding.

Historically, the decision to collect, retain, and release arrest and conviction records has been regarded as almost exclusively within the scope of police discretion. Courts generally have recognized that when such records are compiled following a lawful arrest, their retention in confidential files for use as an investigative tool, including dissemination to other law enforcement agencies for such purposes, is justified in the interest of promoting effective law enforcement.[53] Although records are freely exchanged among law enforcement agencies, certain limits have often been placed on public inspection on the grounds that the public has no right to inspect criminal records maintained by law enforcement agencies.[54]

There are three principal reasons for this judicial concern: (1) increasing public concern over the loss of privacy as a "natural by-product of our modern technology,"[55] (2) the belief that a person with a "criminal record" is more likely than others to be subject to police scrutiny and other governmental disadvantages, and (3) the economic harm that may follow if the arrest of a person becomes known to present or prospective employers and credit reporting agencies.

The primary concern has focused on the harmful effects of a criminal record on employment, whether with governmental or a private concern. Documentation of the use of such records to assist in employment decisions is extensive. Perhaps the best known example is the Duncan Report, which examined employment practices in the District of Columbia and found that information on arrest records was supplied to 350 to 400 persons daily by the D.C. Metropolitan Police Department, and that the use of such records very often resulted in denial of employment.[56]

Another study indicated that 75 percent of New York employment agencies surveyed would not even refer someone with an arrest record to a prospective employer.[57]

Juvenile records may be released pursuant to the general provisions outlined. In addition, the juvenile record of a person who has not reached the age of eighteen at the time the record is requested may be released to his parents, guardian, or other duly authorized custodian.

How long can the justice system keep records? If a person has been arrested and his case has been disposed of other than by conviction, the record pertaining to that arrest is to be designated a closed record five years after the date of the person's last known arrest or conviction, the last known date that the person was released from any prison or jail, or the last known date that the person was subject to probation or parole, whichever event occurred last in time. If a person has been arrested and his case has been disposed of by conviction, the record pertaining to that conviction is to be designated a closed record ten years after the date of the person's last known arrest or conviction.[58]

The purpose of closing a record is to insulate an individual from the liabilities that normally attach simply due to the existence of arrest or conviction records. The principal justification is that careful purging programs would contribute significantly to effective programs of rehabilitation.

Key Supreme Court Decisions

The following cases are court decisions of particular interest to the police.

Identification

Biggers v. *Tennessee,* 89 Sup. Ct. 979 (1968). The victim in a rape case was asked to come to the police station seven months after the rape took place to "look at a suspect." The victim identified the defendant only after he spoke the words of the rapist. The victim had very little opportunity to view the rapist during the assault. The Court reversed the defendant's conviction on the grounds that the totality of circumstances surrounding the identification process was so suggestive and prejudicial as to violate the Fourteenth Amendment.

Simmons v. *United States,* 390 U.S. 372 (1967). Prior photographic identification of a suspect does not taint a subsequent physical identification unless totality of circumstances of the second identification suggests undue prejudice.

United States v. *Wade,* 388 U.S. 218 (6/12/67). Compelling a suspect to appear in a lineup without the aid of counsel does not violate the suspect's right against self-incrimination, but does violate his Sixth Amendment right to counsel. This is not to say that a defendant must consent to a lineup, but that counsel must be present during the lineup to ascertain its fairness.

Search and Seizure

Mapp v. *Ohio,* 367 U.S. 643 (1961). The Fourth Amendment prohibiting unreasonable search and seizure is incorporated through the Fourteenth Amendment, and thus made applicable to the states. Evidence seized in violation of the Constitution is inadmissible in court.

People v. *Gonzales,* 356 Mich. 247 (1959). The Michigan Supreme Court decided that the stopping of a motorist and the issuing of a traffic citation alone was not sufficient grounds for a search of a vehicle.

Bumper v. *North Carolina,* 391 U.S. 543 (6/3/68). Police were admitted to search a premise after telling the defendant's grandmother that they had a warrant, but they did not display or rely upon the warrant in making the search. The court ruled that they could not claim that the search was valid as permitted. The court said that the permission was not voluntary but based on the fact that the grandmother had been told the police had a warrant.

Terry v. *State of Ohio,* 391 U.S. 1 (6/10/68). An experienced police detective observed defendants apparently "casing" a store, approached the defendants, and asked their identity and reason for being there. He was not satisfied with their short reply, "frisked" their outer clothing for weapons, and found two guns, which were admitted in court as evidence. The court said the officer's actions were reasonable and that a "limited weapons search" was justified.

Sibron v. *New York,* 392 U.S. 40 (6/10/68). An officer, having insufficient reason to suspect that the defendant was armed, reached simultaneously into the defendant's pocket and found narcotics. His frisk was held improper even though he suspected narcotics activity.

Peters v. *New York,* 392 U.S. 40 (6/10/68). An off-duty officer noted two suspects "tiptoeing" down a hallway, gave chase with his revolver out, and caught one suspect on a lower floor. His search for weapons and subsequent discovery of burglary tools were upheld on the grounds that he made a valid arrest on "probable cause to believe the suspect was a burglar."

Spinelli v. *United States,* 393 U.S. 410 (1969). An affidavit upon which a search warrant was based, alleging that federal officers had been informed by a reliable informant, was held insufficient to issue the warrant. Reasonable cause did not exist because there was no information to support the allegation that the informant was reliable and because the source of the informant's knowledge was not stated.

Davis v. *Mississippi,* 394 U.S. 721 (4/22/69). In this case, the police detained several possible suspects in a rape case in order (apparently) to take their fingerprints. They were not arrested, but their fingerprints were taken, although not voluntarily. They were released almost immediately. The defendant was later arrested and again printed. The FBI made a positive comparison of his prints, and he was convicted of rape. The Supreme Court reversed the conviction on the basis that the fingerprint evidence was the fruit of an unlawful arrest (not based upon probable cause).

Chimel v. *California,* 395 U.S. 752 (6/23/69). Officers searched an entire house, supposedly incidental to the lawful arrest of an occupant, but without a search warrant. The court held that the search was unreasonable and should have been limited to things within the defendant's reach.

Shipley v. *California,* 395 U.S. 818 (6/3/69). Search of the defendant's residence following his arrest alighting from a car parked ten to fifteen feet away was held not incidental to his arrest.

Evidence

Schmerber v. *California,* 384 U.S. 757 (1966). The properly executed withdrawal of a blood specimen from the defendant, over his objection, did not violate his Fifth Amendment right against self-incrimination, as this right applies only to testimonial utterances.

Gilbert v. *California,* 388 U.S. 263 (1966). The taking of handwriting samples in the absence of counsel did not violate the defendant's Fifth Amendment right against self-incrimination nor his Sixth Amendment right to counsel.

Electronic Eavesdropping

Katz v. *United States,* 389 U.S. 347 (1967). As with other types of searches, eavesdropping, except for a few specifically established and well-delineated exceptions, requires judicial process.

CHAPTER **9**

Contemporary Issues

By the very nature of their job, policemen are faced daily with contemporary social problems and issues. Among the issues that will be discussed in this chapter are the questions of enforcement priorities, politics and corruption, public attitudes toward the police, police attitudes, personnel standards and recruitment, women on the police force, riots and civil disorders, and police-community relations.

Enforcement Priorities

A decision not to arrest in a specific case does not ordinarily come to the attention of the members of the community. Even repeated decisions not to arrest for certain kinds of conduct may be unnoticed. In most situations the decision is known only to those who know of the crime and to the police officer who decides not to arrest. Often the crime is of a kind that involves willing participants or a victim who concurs in the decision not to arrest. Sometimes no victim is involved. In such situations, the offender obviously will not challenge the officer's decision.

Usually the decision not to arrest is made by the individual officer, and seldom is it brought to the attention of a supervisor. Even when a complaint is referred to an individual officer for action, the department may never learn how the officer handled it. Whether or not it does may depend on the type of record kept by the dispatching officer and on how much detail the officer files in a report of his actions. Recording and reporting practices, of course, vary considerably according to the policy of the particular department. The typical police manual suggests that disciplinary action will follow a failure to arrest or to report a crime. However, such disciplinary action is seldom taken. Since the individual officer on the beat is the person who must evaluate a situation and decide whether an arrest is to be made, the officer himself usually determines the enforcement priorities of his department.

In the United States law enforcement agents are expected to engage in suppression of criminality, or at the very least they are charged with the responsibility of apprehending all lawbreakers reported to them. At the same time they labor under a variety of restraints on police practices in the way of rules concerning arrest, evidence, and so on, which render this task difficult.[1] For example, an officer who arrested an individual who had been detained for a misdemeanor by a citizen could, in some states, be guilty of illegal arrest and could be sued by the arrested person, if the officer had not observed the misdemeanor being committed.

Although police chiefs can often be found publicly asserting that their departments enforce all laws equally, the fact is that police enforce criminal laws selectively. This discretionary enforcement is of two kinds. First, certain statutes are not enforced at all. In many localities old laws that were designed for earlier social conditions remain in force but are ignored by the police. And laws go unenforced even though the conditions they are intended to regulate do exist in the community. Second, police may apply laws differentially. That is, police often apprehend some, but not all, of the persons whom they observe violating some statute.

How Priorities Are Determined

Types of crimes are as varied as human behavior in our complex and changing society. There are white-collar crimes such as tax evasion, price-fixing, embezzlement, swindling, and consumer fraud. There are organized crimes like gambling, loansharking, drug traffic, extortion, prostitution, and corruption of officials. There are street crimes against people and property, such as robbery, mugging, burglary, larceny, and murder. And there are also crimes of passion, which include most murders, and some rapes and assaults. But for our purposes, we will simplify all the crimes into two categories—crime with victims and crimes without victims.

Crimes with victims are murder, rape, robbery, mugging, larceny from person, assault, and aggravated assault. In these crimes someone has been victimized by someone else, either physically or through the taking of property unlawfully. These crimes are usually followed by publicity through the news media, and when police action is taken, the public no doubt favors the upholding of *all* the laws to prevent such criminal actions.

Victimless crimes, on the other hand, are on the books as crimes against society, but the crimes themselves do not have specific victims or, when they do, have victims who consented to the act. The most common such crimes are gambling, prostitution, adultery, and intoxication. A good example is prostitution. Prostitution exists in a number of different forms, from the "call girl" to the woman in the house of prostitution to the streetwalker. Prostitution in any of these forms can be a problem, particularly when linked with organized crime. The streetwalker is usually the product of a lower-class neighborhood in a large city and presents the most serious problem. The woman engaging in solicitation in public places, unlike a call girl or a house prostitute, creates a nuisance plainly visible to the public. It is this nuisance aspect of prostitution to which most communities object. In Great Britain the Home Office Report of the Committee on

Homosexual Offenses and Prostitution, in the Wolfenden Report, noted in 1957:

> We are concerned not with prostitution itself but with the manner in which the activities of prostitutes and those associated with them offend against public order and decency, expose the ordinary citizen to what is offensive or injurious, or involve the exploitation of others. . . . We are not attempting to abolish prostitution or to make prostitution itself illegal. We do not think that the law ought to try to do so; nor do we think that if it tried, it would by itself succeed. What the law can do is to ensure that the streets . . . should be saved from what is offensive and made tolerable for the ordinary citizen who lives in them or passes through them.[2]

Even though other forms of prostitution are also criminal, the streetwalker remains the major problem for police. Public knowledge of the existence of streetwalkers results in pressures on the department for action, and the pressure moves from the top down to the policeman on the beat. In brief, the community itself determines the moral standards it wants to impose on its members.

Ideally, all our laws are made to distinguish what is good from what is bad. In practice, however, you cannot make people "good" by passing laws. It is argued that a person's moral standards are fixed and will not be changed by legislation. But laws are not passed to change a person's private beliefs; they are passed to regulate his behavior toward others, particularly his public behavior. Laws define the acceptable standards of conduct in business transactions, public meetings, work relationships, and many other kinds of interpersonal conduct. The need for laws arises when differences of opinion exist about proper standards of behavior, particularly when a few people deviate from the conduct that most people consider proper and when the behavior of these few damages or seriously offends other persons. Laws in a democracy tend to define and publicize the standards of conduct desired by the majority of people.

There may be some truth in the observation that it is difficult to enforce laws with which a large number of people disagree or to which the majority give only mild support. The difficulties of enforcing the Prohibition Amendment and antigambling laws are often cited in this connection.[3] Part of the difficulty arose from the fact that these laws affected private as well as public behavior. People felt that taking a drink or placing a bet was a private matter. People adjust quite readily, however, to laws that affect the public interest rather than just private behavior. Since our society is obviously moving in this direction, the legislatures and the courts have emphasized the necessity for recognizing social and human relations as a matter of public interest. However, when new laws are passed and old laws are broken, it is still the police officer's responsibility to enforce the existing laws to the best of his ability, regardless of what he thinks of them. To do otherwise is to default on one's responsibility as a police officer and on the oath of office.

There is no doubt at all, however, that each police department's predetermined priorities are a major factor in a patrolman's use of discretionary power to make an arrest. Furthermore, it is also generally accepted that it is the duty of the local law enforcement agency to give priorities to the enforcement of those laws that are in the public interest of their own community.[4] In other words, the community's public morals are taken into consideration in effecting local policy. These attitudes reflect a view of the substantive criminal law as something less than a mandate for enforcement in all cases.

There has been no express legislative delegation of discretion to the police, although it is arguable that such a delegation would be constitutional because police are in a position comparable to other administrative agencies. Such a delegation might even be implied, particularly where substantive criminal law is not very clear. However, police have not claimed to have this kind of discretion; rather, they exercise it without attempting to give explicit justification for the practice. Because of this, police currently function differently from other administrative agencies. The common police practice of suspending the effective operation of certain penal statutes or of creating exemptions from them occurs without any standards having been set in advance by the legislature. Priorities are sometimes determined when not enough financial resources are allocated to make possible enforcement of all the laws against all offenders. Resources are ordinarily allocated to enforcement agencies by a municipal body, while the criminal law is defined by the state legislature. A similar conflict occurs when the state legislature appropriates money to a state police unit, since the defining of crime and the decisions regarding enforcement are unrelated even within the same unit of government.

Finally, the exercise of discretion seems necessary in the current criminal justice system, for reasons unrelated to either the interpretation of criminal statutes or the allocation of available enforcement resources.

The Individual Officer

Clearly, a police officer is conditioned by many factors to meet the challenges that face him in his daily performance as a patrolman. It is the patrolman in the discharge of his duties who exercises the discretion necessary to his role in the management of conflict and in part to his role in the suppression of crime. In managing conflict, he must maintain order under circumstances in which the participants and the observer are likely to disagree as to what constitutes a reasonable and fair settlement, and he is likely to be aware of hostility, alert to the possibility of violence, and uncertain that the authority symbolized by his badge and uniform will be sufficient for him to take control of any situation. In suppressing crime, his task is to judge the likely future behavior of persons on the basis of appearance, attitude, and circumstances and to deal with those he considers suspicious under laws that either say nothing about his authority to question and search short of making arrest, or give him ambiguous or controversial powers.[5]

In any case, the patrolman sometimes acts improperly by abusing or exceeding his authority, making arrests or street stops on the basis of personal prejudice or ill temper, or handling a situation differently from the way one of his administrators might handle it. But to say that in a given case the observer or the community could have prescribed a better course of action is not to say that a better course of action, applicable to most situations, could be prescribed in advance. To put it another way, the possibility of deciding in a particular instance that the police behaved wrongly does not mean that one can formulate a meaningful policy as how the police should act in all cases.

The fact that police administrators or the city government cannot prescribe in advance the correct course of action for handling order maintenance or crime suppression situations does not mean that their actions and policies have no effect on the patrolman's behavior. Their influence shapes the policeman's overall style or strategy. In other words, guidelines and policies set by individual departments are more a list of things not to do than a concrete statement of what an officer should do. Negative policies, of course, have their effect, but the control of the organization over the behavior of its members is imprecise, and efforts by a social scientist to explain that behavior are likely to be imperfect. The sources of discretion can be described by the policies of each department, but how officers routinely handle their discretion in the least visible situations can only be stated and explained in approximate terms.

Furthermore, we must take many other possible explanations into consideration. Middle-class officers may behave differently from working-class officers, older officers from younger ones, West Coast officers from East Coast officers. These and other factors will definitely have an effect on each officer's everyday decisions.

With all the training a police officer receives, there are still two factors that will influence his actions. One is his past experiences, and the second is his personal values. The average police officer in the United States comes from a lower-middle-class background and grew up with a traditional respect for authority. Problems arise when he is faced with people who do not readily accept the authority of the police. The officer must be able to respect the views of others even if they are not the same as his own.

Although city governments and police administrators are responsible for the enforcement priorities of the police department, the meaning and value of the entire legal system are determined by the police officer's specific acts or omissions. When the law is that of a democratic society, the conduct of each police officer becomes the living expression of the values, meaning, and potentialities of democracy. If the police officer conforms to law, he becomes one of the most important officials in the structure of government, able to facilitate the progressively greater realization of democratic values.

Democratic societies, like all other societies, require order. But unlike other societies, they need a distinctive kind of order—namely, one that is not imposed by an uncontrolled force. The police in a democracy must not only know the most effective techniques for maintaining order; they must also know techniques that maintain order in a manner that serves to preserve and extend democratic values.

Politics and Corruption

One way for the police to keep their image free from charges of favoritism is to avoid involvement in politics or support of individual candidates. This eliminates an order from the mayor to promote his friends, a request to forget about a traffic citation, or the transfer of a too-vigorous vice squad captain.[6]

Neutralizing local law enforcement is a goal of organized crime. What can the public do if no one investigates the investigators and the political figures are neutralized by their alliance with organized crime? Anyone reporting corrupt activities may be telling his story to the corrupted. In a recent "investigation" of widespread corruption, the prosecutor announced that any citizen coming forward with evidence of payments to public officials to secure government action would be prosecuted for participation in such unlawful conduct.

Organized crime directs its efforts to corrupt law enforcement toward the chief or toward middle-level supervisory officials. The corrupt political executive who forbids police officials to act against organized crime is even more effective for the purposes of the crime organization.

It is impossible to determine how extensive the corruption of police and public officials by organized crime has been. There must be more vigilance against such corruption, and there must be better ways for the public to communicate information about corruption to appropriate government personnel.[7]

Public Attitudes toward the Police

The President's Commission on Law Enforcement and Administration of Justice in 1967 covered in some detail the subject of police-community relations and the effect of public attitudes toward the police.

The National Opinion Research Center conducted a national survey for the commission and found that, contrary to many police officers' beliefs, the public in general hold the police in high regard.

To determine public opinion about the police, they asked such questions as the following:

1. Do you think the police here do an excellent, good, fair, or poor job of enforcing the laws?
   Excellent 22%
   Good 45%
   Fair 24%
   Poor 8%
2. How good a job do the police do protecting people in the neighborhood?
   Very Good 42%
   Pretty Good 35%
   Not So Good 9%
   No Opinion 14%
3. How good a job do the police do on being respectful to people like yourself?
   Very Good 59%
   Pretty Good 26%
   Not So Good 4%
   No Opinion 10%

Sixty-seven percent felt that the police do a good job of enforcing laws; 77 percent felt that the police did either a very good or a pretty good job of providing police protection; and 85 percent thought that the police did a very good or a pretty good job of being respectful.

Members of the public depend on the police for protection. When a law is violated, they expect the police to take some action. If the police fail to respond, or their actions do not satisfy the person who called for them, that person will probably form a negative attitude toward the police.

Views of blacks about the effectiveness of police were more negative than the views of whites. It was found that when the question of community protection by the police was asked, nonwhites gave a "very good" rating only half as often as whites. Also, nonwhites gave a "not so good" rating twice as often as whites to that same question.

In another study, the following question was asked: "Do you agree or disagree that at least half the police department would have to be replaced in order to have a good police force?" The responses were as follows:

	Nonwhite		White	
	Male	Female	Male	Female
Agree	40%	28%	18%	11%
Disagree	40%	52%	60%	62%
No Opinion	20%	20%	22%	27%

Nonwhites show even greater differences from whites in the area of police discourtesy. The following responses were received by the National Opinion Research Center for the commission, concerning the courtesy of police "toward people like yourself."

	White Annual Income		Nonwhite Annual Income	
	$0 to $2,999	$6,000 to $9,000	$0 to $2,999	$6,000 to $9,000
Males				
Very Good	56%	67%	34%	31%
Not So Good	4%	4%	22%	6%
Females				
Very Good	62%	66%	28%	41%
Not So Good	3%	1%	12%	45%

Another study by the commission showed that males below the age of thirty-five were the most critical of police. Fifty-three percent of the young males reported that they had been subjected to insulting language; 44 percent said that they had been rousted, frisked, or searched without good reason; 22 percent reported that they had been subjected to unnecessary force when arrested; and 10 percent said that they had been beaten up by the police while they were in custody.

Mexican-Americans, American Indians, and other minority groups have not had as much attention focused on them in relation to the police, as blacks have, but one survey showed these results regarding how they felt about their police:

One of America's Best Police Departments

White	30.0%
Mexican-American	22.8%
Black	14.4%

Definitely Below Standard When Compared to Other Police Departments

White	8.5%
Mexican-American	14.5%
Black	20.3%

Police Always Respect the Rights of Suspected Criminals

White	34.8%
Mexican-American	21.2%
Black	12.1%

Police Often Conscienceless and Brutal in Performing Duties

White	11.1%
Mexican-American	44.4%
Black	38.2%

These studies show a wide range of opinion among the public toward the police; and the opinion varies with each social, economic, and ethnic group.[8]

No study can be accepted as "gospel truth," mainly because the people asked are only a minute portion of the population. From these studies, however, one can make some reasonable assumptions. People care what the police do and how they do it, and they are more sensitive then ever before about police practices. It is important to know that although opinions about police vary, people—all people—have very definite opinions about police.

The police must recognize this awareness of their actions and keep it in mind when dealing with the public. They must continue to assess public attitudes and look for ways to improve them.

Police Attitudes

A police officer is an individual. There is no standard definition of a "typical police officer," just as there is no standard definition of a typical foundry worker, schoolteacher, garbage collector, or lawyer. Some attitudes are common among police personnel, however. Not all police officers share these views, but they do apply to a high percentage of them. These attitudes reflect on the officer's ability to deal with the public.

The police officer's work brings him into contact with the unpleasant things in life. Death, hate, greed, anguish, and misery confront him daily. As a result, a police officer may become cynical, seeing only bad things and developing a negative attitude toward life. This can harm relations between the police and the public.

A police officer is not only expected to enforce the law; he is also required to live by the law. He conditions himself to be obedient to rules and regulations and respectful of authority and expects everyone to live as he does, often looking down on others who do not meet his standards. This leads to intolerance of people's mistakes and tends to result in a negative view of people in general. The police officer must learn to treat each person he encounters as an individual worthy of his respect, unless that person has done something to force the officer to act differently. The police ask the public not to judge the law enforcement profession by the actions of a few who abuse their authority. The police must also learn not to judge the general public by the actions of the few who violate the law.

When a law is broken, some officers regard it as a personal injury, and their actions in correcting the "injury" may be in excess of what is necessary. Other officers see a disobeyed law as a personal challenge to their authority and assume a superior attitude. As a result, they become further removed from personal contact with the public.

In a study conducted by the International Association of Chiefs of Police, it was found that 73 percent of the experienced police officers interviewed agreed that police did not receive the backing they should from the political power structure in their cities. The problem here is financial. City councilmen, mayors, and managers are reluctant to spend more funds for police services, because it means increased taxes. Police officers, therefore, may feel that their services are not appreciated by the city officials and the public in general.[9]

The notion that a man's occupation determines many of the features of his personality and social life is a familiar one to sociologists. They often assert that the varied conditions under which a man earns a living in a complex society heavily influence general perspectives on life and modes of social participation. Most experts would have to agree that the elements of danger and authority, which are central to police work, lead law enforcement persons to develop certain common personality characteristics.[10] One of these is suspiciousness; another is conservatism. Policemen learn to be especially attentive to unusual situations, for the unpredictable is likely to be dangerous. The police are cast as defenders of the "status quo," so they come to prefer stability to rapid social change. The dangerous nature of their work, and the fact that policemen are engaged in compelling others to obey laws, many of which are unpopular with the citizens, give rise to police solidarity and social isolation from nonpolicemen.

When a person becomes a police officer, his personal life begins changing as well. Because police work requires men on duty every hour of the day, a police officer is required to work shifts on Saturdays, Sundays, and holidays. He will have to give up going to the neighborhood card party on Saturday night, the family reunion on the Fourth of July, the Boy Scout meeting at 7:00 P.M. on Wednesday. His social life begins to decrease; he sees less and less of his friends. When his days off are Monday and Tuesday, he cannot expect to spend an evening out with the couple down the street, since they have to get up early in the morning to go to work.

This often means that the police officer spends more time with those who are available to him—other police officers on the same shift. Eventually he loses contact with many of his old friends and replaces them with new friends from the police department.

He may also find that even when he does have a weekend day off, he is not invited to an event by his old friends. Some people feel uncomfortable "letting loose" in the presence of a police officer, even if he is off duty.

What results is known as the "closed fraternity"—police officers spending their free time with other police officers, being drawn into a group with common needs and desires. The unfortunate part of this tendency is that they lose contact with people in general and may become more closed-minded.

In order for a police officer to be effective in his job, he must identify with the general public and understand people, how they act, and why. There must be more effort on the part of individual police officers to become active in social groups such as the PTA, sports teams, civic groups, and so on. This is the only way the public will see police officers, and the police officers will see the public, as "people." The attitude must be changed from "the" police to "our" police.

Personnel Standards and Recruitment

One of the primary ways to upgrade a police department is to upgrade the quality of police personnel.

Selection of Personnel

Much police activity is relatively simple and does not require extensive training—patrolling school crossings, checking parking meters, directing traffic, and retrieving pets off rooftops. The nature of police work, however, so interweaves the easy and the difficult that an officer today must be prepared for both in order to secure the best possible relations between police and the community. The following events call for a police officer to take action under conditions of high stress: family trouble, an automobile accident, a tavern brawl, a demonstration, a burglar alarm, a desperate psychotic, a traffic jam, and a riot.[11]

The problem of selecting an individual who can perform effectively in such situations is important. Most police departments have a series of tests, and the applicant must pass the first test to go on to the next one. The relatively few applicants who pass all the tests are hired as probationary police officers. After a given period of probation, if he seems to perform effectively, the probationary officer becomes a permanent officer.

The series of tests may include a written examination, a background investigation, a medical examination, an oral interview, a polygraph test, a physical fitness test, and a psychiatric evaluation.

Ideally, a potential policeman is given *all* these tests. Unfortunately, funds available in most police departments limit them to an incomplete testing program. The polygraph test, for example, costs approximately one hundred dollars per applicant. Many police departments save a considerable sum of money by eliminating this test, but undesirable applicants may be accepted as probationary officers, and their actions can greatly injure the relationship of the police to the public.

A bizarre example of the value of polygraph screening is the case of a police applicant who applied for a postion of patrolman in a city police department in June 1961. He passed his entrance examination and a thorough background investigation and had all the appearances of a fine applicant. He was rejected as a result of his polygraph examination, and three years later he killed his wife and three children. Any department would have been considerably embarrassed had this heinous act occurred while the applicant was a patrolman with that department.

The following questions are typical of those asked on a polygraph test for police applicants:

Did you ever commit a serious undetected crime?

Are you attempting to withhold or conceal any derogatory information about yourself?

Did you knowingly give a false or evasive answer on your application?

Did you ever engage in abnormal sexual practices?

Is there anything in your personal life that could embarrass this department?

Did you ever steal anything from a place where you worked?

Have you ever been fired from a job?

Do you have a lot of outstanding debts?

Could you be blackmailed?

Are you seeking permanent employment with this department?

Do you have anything in your personal background which you would like to keep hidden?

Did you ever intentionally perjure yourself in a court of law?

Were you ever court-martialed in the military service?

Have you ever been arrested?

Do you drink to excess?

No test is foolproof, but common sense dictates that future performance can often be based on past performance.

The following is a summary of the first 127 polygraph examinations of applicants conducted by the Kalamazoo Police Department in Michigan. These results gave an indication of future performance and were sources of rejection:

42 admitted falsification of application.
35 admitted being fired from a previous job.
2 admitted serious alimony problems.
3 admitted garnishment of wages and excessive debts.
19 admitted excessive debts only.
82 admitted a total of 226 traffic violations not previously listed.
7 admitted serious drinking problems.
2 admitted breaking and entering.
95 admitted a total of 250 larcenies.
63 admitted a total of 119 traffic accidents not previously reported.
2 admitted being involved in narcotic drugs.
3 admitted having serious gambling problems.
1 admitted a religious restriction.
11 admitted a serious physical defect or handicap not previously known.
2 admitted starting false suits in a court of law.
21 admitted serious military problems.
7 admitted serious mental problems.
5 admitted acts of arson.
3 admitted auto thefts.
74 admitted places of prior employment not previously listed.
4 admitted fostering illegitimate children.
6 admitted being involved in serious cases of assault and battery.
12 admitted previous arrests not otherwise revealed or known.
10 admitted serious cases of venereal disease.
1 admitted an act of abortion.
1 admitted an act of perjury.
1 admitted an act of incest.
1 admitted an act of indecent liberties.
1 admitted the rape of a two-year-old child.
1 admitted numerous cases of identifying himself as a police officer and stopping citizens on a highway.
1 admitted an act of bribery.
28 admitted serious homosexual acts.
2 admitted acts of pyromania.
38 admitted serious acts of abnormal sexual behavior such as bestiality, sodomy, and excessive masturbation (up to 9 times a day).[12]

A police department that believes it cannot afford to give the polygraph test to each applicant should take a good look at the foregoing list. It cannot afford *not* to give this test.

One way to lessen tensions between the police and minority groups is to recruit members of a greater number of racial minorities into the police profession. It is assumed that minority group officers may be able to work more effectively in communities having many minority members. Despite efforts to increase minority group representation in police departments, the number remains low.

The traditional belief that in order to be a good officer a man had to be tall and well built is still held by most police departments. Minimum height requirements range from five feet, eight inches to six feet. This is a major barrier to such minority groups as Orientals and Mexican-Americans, who are usually small in stature. Language is another barrier for many Mexican-Americans. An excellent command of English is a must for applicants to most police departments. People raised in settings where English is not the principal language find themselves facing an impossible hurdle in their quest for an occupation in the law enforcement field. Background investigations for police applicants have the purpose of finding criminal records, bad employment records, a history of bad credit, and so on. The sensitive nature of police work dictates that the police officer should have an exemplary personal background. For a youth growing up in a slum area of a large city, however, these factors are poor indications of personal character. Only rarely can a person grow up in such a poor environment without accumulating a few black marks on his record. These should be seen as an indication of the environment a person was raised in rather than as a measure of his suitability for police work.

Recruitment

In checking recruitment processes nationwide, it soon becomes quite evident that the majority of police departments do not actively recruit, especially not beyond their own local area. Some departments go so far as to require city residency of one year before application for the job. Such requirements have no validity in these days of great mobility and unreasonably demand that an interested applicant give up his old job, move to the city, find temporary employment, and then hope that he will be among those chosen for an opening in the department. This requirement is applied to the prospective officer no matter what his qualifications and is self-defeating to say the least.

Many other departments choose to employ only people they "know." The head of the agency assumes that his knowledge of the applicant or his family is a good starting point from which to build a police department. While this procedure may work, it is certainly not the best procedure when the object is to build the best possible department in regard to skill and competence. Many department heads have never thought about recruiting on a nationwide basis. If they did, they could select from applicants from all over the United States and be able, in effect, to pick "the cream of the crop." Even better applicants can be attracted if recruitment extends to the college campuses and the department actively seeks members of society who have received, or are about to receive, their undergraduate degrees. Because of their exposure to various cultures and ideas, college graduates often make the best and most understanding officers, if they also have the qualities of aggressiveness and curiosity, dedication and a sense of duty that all officers should have.

At this time, however, most departments have at least a state residency requirement before a person is even able to apply. Besides the residency requirement, the applicant must fulfill other minimum requirements before he is eligible. A typical list of minimum requirements is as follows:

Age: Must be between 21 and 30, inclusive, at the time of appointment.

Height and Weight: Must be at least 5′9″ (without shoes), not under 150 pounds and not over 250 pounds in proportion to height.

Residency: Must be a resident of the state and U.S. citizen.

Physical: Must be in good physical condition and pass a medical examination.

Vision: Must have 20/40 vision in each eye without correction. Corrected to 20/20 in each eye with glasses prior to appointment to the department. (Some departments demand only that the eyesight be correctable to 20/20, but the usual requirement is as above.)

Education: Must have graduated from high school or satisfactorily completed a General Educational Development (GED) test. Test results must be presented at the time of submitting application.

Arrest Record: Conviction of any criminal law violation may serve as a basis for disqualification.

Agility Test: Must pass a test of a number of physical agility feats.

Written Tests: Must pass a written test. (Applicants who fail the written examination may take the examination again after an interval of 30 days, then again only after 6 months.)

Many of these requirements differ from department to department, even among neighboring agencies that share common crime problems and draw their officers from the same social and ecomomic communities. Over the years many requirements that might once have had some value are dropped by some departments, while others still continue with the same outdated policies. Since few departments have taken the time to change outdated policies, their personnel officers must operate with unreasonable demands. Only by dropping such limitations as the municipal, county, and state residency requirements prior to appointment, and other requirements that no longer serve any useful function, can agencies expect to interest qualified individuals who would be attracted to jobs with better pay and benefits.

There are many arguments pro and con (as indicated by the large disparity among entrance requirements) over what standards of vision are to be accepted. The trend in more progressive departments is to require only that the individual officer's eyes be correctable to 20/20 vision. Of course, the officer should carry an extra pair of glasses in the patrol car, in case he loses or breaks the ones he is wearing. One argument goes: "What if the officer is hit so hard that it knocks his glasses off and he cannot see anything and cannot work the rest of the shift?" Actually, it is doubtful that *any* officer hit under the same circumstances could see anything, and he would probably be taken off the "road" for the rest of the shift at least, to recover.

Departments that have employed a number of officers with glasses have found that many of the "problems" that are supposed to be encountered with eyeglass wearers just never materialize. The whole point is that each officer should be considered on his individual merits when he is screened for a position with the department. The fact that the prospective officer wears glasses is not and should not in itself be reason to turn down an otherwise desirable applicant.

The same can be said for height requirements. Many officers (presently employed as policemen and skilled in their duties) are turned down for new positions simply because they are—for example—one-quarter inch too short. These officers are denied the opportunity of better pay and benefits simply because of this physical "defect." Yet these same officers work at their present jobs, performing virtually the same duties that, according to the recruitment standards of the new agency, they are unable to perform because they are too short. Again, the total assets and liabilities of each prospective officer should be considered individually before the decision is made whether the person should be hired.

Physical deficiencies alone are not reason to reject anyone who sincerely wants to be a police officer and who applies himself to his duties. It is far better to have an officer who wears glasses and is one-quarter inch too short, yet who is dedicated and conscientious, than to have an officer who meets every physical employment standard, yet turns in a minimum workload, does the very least that is expected of him, and is rarely seen working. By present standards the latter employee seems to be perfect for the job, yet something is missing. The former, while supposedly "lacking" physically, makes a better officer.

In areas of varied ethnic composition, with sizable proportions of minorities in the population, the police department should be representative of the entire population. This is important if for no other reason than community relations, but the reasons and advantages of having a representative department go far beyond that. Many segments of the public feel that unless a member of their own race or group is handling their particular problem, the officer will not be able to understand them fully and that the service to the public will not be as good as it could be.

While this may have merit from the standpoint of community relations, a truly professional department should not and must not have major problems in communication with ethnic groups. Many such problems are nothing more than failure even to try to communicate. However, even professional departments have a strong need for members of minorities on their force, since any department that serves the public should be representative of that same public.

Whenever minority hiring is discussed, one topic that comes up is whether the minimum educational standards should be lowered. In fact, during any police recruitment drive, it is common to hear talk about lowering standards in order to gain a greater number of applicants. Lowering the educational standards, however, is not the answer. For one thing, many members of minority groups can meet the requirements as they stand; furthermore, when the emphasis in the field of criminal justice is to upgrade police educationally and make them true professionals, the answer to any problem is not in the direction of reducing educational standards.

When standards such as education are lowered, the public pays the price in less competent report writing, interviewing, and investigating. The department suffers as a result of lowered public support and esteem, but it is the individual officer with the less adequate education who suffers most. He is the person who must deal with the public face to face, and today, when the general educational level of the public is rising, the officer is disadvantaged in confrontations, especially when someone tries to "flog" the officer verbally. Many less educated officers find the whole situation very disagreeable (it is never pleasant) and do not know how to react except to use force and authority.

Unless the officer is able to deal with the problem adequately, he will not be able to handle other related problems, such as the proper interviewing of victims and questioning subjects under the "stop and frisk" rulings. Through the proper use of interrogatives, the officer should be able to get a great deal of information in any given situation. This ability is the result of training, exposure, and experience. For the officer without the high school diploma, which is the minimum educational level that should be considered, it is difficult to be confident enough to handle personally embarrassing situations.

Any officer who cannot handle himself in a professional manner in a tense situation, in the presence of a crowd, will lose a lot of public respect for himself, his department, and the police profession in general. The salary and other benefits of any police department should be adequate to attract individuals who qualify for the job in all respects. There should be an excess of applicants.

Retention

Once the department has hired an applicant as a patrolman, has sent him through the academy, and has finally promoted him to working on a shift, enforcing laws for the department and community, the matter of the employment of the officer still is not over.

For the community and the department to get the full value from that officer, they must employ him for many years. By retaining policemen over time, the community gains officers who are thoroughly familiar with the area of their jurisdiction—not only with its physical characteristics but also with the modus operandi, crime, and population trends within the community, and with the persons, families, and juveniles with special problems. An officer who is employed for just a few years and then moves on to a department with better pay and benefits will not have the opportunity to learn as much about his community and its people as the officer who remains employed by the same agency.

In order to attract qualified individuals or experienced officers, the agency must offer adequate salaries, benefits, and the opportunity for advancement over the years. The officer would not necessarily need to be promoted, but he has the right to expect to be put in a position that is challenging to him, one that is not boring after a short time. The officer who wishes to put extra effort into his job must be able to work in a field or phase of police work that attracts and holds his interest or he will not feel that his job is worthwhile. No one can work long at any job that does not give him a feeling of accomplishment. In order to attract and retain high-caliber officers, the employing agency must first provide the job opportunities and make available positions that adequately challenge the officer. A properly treated officer who is satisfied with his duties and takes pride in his performance will have a feeling of accomplishment and will be satisfied with his place of employment.

The officer who is employed by an agency, however, also owes a sense of loyalty and duty to his employer. The police officer's job is one of the least supervised of all jobs. It is his duty to fill his shift with steady, quality work. Most good officers will always be able to locate some sort of crime, a stranded motorist, an accident, or another incident while on patrol. Every officer should perform all duties to the best of his ability and within constitutional guidelines. No one should shirk responsibility simply because he does not want to write reports. The officer's and department's attitudes should be such that all persons involved, including the public, have a great deal of pride in their police department and community. When the department and (indirectly) the community send officers to special academies and other schools for further training, the officer owes it to the department and the public to get the maximum from the training, so that the benefit can be passed on to the other officers for the betterment of the community. That is the main reason for sending officers to schools in the first place.

Advancement

With the exception of a small percentage of officers, most policemen look forward to the day when they will be promoted. For the medium-sized and larger departments, the 1967 National Crime Commission recommended that police functions be divided into three levels: the community service officer (CSO), the police officer, and the police agent.[13]

According to the recommendation, the police agent should have at least two years of college, or better still a baccalaureate degree in the liberal arts or social sciences. Persons who cannot attain the degree, but who have shown a definite capability for imaginative and responsible police work were also recommended for the police agent position. The police agent would handle jobs that were complicated, sensitive, and demanding. No matter what function or position the agent was filling—uniform, juvenile, community-relations, and so on—he would be the responsible head of the team and would be knowledgeable in all phases of his assignment.

The police officer would be involved in enforcing the laws and following up minor cases. His duties would not change significantly from those of the patrolman function as it is today.

The CSO would be somewhat similar to the cadet of today's departments, yet he would fill a far greater need within the police community. The CSO would be in a sense serving an apprenticeship, in that he would start at a relatively young age—seventeen to twenty-one—and fill a variety of functions that do not require a sworn police officer. The CSO could work out of the courts and assist on routine investigations and would be especially useful in maintaining liaison with juveniles on the street. The CSO would serve an invaluable function in a police-community relations position. The real benefit of the CSO program is that the departments could employ highly motivated youths who want to be policemen. The youths would be employed by the department at an early age so that by the time they were eligible for employment as police officers, they would have a good working knowledge of the duties of the police profession and would have decided, based on experience, to make a career of the police profession.

The persons of all three levels—agent, officer, and CSO—would work closely together and be familiar with one another's duties and responsibilities; as a result, the lower levels would receive strict and thorough guidance with the overall effect being one of well-planned harmony.

One reason for the difficulty of hiring college graduates is that even if they accept employment in a department with less pay than competitors are paying for the college education, the graduate must in most cases start at the very bottom of the organization, and often the patrolman must serve a fixed number of years before he is eligible to take the promotional tests. The college graduate is not the only person frustrated by the rigid policies of many older departments. These policies originated when there were no police schools, and the only way for an officer to "learn" the law was for him to "put in his time." Again, we see old policies that may once have had some merit continued into present practices and procedures.

When the opportunity for promotion arrives, the promotional tests usually consist of three parts: a written examination, an oral interview, and sometimes a field evaluation. Those who maintain the highest average in all three, without failing any individual one, are promoted. Some departments give "points" based on the number of years the individual officer has been in the department. Others, although very few, give points or other consideration to those with college degrees, so that those officers who are sufficiently motivated to improve themselves, but who cannot compete because of fewer years on the force, are included in promotional considerations.

Under the old system of giving points for seniority, if a young policeman and an older policeman had identical scores on the tests, the older officer would automatically get the promotion. Promotions would also quite possibly go to other "old-timers" with lower scores but with higher total points because of seniority. Many if not most departments at this time give no consideration for college degrees. Fortunately, the trend is changing, and each year more departments give a designated number of points for a two- or four-year college degree.

The written examination should test the officer's knowledge in regard to department policies and procedures, supervision, criminal law, traffic ordinances, juvenile procedures, investigation, and so on, as well as the officer's knowledge of his jurisdiction (roads, streets, alleys, and other crucial physical characteristics). Unless the officer to be promoted to a command rank is thoroughly familiar with the area, he will be unable to formulate plans during a stress call until after he arrives at the scene. Also, unless the officer is familiar with departmental operating procedures and policies, his decisions may not be in accordance with superiors' orders or wishes.

The primary purpose of the oral examination is to evaluate the officer's reasoning and thought processes. The attitude of the officer certainly is a part of the oral examination, but the main purpose is to learn what decisions the officer can make, how he arrives at them, and whether he will stand by them under questioning and pressure. The officer in a command position must be able to make decisions and have the conviction to stand by them unless very reasonable and concrete facts indicate otherwise.

All officers should be evaluated periodically by their superior officers. Evaluations should include attitude, appearance, thoroughness, quality of work, work productivity, safety, decision-making, driving record, and any other factors that affect the officer's performance on a regular basis.

All of these considerations should enter into the decision to promote an officer to a higher position. Officers who expect to be promoted should demonstrate efficiency and proficiency in their daily duties. The efficient officer produces the greatest possible amount of quality work in a given shift with a minimum of defects or mistakes. His arrests are solid and in accordance with Supreme Court rulings. His cases are not frequently dismissed or his suspects acquitted in the courts. All the required forms are submitted along with his complaints and are correctly prepared and complete. This officer has few embarrassing moments in court or elsewhere. Only the officer who knows what should be done and how, and who has demonstrated that he can do the job right, should be put in a supervisory position where he must make sure others follow the correct rules and regulations.

Careers

The field of law enforcement today is just beginning to become a profession. Just recently have colleges increased their offerings of criminal justice courses. In many areas the average police officer is still unable to obtain any special training in his chosen field without having to travel a great distance. The complexities of police work, with legal guidelines, sociological and psychological challenges, and often split-second decision-making, demand great capabilities and knowledge. The field does indeed demand advance specialized study before the officer is truly competent.

If he chooses police work as a professional career, what does the officer expect from the field as he progresses either through the ranks or from agency to agency?

Of primary importance is the matter of seniority. Unless an officer is able to transfer his seniority with him as he leaves one agency for another, he may well lose what would have been half of his retirement benefits and at the same time be required to start at the bottom of the new agency. An ideal situation would be a statewide or, better still, a nationwide retirement system, whereby the seniority of the officer stays with him, so that when the time for retirement comes, the years that the officer has spent in the field will entitle him to a pension at the current agency, based on his rank and total years of service. The officer's rank or position should entitle him to take competitive examinations in other departments for the same position, and if the officer were to be accepted, his seniority should go with him (his experience certainly does).

Currently, the officer loses his rank, seniority, and often his pension every time he switches departments. Since the officer is required to suffer this loss of security, the law enforcement profession loses its ability to be competitive and, as a result, ceases to grow professionally to its maximum extent.

Unless officers are forced to better themselves in order to attain a desired position, they will not improve themselves and will merely progress as a result of political considerations or by "putting in their time." Either method is totally unsuitable and inexcusable as a system of filling the command slots that demand broad expertise. One cannot imagine the medical or legal profession operating in such a fashion.

State Licensing

An obvious answer, which helps reduce the problems of promotion, pensions, employment, and competence, is state licensing. Under this system, each officer within the state would have to meet and maintain a designated set of standards. These standards would be comprehensive and would test all phases of law, police work, first aid, and physical fitness, as well as efficiency and proficiency. Once the officer were licensed by the state (the only way that he could hold the position), it would be up to the officer to maintain his level of competence and proficiency. Each year, or every two years, the officer would be retested and would be expected to maintain at least a passing score. If the officer were to fail, his license would be suspended, and he would be retested again. If he then passed, his license would be reinstated, and he would once again be a police officer. The terms may seem harsh, but officers who are sincere in becoming professionals will work toward these goals.

Career Orientation to Law Enforcement Fields

Nationwide, there are many varied positions with local law enforcement agencies. These include village, township, city, county, and sometimes metropolitan departments. With rare exceptions, the four-year college degree is not needed. The requirements vary from department to department, being very similar to the ones given earlier in this section. State police agencies also have a variety of jobs with certain departments. State police do not require a four-year degree at this time, but they do have very high personal standards for recruitment. Many agencies are very selective and thorough in the recruitment of their personnel and have rigorous academies in which the less devoted "police buffs" are eliminated. Only dedicated and competent individuals who really want to be policemen will still be in the academy at graduation. In such a highly selective process, fewer policemen usually leave the field after they are sworn in.

As discussed, many federal agencies have police duties and powers of various types. The main ones are the Federal Bureau of Investigation, the Drug Enforcement Administration (DEA), the Bureau of Alcohol, Tobacco and Firearms (BATF), the Secret Service (SS), and the Defense Investigative Service (DIS). Federal agencies, with the exception of BATF, SS, and DIS, require the four-year college degree. With DIS and SS, however, a degree is helpful in getting a supervisory position. The BATF will take agents with four years' police experience in lieu of the four-year degree, but it prefers the degree. The FBI used to require a degree in either law or accounting, but recently it has been recruiting persons with four-year degrees in criminal justice and other majors. However, the applicant must then have two years' experience in police work after completion of the degree prior to applying for a position as an FBI special agent.

Also on the federal level are law enforcement positions in the military. For the U.S. Army, law enforcement is known as the Criminal Investigation Division (CID). To be a criminal investigator, the person must be a warrant or commissioned officer with a four-year degree. Assistant criminal investigators are enlisted men who may or may not have a degree in criminal justice. The CID branch handles serious misdemeanors and all felonies. The Military Police handle regular traffic and enforcement functions and do the initial investigation on felonies. The requirements for military policemen are the same as those for other servicemen. The counterpart of CID in the U.S. Navy is the Naval Investigative Service (NIS), formerly the Office of Naval Investigation (ONI), and in the Air Force, the Office of Special Investigation (OSI). Both the Navy and Air Force have requirements similar to those of the Army.

Another option is available for persons not wishing to become local, state, federal, or military investigators or policemen; they may become private investigators or security guards.

Although licensed by the state, the private investigator is either self-employed or works for a small firm of investigators or attorneys. Some staffs of prosecuting attorneys also employ civilian investigators in such fields as consumer fraud. These investigators are directly under control of, and responsible to, the prosecuting attorney.

The security guard, too, has several options. He can work for a large industrial complex, for example. Many retired military personnel and others of younger age turn to the security guard business and find themselves guarding stores, work sites, and other places that are subject to theft or vandalism.

As can be seen, a multitude of jobs are open to the individual who is interested in a career in the field of law enforcement if he seeks the position that fills his needs and prepares himself appropriately.

The Policewoman

Many Americans still hold to the old tradition that it is basically a man's world. People can go to great lengths to find arguments why women should not be in some professional fields such as law enforcement, but there are many more reasons why women *can* be in law enforcement.

Some women have broken down the barriers of tradition and have become involved in police work. One such woman was Lola Baldwin. Although not well known, she had a historical role in law enforcement. She was the first woman to be given the right to arrest people who threatened young girls and children in the Lewis and Clark Expedition in 1805.[14]

Women were filling positions in the Los Angeles, California, Police Department as early as 1910. The first woman hired was one Alice Stebbins.[15] At that time policewomen primarily worked with runaway girls and warned children and young girls of the social ills of gambling and drinking.[16] They were forerunners in crime prevention programs.

Policewomen of the early 1900s were pushed into the criminal justice system by a movement of social reform to stop the abuse of women and children by police officers.[17] It was thought that a policewoman could better guide and reform children and other women.

By 1924 most large city police departments hired women, but only for the women's bureau. Policewomen could not compete against men for positions; they could compete only against women within the women's bureau.[18]

In the 1930s, the mobility of policewomen changed very little. They were still performing counseling duties, but they were not allowed to investigate crimes that involved women and children.[19]

During the Second World War, when the United States was faced with shortages of manpower, more and more women took over men's jobs, including policemen's positions in identification, criminalistics, communications, and juvenile work.[20]

Women are now employed by large police departments throughout the country. The number of women in police departments has risen, but the figure is still minimal. Some of the large police agencies that employ women in their departments are Miami, New York, Boston, Ann Arbor, Detroit, Washington, D.C., and Los Angeles. In many of these cities, women are assigned to narcotics, gambling, patrol, and shoplifting units. Yet in many departments, women still are confined to juvenile delinquency, matron tasks, and clerical work.

Washington, D.C., opened the door fully to policewomen on an experimental basis in 1972. The ninety-five policewomen were assigned to police duties of all kinds. The program was so successful that many other police agencies across America soon opened their doors to women, too.

Women still meet with resistance, however.

Among the traditions that have been carried down through the years by men is the belief that women are the weaker sex; what men really mean is that they view women as being inferior, unstable, and possessing lower IQ's. Yet a study done by Dr. James B. Hamilton shows that women can tolerate every day stress better than men.[21] (This may be why women live longer than men.)

It has often been concluded that men have higher IQ's than women, but actually there is little difference between the IQ's of the sexes.[22] It is true that there are more men in professional fields than women, but women have been stereotyped and discouraged from many occupations. Women who have gone into professions have been channeled into positions as teachers, secretaries, and librarians.

For years, men have laughed at women's driving abilities. Many people do not believe that women could pursue a fleeing offender at high speeds. There is no evidence showing that women are worse drivers than men, however, and the quality of personnel should not be determined by their ability to start and stop a vehicle.[23]

Patrolmen often have negative attitudes toward policewomen and prefer not to be placed on patrol duty with them. Many believe that women are unstable and that their emotions would overpower them so they would attend a victim and allow an offender to flee. Patrolmen generally believe that a woman could not provide adequate assistance if in danger. Many more black police officers feel that women should be put on patrol than do white officers. This may partially be due to blacks' understanding of minority status. Many patrolmen, particularly older ones, feel that their wives would be opposed to their having female partners on patrol.

A 1972 survey in Washington, D.C., concluded that there are few differences between the performance of patrolmen and women during general patrol procedures.[24] Both men and women were rated equal on general patrol performance. Still, many police departments are very traditional with regard to their employment of women. Men are put directly on patrol after training and later are able to compete for positions such as vice officer, detective, and sergeant. Women are met with great opposition if they want to be placed on patrol. Instead, policewomen go directly from training to jobs such as clerical work and juvenile delinquency with very little future mobility.[25]

Despite resistance within departments, many citizens believe that patrolmen and patrolwomen should respond to the same calls. They also feel that using both sexes is advantageous. Some believe that patrolwomen are more understanding and show more compassion than patrolmen, allowing them to gather more crime information and attract fewer insults.[26]

Many police patrol calls deal with domestic problems such as marital troubles, alcoholism, assistance, family disputes, and other noncriminal matters. Patrolmen used to be called to settle family disputes and marital problems in cities, but now many departments are sending women to be the truce-makers. Some patrolwomen are better attuned to handle such calls because they try to get to the bottom of the problem[27]

Patrolwomen also are better suited for particular patrol operations than men, such as cases of abortion, rape, destitution, nonsupport, false advertisement, child neglect, disorderly females, and young girls with problems.

For such problems, policewomen have always been associated with children's problems, including those of neglected and abused children. Often a policewoman is in a better position than a man to deal with children and put them at ease. Some special problems that a policewoman must deal with are the medical examination in a rape case, contributing to the delinquency of a minor, and sex crimes involving minors. Women often have the necessary personality traits—understanding, observation, respect, compassion, leadership, stability, and persuasiveness.[28]

The policewoman also can provide good human relations between her department and the community. She can talk to luncheon groups, church groups, guilds, the YWCA, and school groups and can sometimes help break down the barriers between the police and the community. She can perform a service to women of the community by teaching them what to do in case of rape or purse-snatchings and telling them what they should know about self-defense. She may reach people who are hostile to the authority figure of a policeman.

The policewoman also has a legal role to perform. The Civil Rights Act of March 1972 prohibits discrimination on the basis of race, creed, color, sex, or national origin. This act pertained to public and private employers, which include government and police agencies. Police agencies that did not hire women had to prove that there was a difference in job performance between the two sexes. This issue is an important one for all police agencies, which fear that discrimination against women on the force may mean legal and political problems within the agency.[29]

The physical standards for policewomen are different from those of policemen. Good health is essential for both sexes. Weight and height requirements are not the same, however, since women are usually smaller in size and weight. Physical training for both sexes is usually the same. Policemen and policewomen are taught the same basic patrol procedures, self-defense, law, and proper gun use. Policewomen may lack in physical size, but they can learn to use a gun as well as a man. In physical testing, the policewoman is not tested in as many events as the policeman.[30]

Educational standards vary between policemen and policewomen. Women are sometimes required to have a college education even when men are not. Policemen were not required to have a college education in the past, but recently more police departments are beginning to require a college degree of officers of both sexes.[31]

Selection of policemen and policewomen for employment varies. It is true that members of both sexes have to take the civil service test, have their history reviewed, and have a personal interview.[32]

Policewomen should not be denied job opportunities and mobility because of sex. Since both men and women have advantages in patrol work, both should be allowed on patrol. Women should not be restricted to specific duties; they are not less knowledgeable, trained, or resourceful than men in police work. Men and women in police work should be equally effective on the job.

All officers should be allowed to compete for positions on the basis of their qualifications, standards, and responsibilities. Many policemen are afraid that policewomen will rise to supervising positions and pose threats to men. But all officers who are qualified should be allowed to compete for command positions.

The competent policewoman of the future should perform the same duties as a policeman. Her functions will have to be redefined to include routine patrol, vice squad, investigation, police-community relations, and many other police functions with opportunities for specialization at higher educational levels in such areas as police administration, intelligence, and polygraph examinations. All police organizations can make full use of women employees.

Women make up almost half the population of the United States, yet the number of women in police agencies is relatively small. It is not realistic to close out half the population as potential law enforcement professionals in the future.

National Crime Commission Recommendations

The 1967 National Crime Commission (the President's Commission on Law Enforcement and Administration of Justice) made a number of recommendations concerning the police in the fields of community relations, personnel, organization and operations, and finally, the pooling of resources and services.[33]

The first recommendation in the area of community relations concerned the establishment of community relations groups or officers in areas with a large proportion of minority population. The primary purpose of such a group would be to ease tensions between the public and the police and also to promote greater understanding between the two groups. The community relations officer or group is not the same as a public relations officer. In community relations the task is not only to "sell" the department; it is to find and attempt to correct the problems that the police and community are experiencing through daily contacts. The task of community relations is not a one-man or two-man job, either. To be effective, community relations should involve everyone in the department, from the chief down to the newest recruit.

In order for such a program to work, the personnel must be objective and professional. Only through professionalism can any type of police work succeed, and this is especially true in something as sensitive as community relations. The commission also felt that departments in areas with sizable minority populations should employ a larger percentage of minority group members. This, of course, helps the department in the field of community relations in two ways. First, the greater the number of minority policemen, the less the friction through misunderstanding of the community. Second, minority officers and officers from the majority group get the opportunity to exchange conversations and ideas; the resulting direct understanding gained in the squad room and patrol car may be passed on to the public. Community relations also should be made a part of all training and operational procedures. What the officer is taught as a part of his training should be utilized whenever the opportunity presents itself, and community relations is no exception.

Another commission recommendation was the organization of adequate procedures to process citizens' grievances against public officials. Every department should have a provision and capability to investigate impartially and professionally all citizen complaints against officers. The department should set guidelines for the conduct of officers, and when an officer violates those guidelines, he should be held accountable. It is the responsibility of the police agency to investigate all charges and determine whether, in fact, there was a violation of either the department policy or the citizen's rights. The commission further held that not only the police but all public employees whose jobs affect the public welfare should be held responsible for incompetence or other unjustifiable action. It is not necessary for civilians to sit on the police review board or grievance committee, since the citizen can contact a number of civilian agencies and offices in regard to his particular problem if he is not satisfied with the decision of the police department.

In the area of personnel, the commission had many recommendations. As mentioned earlier, it recommended three levels of entry and promotion—the community service officer (CSO), police officer, and the police agent. Active recruitment on college campuses and among minorities in the inner cities was also recommended.

The commission recommended that salaries be raised to the point where they are competitive, and further, that police salaries be separate from those of other municipal departments. The commission believed that identical pay scales for employees with "widely differing functions are unfair and unwise."[34] The attainment of a baccalaureate degree for all supervisory personnel and a goal of a baccalaureate degree for all general enforcement officers was recommended. Of great significance to the officer who has improved himself educationally through self-motivation is the recommendation that lateral entry to supervisory or specialist grades be encouraged.

The commission felt that a probation of from twelve to eighteen months for a recruit was needed in order to obtain, select, and retain the best police personnel.

In the area of organization and operations, the commission had a number of worthwhile recommendations. The first one, which should be a part of every department at this time, was the development of policy guidelines to cover operational procedures of the department and the matter of law enforcement discretion. Unless these matters are set down in writing for the review of all members of the department, especially command officers, the officers cannot know what is expected of them under a given set of circumstances. Of great importance was the recommendation that the police be included in matters of community planning. Obviously, if the police must enforce laws and ordinances and look out for the public welfare, they have a good idea where the problems are in the community at a given time and offer concrete ideas regarding future projects.

The use of legal advisers in the police department is important. Not only should an attorney help establish legal guidelines in departmental policies, but he should be employed in training programs with the officers, so that they, too, may take advantage of his legal background and training. With the many recent Supreme Court decisions and new ones on the way, a lawyer working for the department could screen the decisions and give guidelines for changing departmental procedures to conform with them.

In the area of pooling resources and services, the commission made several important points. The first dealt with the matter of providing areawide communications and records systems. Such a system is very practical and generally more economical than a series of independent dispatching and identification bureaus maintained by individual departments. Small departments do not have the money to maintain a dispatch system, with its equipment and personnel, and in all probability they cannot justify its existence on the basis of workload. The same applies to maintaining a records or identification bureau. One agency within the county—the sheriff's department, for example—could maintain an identification bureau with all the departments contributing records and reports. The bureau then would be able to justify assigning employees to that phase full-time. At the same time the area would have a useful, well-coordinated, comprehensive system from which all departments would get information that could help combat crime in their own areas but that used to be locked away and forgotten in a small department's files.

Much the same thing could be said for pooling resources to fund and coordinate laboratory services. It is a waste of time and money to train officers for specific, complex phases of investigation when the workload or requirements of a given area do not justify such expertise. That is a very expensive way to maintain a "title." However, such a position could be justified if the person served a large enough area. In remote areas it is often a good idea to combine and pool several small police departments in order to gain experience and justify special training. Often a given area cannot afford a police department, but by sharing costs it can provide police protection.

American Bar Association Recommendations

The 1967 National Crime Commission has not been the only group to investigate and comment on police problems and possible remedies. The American Bar Association (ABA) made a study in the early 1970s. (The ABA recommendations appear in the Appendix.) One of the best parts in the study dealt with the need for positive approaches, specifically the matter of eliminating police responsibilites where there is no legal authority for the police to act. The ABA believed, and with cause, that either the responsibility should be removed or the needed authority should be given.[35] This is one phase of police work that really does promote bad community relations. The public has a problem and wants the police to do something about it; yet the police do not have the authority to act. Therefore they either do not act, or they act without benefit of law. The public, failing to see the dilemma, then loses faith in the police.

The ABA also believed that in communities where a tort immunity protected the police from court action for illegal conduct and other activities, such laws should be repealed and the officers held accountable for their actions. This is in essence what the National Crime Commission had to say in the section concerning community relations and grievance committees.

The ABA study also covered the matter of police unions. The ABA said that the police should have a bargaining agency to work on such problems as wages, length of work week, pension, and other fringe benefits. However, in view of the fact that civilian control over department policy-making is essential, the matter of law enforcement policy should not be a matter of collective bargaining. Also, it was noted that local policy should not be influenced by a national police union. Most of the other ideas mentioned in the ABA report were also covered by the 1967 commission.

In the appendix of their book, *The Honest Politician's Guide to Crime Control,*[36] Norval Morris and Gordon Hawkins have included a comprehensive summary of the ABA study with all major recommendations. In the book, the authors also cover a series of issues in the realm of law enforcement that directly affect community relations and the public's attitude and reaction toward law enforcement. These issues concern a number of acts that should not, according to the authors, be criminal. These acts include drunkenness, narcotics and drug abuse, gambling, disorderly conduct and vagrancy, abortion, certain kinds of sexual behavior, and juvenile delinquency. It is the authors' contention that the elimination of these offenses as crimes would reduce the workload of police departments by more than half, so the serious crimes could receive more attention. Two of the crimes listed demand clarification to prevent undue concern: narcotics and drug abuse and sexual behavior.

Selling narcotics and dangerous drugs, as evidenced by a quantity in possession, would still be a crime and would be dealt with as it is now. However, the purchase of, addiction to, or use of narcotics and drugs should not be considered criminal. In the second area, sexual behavior, such crimes as child molesting, rape, and public indecent exposure would still be considered criminal, but such offenses as adultery, homosexuality, prostitution, and statutory rape would not. These acts are between consenting persons, and if not committed in public should not be considered criminal.

Riots and Civil Disorders

Since the 1800s lynchings, mobs, and riots, often sparked by prejudices, have been part of American history. Negroes during the 1800s largely fell prey to the white population as they were robbed, burned out of their homes, abused, and exploited.

In the 1860s Negroes met opposition through job competition, lowered wages, and poor housing, and in many cities such as Detroit, Chicago, Cleveland, Philadelphia, and New York, they were the objects of many shooting incidents, lynchings, and drownings in efforts to stop their perceived threat to the white race.[37]

Many Negroes from the South migrated to the North, where industry provided greater job opportunities than existed in the South. World War I broke out, increasing the demand for goods and cheap labor. Many Negroes believed that the North was the promised land, but they were disillusioned when they were subjected to overcrowded cities with poor housing.[38]

Violence against the American Negro continued in the early 1900s. The Washington riot of 1919 was provoked when whites believe that crimes against white women were on the increase. It was believed that Negro males were attempting to rape white women, but in truth there was only one black male who was attempting assaults on white women to annoy them. This situation eventually led to a full-scale riot in which four hundred to five hundred whites were trying to seek revenge on the Negro males.[39]

Because the number of white police officers far outnumbered black ones, leaving blacks feeling unprotected, they armed themselves for protection. The riot was finally put down with the help of the marines, the infantry, and the cavalry, with only seven fatalities.[40]

Another riot during 1919 was the Chicago riot, which was sparked by the increased overlapping of the nonwhite community with the white community. Competition was strong because of too few jobs and too little housing. In addition, Negroes were voting Republican, which brought fear to the Democrats. Many homes were bombed by whites or received random sniper fire. Many other incidents in which one member of a group was singled out and killed brought retaliation by one group upon the other.[41] Many small outbreaks preceded the major riot, which left the city with a toll of 38 deaths and 557 injuries, the majority of these being Negroes.[42] (The *Chicago Tribune* and the *Chicago Daily News* reported that Negroes were in the lead and were subduing white attacks. Whites then furthered their war against the Negroes, accounting for the fact that twice as many Negroes than whites were killed, injured, or charged with crimes.)

The attitude of the police was not justifiable. Many police officers participated in the riot, and they arrested very few whites.[43] The conduct of the militia was probably better. The militia did not heighten the disorder, but aided in diminishing it.[44]

After World War I there was widespread unemployment when white soldiers returned from the war to find their jobs occupied by Negroes, and the lack of trust by both races continued.

World War II brought many Negroes and whites into closer relations. During the war the Negro was pressured and subjected to many indignities. The final blow was the shooting of a black soldier by a white police officer. This touched off one of a series of riots in the 1940s—in Harlem and across the United States.[45]

Minorities in America are still plagued by many problems—discrimination, overcrowded living conditions, poor housing, psychological struggles, class struggles, separatism, segregation, lack of police protection, poor police-community relations, public attitudes, rumors, physical and verbal abuse, inadequate news coverage, lack of communication, unemployment, and idleness. These factors have aided in creating violence as an alternative means of coping. American society as a whole contributed toward riots in Harlem, Watts, Newark, Atlanta, and Detroit during the 1960s.

Who rioted in the 1960s? We sometimes envision a rioter as an ex-convict, a criminal type, an outside agitator, or a revolutionary, but actually the majority of the rioters were between the ages of fifteen and twenty-four, black, and unmarried. The typical rioter had lived in the riot city all his life. He was typically a high school dropout and worked at a low-status job part time.[46] The rioter typically felt deprived because of discrimination. He felt supremacy over whites and was usually antiwhite. He was not attuned to the black middle class, politics, and political leaders, but he was involved in black rights.[47]

Many youths who did riot were in small gangs, and the older gang members were more involved than younger ones. Most girls refrained. Youths did not premeditate the rioting but became involved after an incident occurred. Once a riot was in process, they made plans to take revenge on a store owner or to loot something that the rioter felt was owed to him.[48]

Very few members of the middle class participated in rioting; in fact, many of them were trying to prevent the riots, creating friction between themselves and the lower-class rioter. Race was not as strong a tie as social class in many riots.[49]

A profile of a riot can be seen by looking at Newark, New Jersey. The flight of the white middle class and the increase in black, Puerto Rican, and Cuban populations was common in many cities, including Newark. Although the city was occupied by blacks and other minorities, it was still controlled by whites. This situation brought considerable opposition by minority groups and the lack of blacks in the police department brought many accusations of "police brutality."[50]

The lack of money and its appropriation presented a serious problem. Taxes and health costs were up. The city government wanted to build a medical and dental college and extend the city airport. There was little money being appropriated for urban renewal, education, and recreation for minority groups. The crime rate was also a problem. Many crimes were drug-related, involving organized criminals and blacks. Activist groups were common in the Newark area but had little influence. The majority of the police department was of Italian descent.[51]

The riot was touched off by a rumor that a black cab driver had been beaten by a policeman. When the riot ended, twenty-one blacks and two whites were dead.[52]

In American history a few black leaders have emerged to work for cooperation. One such leader was the Reverend Martin Luther King. In the mid 1950s the segregation of whites and blacks on buses became an issue. A boycott of the bus line in Montgomery, Alabama, was organized by Dr. King. King was an advocate of nonviolence, and the majority of his followers refrained from engaging in violent acts. However, many black leaders were arrested on charges of plotting to bankrupt the bus company. The strike lasted a year and ended with a Supreme Court decision that Montgomery's buses should be desegregated. The nonviolence movement was primarily active in the South, but it spread to the North in some cities. The movement was used in issues of accommodation, voting, transportation, and housing.[53]

The nonviolence movement worked not only for blacks, but also for other minority groups that were victims of discrimination. In the 1950s the Supreme Court handed down many decisions in favor of civil liberties and civil rights, not just for blacks, but for all of society. The injustices that the blacks and other minority groups were experiencing led to protests, marches, demonstrations, and sit-ins. Some of these actions were successful in changing policies, while others failed. One of the changes they did accomplish was to take the demonstration off the street and put it in the courtroom, creating a favorable climate for the Voting Rights Act of 1965.[54]

The significance of the nonviolence movement was that it was conducted and supported by both whites and blacks, young and old. The movement interested many people because it often centered around the church. One theme of the movement was love and sacrifice.[55]

In later years King's Southern Christian Leadership Conference was failing. No longer were people as sympathetic as they had been a few years before. The unity of the black people was shaken. Many young people left the group to protest the war in Viet Nam. Some people left the movement because promises made to blacks were not fulfilled, causing them to engage in other actions.[56]

In the North, black nationalism was rising in the early 1960s; at the same time, the nonviolence movement was at a peak in the South. Blacks who had been attracted to the large cities of the North were squeezed into small communities plagued by deprivation. Trade unions aided the lower-class white population, but did little to aid the black population. There was a revival of sentiment toward black freedom and independence that boosted the cause of black nationalism even further.[57]

The Black Muslims were seen as antiwhite. They believed in a new and better way of life for blacks. One of the leaders that emerged from the Black Muslim movement was Malcolm X, a minister from Harlem. By 1966 some blacks were giving up on integration and deciding to start their own society.[58]

In the mid-1960s, many blacks were tired of continuing inaction. In 1966 Stokely Carmichael became the head of the Student Non-Violent Coordinating Committee, which no longer preached pure love, but "black power," by which blacks would be separate from whites, having their own schools, churches, and businesses. The nonviolence movement was dropped and calls of "strike back" predominated. The Student Non-Violent Coordinating Committee gained much attention, attracting people from the New Left. The Congress of Racial Equality was feeling the wave of change and also advocated violence and separatism. The National Association for the Advancement of Colored People and the Urban League still stood for integration and nonviolence.[59]

With each new generation a new wave of action is needed to correct the old injustices. The civil rights movement was concerned with extending civil rights to those who had been deprived of them. The movement acted through legislation, marches, sit-ins, boycotts, demonstrations, and organizations.[60]

The youth movement of the 1960s was concerned with American involvement in Viet Nam, the deprivation of blacks, political movements, drug cultures, outdated morals, turmoil on college campuses, and power struggles such as black power and student power. An example of the youth movement could be seen in 1964 on the University of California campus. The right to free political expression was the issue. Another famous student uprising was in 1968 at Columbia University. It was caused by the association of the university with war policy and led to students' taking over several university buildings.[61]

The aftermath of the riots, civil disorders, and other movements left mixed feelings about their accomplishments. Some people felt that they had brought a new awakening, while others felt that they were senseless and had accomplished very little. The area that the protests improved the most was probably the riot-torn cities. The riot cities were subjects of many surveys, and they proved to be different from nonriot cities. Federal programs such as welfare, housing, and employment had not reached those cities adequately.[62]

We can now point out mistakes that were made in controlling the riots. During the riots of the 1960s, it was shown that the police were ill-trained and ill-equipped. In New York the police department had only a few shotguns. In Detroit the police withdrew when citizens were looting, bombing, and burning, and did little to keep people off the streets. In Washington, D.C., the police did not get involved on the first day of rioting, but waited until the next day to take action. The police officers on regular patrol the first day in most cities were defenseless.[63]

There has been a great resentment within the black community and among other minorities toward the police. To them, the police are not a symbol of justice and peace, but a symbol of frustration and bitterness. The police serve dual roles. In the black community they are viewed as "out to get the blacks" in a white world. In the white community the police are viewed much differently, even though the policeman has the same duty in both communities to protect life and property and has to rely heavily on his own discretion to make decisions.

When patrolmen answer what appears to be a routine call, the situation can flare up into civil disorder or a full-scale riot. During the summer months, especially in urban areas, when the heat has forced many people outside on the streets and when many youths are idle, patrolmen become more cautious about their conduct. The patrolman may already be a target of hostility before he reaches the scene of an incident. A patrolman answering a call often attracts a crowd. He has to have proper patrol tactics and training to enforce the law without causing disorder. The fact that a patrolman has arrived at the scene of an incident may start rumors that will lead to disturbances.[64]

Most new recruits are trained for riot control for an average of only eighteen hours. Natonal Guard members receive a minimum of thirty-two hours of such training, while command training for National Guard officers is only sixteen hours. The training is usually inadequate, because it is focused on a small scale in terms of people and area. When a riot does occur, it involves a large number of people and a large area, which the patrolman or National Guardsman is unprepared to cope with.[65]

Police discipline is an important factor in many riots. Many men have panicked, which has led to the deaths of some innocent people. Commanding officers should be in control of police and National Guard troops. At the time of the 1967 riots, communications were not as good as they are today, but still communication needs to be improved among citizens, police and guardsmen.[66]

To suppress a riot, it is important to have enough manpower to control the disturbance. There is also a time factor.[67] When delays occur in putting down a riot, they only lead to more skirmishes. Whatever tactics the police use, they must act swiftly to stop violence before it spreads. Prompt opposition occurred when radical leader Rap Brown was inciting rioters to "burn baby burn" in his speech to a group in Jersey City. A second speaker spoke to the would-be rioters, telling them that if they tried to burn the town down, they would be met with gunfire. The crowd quickly dispersed.[68]

At times during the riots there was overreaction, and at other times there was lack of action. Much controversy occurred over the shooting of looters and the consequent killing of innocent people. Some alternatives could have been used, such as shooting into the pavement, shooting above the crowds, or using birdshot instead of heavy ammunition. The use of bullhorns to move people off the streets should be another priority.[69]

The preservation of civil peace is not the responsibility of the police alone, but of the community and all of American society as well. The close association among city leaders, the police, and citizens can help suppress a disorder.[70]

The duty of the government is to preserve civil peace at all times. The rule of law should always be maintained. Yet peaceful demonstrations should be viewed as lawful and possibly as an outlet. The demonstrator should not be denied his constitutional rights.[71]

Police-Community Relations

What is police-community relations? One police administration professor writes:

> Police-community relations means the variety of ways in which it may be emphasized that the police are indeed an important part of, not apart from the communities they serve. Properly understood, police-community relations is a concept for total police organization, functionally speaking—a total orientation, not merely the preoccupation of a special unit, or bureau within the department.[72]

Definition of Police-Community Relations

Police-community relations is difficult to define. It measures the most important quality of police service—the total of all the communications and contacts, of all the attitudes and points of view that run between the police and the community they serve, what every element of the community knows and thinks of police services, and most important, what is done in light of that knowledge and opinion.

Police-community relations is not a public relations program to sell the police image to the people. The relationship must include an exchange of ideas. It is not enough for the people to listen to the police; the police must also listen to the people in order to obtain trust, respect, and support.[73]

Police-community relations is a long-range, full-scale effort to make the police and the community aware of each other's problems and to initiate action aimed at solving them. This relationship is not the exclusive business of a special unit, but the business of the entire department. It is not confined to special programs, but touches on all phases of police activity. Police-community relations includes all the formal and informal associations of the police with the community.

Police-community relations was evident in Sir Robert Peel's time in the 1800s. He stated, "No quality is more indispensable than a command of temper; a quiet determined manner has more effect than violent action."[74] Although the need for police-community relations was evident then, it was not prominent and did not reappear until the mid-1900s.

The migration into large cities brought much tension within the urban areas. There was a need for understanding between the citizens and the police that first developed in such large cities as New York, Los Angeles, Philadelphia, and Boston. During the 1950s there was a great interest in police-community relations in small police departments as well.

A great emphasis on police-community relations programs began as a result of the establishment of the National Center of Police and Community Relations, and the National Conference of Christians and Jews in 1955.[75] When these community relations programs first began, they were directed toward crime prevention, but later they were directed toward the whole community and the solution of crime, delinquency, and abnormal behavior.

It was not until 1957 that the Metropolitan Police Department in St. Louis, Missouri, established the first program in police-community relations.[76] The goals of this program were to bring about better relations among the public, minority groups, youth groups, schools, and neighborhood groups.

When police-community relations began, it was called public relations. Public relations is a one-way communication system in which the police do the talking and not the listening. The police agencies tell the public what they are doing to make the community better and try to "sell" themselves to the public. The police who engaged in public relations were not concerned with the tensions between themselves and the public. The emphasis was on gaining public support. Public relations did little to try to bring change in the police agency or the community. There was little feedback and little true progress.

Police-community relations is a two-way communication system in which the police go into the community to hear what the community views as problem areas. Today we have police-community relations that is better and more realistic than public relations. Police-community relations involves public relations goals, but many more goals in addition.

Police-community relations, although still new, has had in its short life a dynamic impact on both the police and the public. Police-community relations is such an important aspect of police work today that it is encouraged by the United States Department of Justice. The Department of Justice has emphasized it so highly that it has established special grant programs for large cities to begin programs in their police agencies.[77]

Police agencies can improve police relations within the community by extensive training. This training goes beyond such public relations skills as politeness, service attitudes, and methods of dealing with individuals the police will contact in the community.[78]

Education in basic psychology, sociology, criminology, criminal law, juvenile delinquency, and child psychology may all help the police officer understand the people with whom he will have to deal. Through education and training, attitudes may change and prejudices be reduced. Police officers often identify criminals by race, nationality, and even religion.

Recruit training usually involves less than twenty hours of police-community relations training. The number of hours will have to be drastically increased. Police-community relations classes should be made available in universities and local colleges, particularly for officers who do not have backgrounds in psychology and sociology. Specialized training should be made available for police officers in non-English-speaking neighborhoods. In large cities police are handicapped when they cannot communicate due to a language barrier.

The police contact with any one person usually lasts for only a short time. The public has to cooperate with the police and the police with them. The police do not generally view the public as cooperative. The citizen often fails to give information or share his knowledge about criminal incidents. Public lack of cooperation with the police may be due to such factors as sex, race, age, distrust, or noninvolvement. A black police officer can more readily obtain information in a black community than can a white officer.[79]

In order to have communication between the police and the public, we must have understanding by both groups about each other's roles, duties, and performances. Some policemen do not seem to care whether the public understands them or their organization. What needs to be done is to educate the public as to the role of the police in relationship to the community. The police not only provide services and enforce laws, but they also try to make the public more knowledgeable about the law.

The contact between a policeman and a member of the public, no matter how large or small the community or the problem, must be favorable. The favorable contact may be only a smile, a word, or even an act of courtesy. The police officer has the best opportunity to make a good impression on the public because he is a symbolic figure. On matters of courtesy, the police officer is on his own without any rule books to follow. When situations arise he must use his good judgment.[80]

The success of the police force depends on its acceptance by the public, and there are many advantages of a strong, friendly relationship between the community and the police department. The public measures police performance daily. They should be made to feel that the police are not an enemy, but a friend.[81]

It gives a policeman a sense of security to be accepted by the public, but when the police are constantly facing hostility, it degrades the policeman himself, affects his job, and even has an impact on the recruitment of new policemen and policewomen.[82]

Minority Groups

The United States has been referred to as a "melting pot" because it includes people of many cultures and nationalities, who in many cases have easily assimilated into the national population. However, some groups have been forced to live as "second class citizens" due to years of discrimination and prejudice. These people, as a result, live in the ghettos and slums of the major cities and face serious economic and social problems. These people are the ones who have come into the most conflict with the police.

Racial intolerance in the United States is symbolized by the treatment of the American Negro. The Civil War was fought over one hundred years ago to provide Negroes with full rights and privileges. Equality did not become a reality in 1865 and still is not a reality today.

When Negroes came to the city, they generally were relegated to jobs that others would not take and were paid too little to be able to save money. A steady rise in the cost of living and the existence of segregation denied blacks the opportunity to move out of the ghetto.[83]

The policeman in the ghetto is the most visible symbol of a society from which many ghetto blacks are becoming increasingly alienated. Many blacks see the police officer as a soldier of an occupying army rather than someone there to serve and protect him.

Five basic problem areas must be dealt with in order to improve the relationship of the police and ghetto dwellers:

1. The need to insure proper conduct by individual officers and to eliminate abrasive practices
2. The need for more adequate police protection in ghetto areas to eliminate the high sense of insecurity to person and property
3. The need for effective mechanisms for resolving citizen grievances against the police
4. The need for policy guidelines to assist in areas where police conduct can create tensions
5. The need to develop community support for law enforcement

Physical abuse is only one type of aggravation in the ghetto. Police harassment of interracial couples, dispersal of social street gatherings, and the stopping of blacks on foot or in cars without obvious basis, together with verbal abuse, have a great impact on ghetto dwellers' impressions of the police.[84]

The second largest minority group in America is the Mexican-Americans. They, too, have not fully assimilated into American society, and many feel the police officer is in his community to enforce the "white man's law."

The police officer in a minority neighborhood often becomes defensive and hostile. He realizes that he is an unwelcome intruder in a world he does not fully understand. His displeasure at being there is felt by the residents through his actions and attitudes. He becomes overly sensitive to criticism and translates his hostile feelings into acts that are sometimes discriminatory and prejudicial.[85]

Many other types of minority groups in America also hold the police in contempt and are therefore a problem for police-community relations. One of the largest such groups is young people. Many contacts between youth and the police today are negative ones. Young people frequently become exposed to the police for the first time when they have done something wrong. This situation does not encourage warm, friendly interaction and results in suspicion and distrust of the police.

Young people in America compose a large part of the population, but they do not have the power or the money to make the changes they would like. Because of this, they feel oppressed, and once again the police are seen as representatives of the establishment, and therefore the oppressor.

As large cities become more heavily populated with minority groups, it becomes necessary to increase the number of policemen and policewomen from these groups. This does not mean that police recruitment standards should be lowered to allow minority members to enter. It means that better relations between the police and minority groups could and should be improved if both parties desire to modify relations.

Youth Programs

Being young was never easy. Today it is harder than ever. The young person of today is trying to find himself or herself in a world full of noise, pollution, strangers, and general complexity. We live in an environment largely of our own making but largely beyond our control. America's young see the immense opportunities this country offers but are desperately aware of the difficulties and frustrations in achieving them.

Most crime is committed by minors. Almost two-thirds of all people arrested for serious crime are under twenty-one. Because of this fact, and because youth is when character is forming, when an individual begins to know himself, it is apparent that the police must concentrate more effort toward dealing with the youth of the community—not only the juvenile offender, but also the law-abiding young.

Some police programs for youth are concerned with the prevention of juvenile delinquency. Others are aimed at improving understanding by young people of the police mission and role.

Delinquency prevention programs involve young people who have been in trouble with the law or are in danger of becoming involved in delinquent acts. The objective of these programs is to redirect the energy of these young people into activities that will lead to more productive lives. These include athletic activities, involvement programs such as "ride-along" programs, and employment programs in city recreational areas.

Since schools serve as the basic learning ground where behavior patterns are molded and attitudes formed, the police have turned their attention to schools in an attempt to reach young people. School programs include the assignment of a police officer to a school to act as a counselor, give safety talks, and be available for "rap sessions."

The police officer must keep in mind that how he treats the youth of today will play a major role in the police-community relations of the future as well as the present.

The contact between the police and youth can sometimes be a lasting one. In the elementary school and the middle school, the police officer usually appears and gives pedestrian and bicycle safety instructions. At this age the child usually has positive attitudes and respect for the police officer.

Somewhere between the end of middle school and the beginning of high school, disapproval of the police grows. In high school, students do not often come in contact with the police, yet ill feelings toward police exist. High school students sometimes view the police as authority figures who are "out to get them."

Youths can be taught to respect law enforcement and also taught the law. Perhaps there should be more contact between police and youth to reduce juvenile delinquency and to improve relations with the citizens of tomorrow.

Good police-community relations aids the police officer in his efforts to perform in accordance with the Law Enforcement Code of Ethics. It allows the police officer to exercise rather than just read the code.[86]

The utilization of police-community relations programs depends on citizens and thorough planning. The citizens could set up a program much like the one in St. Louis, Missouri. The community relations division consists of a director, a manager, an assistant, a representative, and a sociologist. The director deals with media, handles the publication of a monthly magazine, brochures, and speaking engagements. The manager is responsible for coordinating and scheduling police-community relations programs. He attends various police-community relations meetings and proposes new projects for the future. A representative is usually a respected person in the community who attends civic, youth council, and women's group meetings and discusses police procedures and programs.[87] A district committee made up of citizens and police meets in subcommittees to discuss problems of the future. The program in St. Louis has been a forerunner of programs in other cities.[88]

Should police-community relations programs be implemented by specialized units or by the entire personnel of the police agency? The better police agencies would require that all personnel be part of the police-community relations program. Although policemen have other assignments, this task cannot be ignored, regardless of the size of the department or the number of employees.

Large police agencies have a specialized police-community relations unit. Smaller agencies can have one or two employees assigned to police-community relations. It may be wise for smaller agencies to have representatives from larger agencies come and help them develop programs.[89]

The type of police-community relations program that is created depends on the size of the community, the size of the police agency, available resources, and many other factors. Regardless of the type of program, however, it must be well coordinated. Each individual in such a unit must know his or her responsibility.[90]

The public and the entire police agency should work in unison to identify problems in order to reconcile differences. An evaluation of the effectiveness of the program should be made. Evaluation questions such as the following could be helpful:

1. What is the number of favorable police relations?
2. What is the police attitude toward citizens?

3. How many citizens assist the police?
4. How many assaults are made upon citizens by police?[91]

The police-community relations unit should become acquainted with such groups as the PTA, the Rotary Club, and other service, church, and civic groups. However, too often it seems that the only people who hear about police programs and who are reached by police representatives are those from the upper and middle classes. Police-community relations programs do not sufficiently relate to addicts, gay liberation groups, gang members, skid row people, and other "unpopular" groups. It may be hard for a white middle-class person to mix with members of these groups. The problem here is that the police relate primarily to the people who already accept them. Police-community relations is more vital and essential in relation to the groups who do *not* accept them.

Community tension cannot be blamed solely on the police, of course. The everyday pressures of city life have added to the mounting unrest. Community tension grows in part out of unresponsiveness of government, including the entire criminal justice system. Years ago, the public was basically in the dark about local and nationwide affairs. Today the media keep us increasingly informed.

Police Relations with the News Media

The news media bring news events and other information to the public. They include radio, television, newspapers, and magazines. The news media have played an increasingly important role in police-community relations due to public demand for knowledge of police activities.

The media have an obligation to report events to the public with complete accuracy. Unfortunately, sensationalism, inaccuracy, and erroneous reporting of police incidents do occur and they greatly hamper good police-community relations.

Stories of police using physical force, pictures of officers holding people back with a German shepherd dog, and articles about officers being suspended for wrongdoing may appear as front-page news. The same paper may report an officer's graduation from

Several police departments have started programs for the safety of women. This is done through demonstrations, discussions, and informative booklets. They provide tips such as the following:

1. At home
   a. Provide good lighting around the entrance.
   b. Check through the peep hole before opening the door.
   c. Use initials rather than first name on the mailbox and in the phone book.
2. On the phone
   a. Never let the caller know that you are home alone.
   b. Keep a list of emergency numbers.
   c. Upon receiving an obscene telephone call, hang up at once, notify the police and telephone company.
3. On the street
   a. Guard your purse. Carry it close to your body with the latch facing in.
   b. If approached by a suspicious-looking person, cross the street or change direction.
   c. Avoid walking in alleys and deserted areas, especially at night.[98]

"Operation Identification" is one of the best home protection programs in existence. The police provide electric marking pens without charge for people to use to engrave their driver's license number on all items of value. A sign is placed on the doors of the house stating that the contents are protected by Operation Identification. This serves to discourage thieves, as the items are easily identified and difficult to dispose of.

Business establishments are visited by police officers who recommend the best type of alarm system (not by name brand). The officers also talk to employees concerning what to do and what not to do in case of robbery, shoplifting, bad checks, and so on. Other crime prevention programs, too, are designed to alert the citizen to suspicious incidents and advise him what to do.

Education plays an important part in police-community relations programs, as police personnel with college backgrounds have fewer prejudices toward social, economic, and cultural groups.[99] Improved police-community relations should be attained with higher education. Many unskilled, uneducated police officers try to "crush violence with violence." Many differences between the college, a police-sponsored baseball team, or a police officer's hospitalization as a result of a job-related injury, but these would be found in the back pages. The reason is that sensational articles interest readers and sell papers. The public trust and confidence destroyed by these articles is hard to measure, but it is great.

The press has no obligation to explain the police, any more than it has a right to try to blame them for society's problems. The police must respect the duty of the press and should not try to manage the news by screening what is to be published.

Police secrecy about their operations is harmful to understanding between the public and the police. If the police are to be accepted by the public, they must prove that they have nothing to hide and be open about their operations. This, naturally, does not include such things as making public the identities of informants or the location of a stake-out operation on a suspected dope house.

Although in given situations the media can be harmful to the police image, they can also, through cooperation between police and media, be a big help toward promoting a positive police-community relationship.

The public can be made aware of the problems the police face and can better understand why the police fail to do certain things expected of them. If they gain better understanding of police operations, the public is more likely to support needed improvements.

A good method to insure cooperation between the police and the media is to establish a liaison office. This unit could make its services available to the news-gathering agencies and help solve problems involving the press and the department. It could also appear at the scenes of emergency situations to assist the media.[92]

One thing the police can do to further police-community relations is anticipate community tension and gather information about trouble-producing incidents.[93] There are many techniques the police can use to decrease community tension, including taking surveys, polls, and interviews, listening to complaints by citizens, and having studies conducted by sociologists.[94] All of these activities and programs can help improve the relationship between the police and the public.

Meeting the Public

Most police departments are aware that giving talks and becoming involved in discussions with community groups is beneficial to them in their quest for better police-community relations.

They readily send officers to church groups, the PTA, the Knights of Columbus, the Lions Club, and so on. These groups already have a pro-police attitude, and the policemen's appearances reinforce that attitude.

It is seldom that a police officer is sent to talk with such groups as the Hell's Angels, the Black Panthers, or SDS. In some cases such a group would not have any desire to talk over differences with the police. But there have been cases of some such organizations wanting to exchange ideas. Unfortunately, polite excuses are usually made, and the meeting never takes place. If the police are to improve relations with the community, they must reach out to the entire community.

An example is an antidrug campaign launched by a California chapter of the Hell's Angels Motorcycle Club. They asked the Los Angeles Police Department for funds to help finance antidrug bumper stickers. A spokesman for the police department informed the Hell's Angels that they agreed with the program but would in no way help them, as the department did not want any link whatsoever with the motorcycle club.

Police-community relations centers must be located where they will be accessible to all in the community, particularly where police-community relations are the poorest.

When police-community relations centers are not available to all, they may have to become mobile. In South Bend, Indiana, the police-community relations center is a mobile unit—an eight-foot by nineteen-foot trailer that is pulled by a police station wagon. The center can be made available throughout the city.[95]

Police-community relations programs are many; they pertain to different groups of people of all ages and are called many different names. The programs deal with getting to know the police on the job or off the job. Some of the programs and activities are the ride-along program, Law Enforcement Day, tours of police departments, police athletic leagues, Operation Hi, workshop programs, public information letters, public information projects crime prevention programs, crisis intervention, Head Start, and Boy Scout Explorer Troops, to mention only a few.[96] The list goes on and on, but there can never be enough of these programs.

Crime Prevention Programs

Crime prevention programs encourage public participation in the police role of preventing crime. They help the police because they insure a degree of cooperation from the public. The community is more supportive due to the reduction in crime, and the people are more aware of the police effort in safeguarding lives and property.

In order for the police to protect the public from criminal acts, they must rely on the help of the members of the community and teach the citizens to protect themselves. Crime prevention programs can be made to fit the unique needs of the people to prevent almost any type of crime.

In crime prevention programs individual officers must come in contact with individual citizens for a common cause. Such mutual dependency and personal contact often result in better mutual understanding and better police-community relations.

"Crime in the streets" has become a major concern of the American public. The Federal Bureau of Investigation reported that between 1966 and 1971, crimes of violence increased 90 percent.[97] Accordingly, the police have turned their attention to programs aimed at increasing personal safety.

The Block Parent Program was organized in 1962 in Oakland, California. Responsible parents (checked by the police and the school) offer protection to children while going to and returning from school. Their houses have easily identified signs in the front window. Any child in trouble can go to these houses for help. The principal function of the "block parents" is to act as the eyes and ears of the police.

They are on call when children are normally on the street. They keep a list of emergency phone numbers and report incidents immediately to the proper authorities.

police and the community are ignited by police agencies hiring inferior personnel.[100]

The goals of police-community relations must be set and followed through by implementing specific programs. The goals can be met if the police and community seriously seek cooperation. The needs of good community relations and of effective law enforcement will not be identical at all times. While immediate law enforcement considerations may take precedence, it should be kept in mind that in the long run, sound community relations are essential to effective law enforcement.[101]

Preparation for the Future

The nation's interest in the police and their activities and the desire of the police to become professional are relatively recent developments. At the present time police in general are not truly professional, although there are many individual professional officers.

Effective police-community relations will not happen by itself; it is something for which the police and the public must work together. If the community wants a better police department, they must be willing to work and pay for it.

A better police department depends not on bigger guns and faster cars, but on the individuals selected to be police officers. More than quick reflexes, law enforcement know-how, and devotion to duty, the police officer of today needs better education. Police candidates must be sought in the colleges, especially among liberal arts and social science students. There should also be more effort toward recruitment in inner-city neighborhoods. Modification of requirements on age, height, weight, visual acuity, and prior residence should be enacted, and at the same time, there should be more emphasis on education, background, character, and personality of the candidate for police service. Lateral entry of officers from one department to another would result in better supervision.

The training of police officers should continue throughout their careers. The programs should provide instruction in subjects that prepare the police to exercise discretion properly and to understand the community, the role of the police, and what the criminal justice system can and cannot do.[102]

Traditional police organizational concepts that have earmarked the occupation must be reexamined and their effectiveness reevaluated. As new duties and responsibilities are thrust upon the police, the structure of the police organization must be modified in order to accommodate these changes.

The police must commit themselves to a philosophy that they have a unique and vital service to provide to the public, and that it is by the quality of this service that they will be judged. Indeed, it is by the quality of such services that the worth of the entire society may be measured.

When the police and the community become willing to listen to each other and work on their mutual problems together, then—and only then—the people will be the police and the police will be the people.

Appendix

The American Bar Association's Standards Relating to the Urban Police Function*

Part I. General Principles

1.1 Complexity of police task.

(a) Since police, as an agency of the criminal justice system, have a major responsibility for dealing with serious crime, efforts should continually be made to improve the capacity of police to discharge this responsibility effectively. It should also be recognized, however, that police effectiveness in dealing with crime is often largely dependent upon the effectiveness of other agencies both within and outside the criminal justice system. Those in the system must work together through liaison, cooperation, and constructive joint

* "Approved Draft of Standards," pp. 1-20. Reprinted with permission of the American Bar Association.

The ABA Standards are printed in seventeen volumes. They may be ordered from ABA Circulation Department, 1155 E. 60th Street, Chicago, Illinois 60637. Cost is $3.25 for a single volume; $38 for a set of 17 volumes; $2.25 each for bulk orders of 10–24 of the same title; or $1.75 each for 25 or more of the same title.

effort. This effort is vital to the effective operation of the police and the entire criminal justice system.

(b) To achieve optimum police effectiveness, the police should be recognized as having complex and multiple tasks to perform in addition to identifying and apprehending persons committing serious criminal offenses. Such other police tasks include protection of certain rights such as to speak and to assemble, participation either directly or in conjunction with other public and social agencies in the prevention of criminal and delinquent behavior, maintenance of order and control of pedestrian and vehicular traffic, resolution of conflict, and assistance to citizens in need of help such as the person who is mentally ill, the chronic alcoholic, or the drug addict.

(c) Recommendations made in these standards are based on the view that this diversity of responsibilities is likely to continue and, more importantly, that police authority and skills are needed to handle appropriately a wide variety of community problems.

1.2 Scope of standards.

To ensure that the police are responsive to all the special needs for police services in a democratic society, it is necessary to:

(i) identify clearly the principal objectives and responsibilities of police and establish priorities between the several and sometimes conflicting objectives;

(ii) provide for adequate methods and confer sufficient authority to discharge the responsibility given them;

(iii) provide adequate mechanisms and incentives to ensure that attention is given to the development of law enforcement policies to guide the exercise of administrative discretion by police;

(iv) ensure proper use of police authority;

(v) develop an appropriate professional role for and constraints upon individual police officers in policy-making and political activity;

(vi) provide police departments with human and other resources necessary for effective performance;

(vii) improve the criminal justice, juvenile justice, mental health, and public health systems of which the police are an important part;

(viii) gain the understanding and support of the community; and

(ix) provide adequate means for continually evaluating the effectiveness of police services.

1.3 Need for experimentation.

There is need for financial assistance from the federal government and from other sources to support experimental and evaluative programs designed to achieve the objectives set forth in these standards.

Part II. Police Objectives and Priorities

2.1 Factors accounting for responsibilities given police.

The wide range of government tasks currently assigned to police has been given, to a great degree, without any coherent planning by state or local governments of what the overriding objectives or priorities of the police should be. Instead, what police do is determined largely on an ad hoc basis by a number of factors which influence their involvement in responding to various government or community needs. These factors include:

(i) broad legislative mandates to the police;
(ii) the authority of the police to use force lawfully;
(iii) the investigative ability of the police;
(iv) the twenty-four-hour availability of the police; and
(v) community pressures on the police.

2.2 Major current responsibilites of police.

In assessing appropriate objectives and priorities for police service, local communities should initially recognize that most police agencies are currently given responsibility, by design or default:

(i) to identify criminal offenders and criminal activity and, where appropriate, to apprehend offenders and participate in subsequent court proceedings;

(ii) to reduce the opportunities for the commission of some crimes through preventive patrol and other measures;

(iii) to aid individuals who are in danger of physical harm;

(iv) to protect constitutional guarantees;

(v) to facilitate the movement of people and vehicles;

(vi) to assist those who cannot care for themselves;

(vii) to resolve conflict;

(viii) to identify problems that are potentially serious law enforcement or governmental problems;

(ix) to create and maintain a feeling of security in the community;

(x) to promote and preserve civil order; and

(xi) to provide other services on an emergency basis.

2.3 Need for local objectives and priorities.

While the scope and objectives of the exercise of the government's police power are properly determined in the first instance by state and local legislative bodies within the limits fixed by the Constitution and by court decisions, it should be recognized there is considerable latitude remaining with local government to develop an overall direction for police services. Within these limits, each local jurisdiction should decide upon objectives and priorities. Decisions regarding police resources, police personnel needs, police organization, and relations with other government agencies should then be made in a way which will best achieve the objectives and priorities of the particular locality.

2.4 General criteria for objectives and priorities.

In formulating an overall direction for police services and in selecting appropriate objectives and priorities for the police, communities should be guided by certain principles that should be inherent in a democratic society:

(i) The highest duties of government, and therefore the police, are to safeguard freedom, to preserve life and property, to protect the constitutional rights of citizens and maintain respect for the rule of law by proper enforcement thereof, and thereby, to preserve democratic processes;

(ii) Implicit within this duty, the police have the responsibility for maintaining that degree of public order which is consistent with freedom and which is essential if our urban and diverse society is to be maintained;

(iii) In implementing their varied responsibilities, police must provide maximum opportunity for achieving desired social change by freely-available, lawful, and orderly means; and

(iv) In order to maximize the use of the special authority and ability of the police, it is appropriate for government, in developing objectives and priorities for police services, to give emphasis to those social and behavioral problems which may require the use of force or the use of special investigative abilities which the police possess. Given the awesome authority of the police to use force and the priority that must be given to preserving life, however, government should firmly establish the principle that the police should be restricted to using the amount of force reasonably necessary in responding to any situation.

2.5 Role of local chief executive.

In general terms, the chief executive of a governmental subdivision should be recognized as having the ultimate responsibility for his police department and, in conjunction with his police administrator and the municipal legislative body, should formulate lawful policy relating to the nature of the police function, the objectives and priorities of the police in carrying out this function, and the relationship of these objectives and priorities to general municipal strategies. This will require that a chief executive, along with assuming new responsibilities for formulating overall directions for police services, must also:

(i) insulate the police department from inappropriate pressures including such pressures from his own office;

(ii) insulate the police department from pressures to deal with matters in an unlawful or unconstitutional manner; and

(iii) insulate the police administrator from inappropriate interference with the internal administration of his department.

Part III. Methods and Authority Available to the Police for Fulfilling the Tasks Given Them

3.1 Alternative methods used by police.

The process of investigation, arrest, and prosecution, commonly viewed as an end in itself, should be recognized as but one of the methods used by police in performing their overall function, even though it is the most important method of dealing with serious criminal activity. Among other methods police use are, for example, the process of informal resolution of conflict, referral, and warning. The alternative methods used by police should be recognized as important and warranting improvement in number and effectiveness; and the police should be given the necessary authority to use them under circumstances in which it is desirable to do so.

3.2 Avoiding overreliance upon the criminal law.

The assumption that the use of an arrest and the criminal process is the primary or even the exclusive method available to police should be recognized as causing unnecessary distortion of both the criminal law and the system of criminal justice.

3.3 Need for clarified, properly limited authority to use methods other than the criminal justice system.

There should be clarification of the authority of police to use methods other than arrest and prosecution to deal with the variety of behavioral and social problems which they confront. This should include careful consideration of the need for and problems created by providing police with recognized and properly-limited authority and protection while operating thereunder:

(i) to deal with interferences with the democratic process. Although it is assumed that police have a duty to protect free speech and the right of dissent, their authority to do so is unclear, particularly because of the questionable constitutionality of many statutes, such as the disorderly conduct statutes, upon which police have relied in the past;

(ii) to deal with self-destructive conduct such as that engaged in by persons who are helpless by reason of mental illness or persons who are incapacitated by alcohol or drugs. Such authority as exists is too often dependent upon criminal laws which commonly afford an inadequate basis to deal effectively and humanely with self-destructive behavior;

(iii) to engage in the resolution of conflict such as that which occurs so frequently between husband and wife or neighbor and neighbor in the highly-populated sections of the large city, without reliance upon criminal assault or disorderly conduct statutes;

(iv) to take appropriate action to prevent disorder such as by ordering crowds to disperse where there is adequate reason to believe that such action is required to prevent disorder and to deal properly and effectively with disorder when it occurs; and

(v) to require potential victims of crime to take preventive action such as by a legal requirement that building owners follow a burglary prevention program similar to common fire prevention programs.

3.4 Legislative concern for feasibility of criminal sanction.

Within the field of criminal justice administration, legislatures should, prior to defining conduct as criminal, carefully consider whether adequate authority and resources exist for police to enforce the prohibition by methods which the community is willing to tolerate and support. Criminal codes should be reevaluated to determine whether there are adequate ways of enforcing the prohibition. If not, noncriminal solutions to all or a portion of the problem should be considered.

Part IV. Law Enforcement Policy-making

4.1 Exercise of discretion by police.

The nature or the responsibilities currently placed upon the police requires that the police exercise a great deal of discretion—a situation that has long existed, but is not always recognized.

4.2 Need for structure and control.

Since individual police officers may make important decisions affecting police operations without direction, with limited accountability, and without any uniformity within a department, police discretion should be structured and controlled.

4.3 Administrative rule-making.

Police discretion can best be structured and controlled through the process of administrative rule-making by police agencies. Police administrators should, therefore, give the highest priority to the formulation of administrative rules governing the exercise of discretion, particularly in the areas of selective enforcement, investigative techniques, and enforcement methods.

4.4 Contribution by legislatures and courts.

To stimulate the development of appropriate administrative guidance and control over police discretion, legislatures and courts should actively encourage police administrative rule-making.

(a) Legislatures can meet this need by delegating administrative rule-making responsibility to the police by statute.

(b) Courts can stimulate administrative development in several ways including the following:

(i) Properly-developed and published police administrative policies should be sustained unless demonstrated to be unconstitutional, arbitrary, or otherwise outside the authority of the police;

(ii) To stimulate timely and adequate administrative policy-making, a determination by a court of a violation of an administrative policy should not be a basis for excluding evidence in a criminal case unless the violation of administrative policy is of constitutional dimensions or is otherwise so serious as to call for the exercise of the superintending authority of the court. A violation per se should not result in civil liability; and

(iii) Where it appears to the court that an individual officer has acted in violation of administrative policy or that an administrative policy is unconstitutional, arbitrary, or otherwise outside the authority of the police, the court should arrange for the police administrator to be informed of this fact, in order to facilitate fulfillment by the police administrator of his responsibility in such circumstances to reexamine the relevant policy or policies and to review methods of training, communication of policy, and supervision and control.

4.5 Method of policy-making.

In its development of procedures to openly formulate, implement, and reevaluate police policy as necessary, each jurisdiction should be conscious of the need to effectively consult a representative cross-section of citizens in this process.

Part V. Control Over Police Authority

5.1 Need for accountability.

Since a principal function of police is the safeguarding of democratic processes, if police fail to conform their conduct to the requirements of law, they subvert the democratic process and frustrate the achievement of a principal police function. It is for this reason that high priority must be given for ensuring that the police are made fully accountable to their police administrator and to the public for their actions.

5.2 Need for positive approaches.

Control over police practice should, insofar as possible, be positive, creating inducements to perform properly rather than concentrating solely upon penalizing improper police conduct. Among the ways this can be accomplished are:

(i) Education and training oriented to the development of professional pride in conforming to the requirements of law and maximizing the values of a democratic society;

(ii) Inducements to police officers in terms of status, compensation, and promotion, on the basis of criteria that are related as directly as possible to the police function and police goals;

(iii) Elimination of responsibilities where there is a community expectation that police will "do something," but adequate lawful authority is not provided. Either the needed authority should be given or the police should be relieved of the responsibility;

(iv) Systematic efforts by prosecutors and judges to encourage conforming police behavior through: (a) a more careful review of applications for warrants and (b) formulation of new procedures to simplify and otherwise provide easy access for judicial review of applications for warrants, thereby encouraging maximum use of the formal warrant process;

(v) Requirements that police develop administrative policies controlling police actions which, if reasonable, would be sustained and utilized by the courts; and

(vi) Effective involvement of the community in the development of police programs.

5.3 Sanctions.

Current methods of review and control of police activities include the following sanctions:

(i) the exclusion of evidence obtained by unconstitutional means;

(ii) criminal and tort liability for knowingly engaging in unlawful conduct;

(iii) injunctive actions to terminate a pattern of unlawful conduct; and

(iv) local procedures for handling complaints against police officers, procedures which usually operate administratively within police departments.

Each of these should be continually reevaluated and changed when necessary to achieve both effective control over the exercise of police authority and the effective administration of criminal justice.

5.4 Need for adminstrative sanctions and procedures.

In order to strengthen administrative review and control, responsibility should formally be delegated to the police for developing comprehensive administrative policies and rules governing the duties and responsibilities of police officers together with procedures and sanctions for ensuring that these duties and responsibilities are met. Police administrative rules and procedures should establish effective investigative, hearing, and internal review procedures for alleged violations. Such procedures should include provisions for handling, monitoring, and reviewing citizen complaints in such a way as to ensure diligence, fairness, and public confidence. In developing such rules and procedures, recognition must be given to the need to comform procedures to administrative due process requirements, to develop means for ensuring impartial investigations, and to keep the public informed of all administrative actions as they are taken.

5.5 Tort liability.

In order to stengthen the effectiveness of the tort remedy for improper police activities, governmental immunity, where it still exists, should be eliminated, and legislation should be enacted providing that governmental subdivisions shall be fully liable for the actions of police officers who are acting within the scope of their employment. Neither tort liability nor costs attendant to the defense of a tort action should be imposed upon a police officer for wrongful conduct that has been orderd by a superior or is affirmatively authorized by police rules or regulations unless the conduct is a violation of the criminal law. Instead, liability and incidental costs and expenses in such cases should be borne by the governmental subdivision.

Part VI. Police Unions and Political Activity

6.1 Collective interest of policemen and limitations thereon.

(a) Policemen have a proper collective interest in many aspects of their job such as wages, length of work week, and pension and other fringe benefits. To implement this interest, the right of collective bargaining should be recognized. However, due to the critical nature of the police function within government, legislation should provide that there shall be no right to strike. Effective alternatives to the right to strike should be made available as methods by which policemen can pursue their collective interest; and model procedures governing this important matter should be developed.

(b) The right of police to engage in collective action, however, should be subject to the following limitations:

(i) The preservation of governmental control over law enforcement policy-making requires that law enforcement policy not be the subject of collective bargaining.

(ii) The need to preserve local control over law enforcement and over the resolution of law enforcement policy issues requires that law enforcement policy not be determined by a police union or other police employee organization.

(iii) The maintenance of police in a position of objectivity in engaging in conflict resolution requires that police not belong to a union which also has nonpolice members who may become party to a labor dispute.

(iv) The maintenance of proper control by the police administrator over his department requires that collective action not interfere with the administrator's ability effectively to implement the policies and objectives of the agency.

6.2 Police officer contribution to police policy.

Policemen, as individuals and as a group, have a proper professional interest in and can make significant contributions to the formulation and continuing review of local law enforcement policies within individual communities. Methods should be developed by police administrators, therefore, to ensure effective participation in the policy-making process by all ranks including the patrolman who, becuase of his daily contact with operational problems and needs, has unique expertise to provide on law enforcement policy issues.

6.3 Political activity by policemen.
Policemen share the individual right to engage in political and other protected first amendment activity. However, police should not use their authority or the indicia of office, such as the uniform, for this purpose because of their possible coercive effect nor should they engage in collective political activity which compromises their ability to view objectively conflicts with which they may be called upon to deal.

Part VII. Adequate Police Resources

7.1 Variety of police methods.
Police should be provided with effective methods for carrying out the full range of governmental responsibilities delegated to them. Adequate development of such methods requires:
(i) a variety of skills in individual police officers;
(ii) arrangements for police officers to make referrals to the various private and public services and resources available in the community, and the existence of sufficient resources to meet community needs; and
(iii) broad use of informal means of resolving conflict.

7.2 Important function of patrolmen.
The nature of police operations makes the patrolman a more important figure than is implied by his rank in the organization. He exercises broad discretion in a wide array of situations, each of which is potentially of great importance, under conditions that allow for little supervision and review. Even with the controls recommended in these standards, in the interest of developing a police profession as well as in the interest of improving the quality of police operations generally, the patrolman himself should understand the important and complex needs of policing in a free society and have a commitment to meeting those needs.

7.3 Recruitment.
In view of the broad diversity of the police role, experiments should be conducted which make use of different levels of entry for personnel and standards particularly relevant for the various levels. Such recruitment standards should be related directly to the requirements of various police tasks and should reflect a great degree of concern for such factors as judgmental ability, emotional stability, and sensitivity to the delicate and complicated nature of the police role in a democratic society.

7.4 Training.
Training programs should be designed, both in their content and in their format, so that the knowledge that is conveyed and the skills that are developed relate directly to the knowledge and skills that are required of a police officer on the job.

7.5 Recruitment of college graduates.
College graduates should be encouraged to apply for employment with police agencies. Individuals aspiring to careers in police agencies and those currently employed as police officers should be encouraged to advance their education at the college level. Communities should support further educa-

tional achievement on the part of police personnel by adopting such devices as educational incentive pay plans and by gradually instituting requirements for the completion of specified periods of college work as a prerequisite for initial appointment and for promotion. To increase the number of qualified personnel, police departments should initiate or expand police cadet or student intern programs which subsidize the education and training of potential police candidates.

7.6 Police education.

Educational programs that are developed primarily for police officers should be designed to provide an officer with a broad knowledge of human behavior, social problems, and the democratic process.

7.7 Importance of police administrator.

In addition to directing the day-to-day operations of his agency, the police administrator has the responsibility to exert leadership in seeking to improve the quality of police service and in seeking to solve community-wide problems of concern to the police. The position of police chief should be recognized as being among the most important and most demanding positions in the hierarchy of governmental officials.

7.8 Authority of police administrator.

A police administrator should be held fully responsible for the operations of his department. He should, therefore, be given full control over the management of the department; and legislatures, civil service commissions, and employee associations should not restrict the flexibility that is required for effective management.

7.9 Qualifications for police administrator.

In the screening of candidates to assume leadership roles in police agencies, special attention should be given to the sensitivity of the candidate to the peculiar needs of policing in a free society; to the degree to which the candidate is committed to meeting the challenge of achieving order within the restraints of the democratic process; to the capacity of the candidate to deal effectively with the complicated and important issues that police administrators must confront in the decision-making processes that affect police operations; and to the overall ability of the candidate to manage and direct the total resources of the agency. A community should employ the best qualified candidate without regard to his present location or departmental affiliation. Because of the fundamental importance of the objectives set forth in section 10.1, the police administrator should be given the necessary support, job security, and procedural safeguards to allow him to achieve these objectives.

7.10 Police department organization.

More flexible organizational arrangements should be substituted for the semimilitary, monolithic form of organization of the police agency. Policy administrators should experiment with a variety of organizational schemes, including those calling for substantial decentralization of police operations, the development of varying degrees of expertise in police officers so that specialized skills can be brought to bear on selected problems, and the substantial use of various forms of civilian professional assistance at the staff level.

7.11 Research.

A research capability should be developed within police agencies that will aid the police administrator in systematically formulating and evaluating police policies and procedures and that will equip the administrator to participate intelligently in the public discussion of important issues and problems involving the police.

7.12 Need for in-house police legal advisor.

Given the nature of the police function, police administrators should be provided with in-house police legal advisors who have the personal orientation and expertise necessary to equip them to play a major role in the planning and in the development and continual assessment of operating policies and training programs. The police legal advisor should be an attorney appointed by the police administrator or selected by him from an existing governmental unit.

7.13 Relationship of legal advisor to police administrator.

In view of the important and sensitive nature of his role, a police legal advisor or the head of a police legal unit should report directly to the police administrator. The relationship of a police legal advisor to a police department should be analogous to that of house counsel to a corporation. The police legal advisor should provide independent legal advice based upon his full understanding of the police function and his legal expertise, and should anticipate as well as react to legal problems and needs.

7.14 Priority tasks for legal advisor.

Among the range of tasks that may be performed by police legal advisors, priority should be given to assisting police administrators in:

(i) formulating the types of administrative policies that are recommended in these standards;

(ii) Developing law-related training programs pertinent to increased understanding of the nature of the police function, of departmental policies, of judicial trends and their rationale, and of the significant role of the police in preserving democratic processes;

(iii) formulating legislative programs and participating in the legislative process;

(iv) maintaining liaison with other criminal justice and municipal agencies on matters primarily relating to policy formulation and policy review, and assessing the effectiveness of various agencies in responding to common legal problems; and

(v) developing liaison with members of the local bar and encouraging their participation in responding to legal problems and needs of the police agency.

Part VIII. Police Performance in the Criminal Justice System

8.1 Relationship of the criminal justice and other systems to the quality of police service.

(a) To the extent that police interact with other governmental systems such as the criminal justice, juvenile justice, and public and mental health systems, police effectiveness should be recognized as often largely dependent upon the performance of other agencies within these systems.

(b) For these standards to be of value in the criminal justice system, other parts of the system must operate, as a minimum, in such a manner that: (i) criminal cases are speedily processed; (ii) prosecutors and judges carefully review applications for warrants and use simplified procedures and otherwise provide easy access for impartial review of applications for warrants; (iii) the lower trial courts, especially in the larger cities, are conducted in a dignified and orderly manner, considerate of and respectful toward all the participants; and (iv) sentencing alternatives and correctional programs are as diversified and effective as possible.

Part IX. Public Understanding and Support

9.1 Contribution of legal profession.
Members of the legal profession should play an active role, individually and collectively, in developing local government policies relating to the police, in supporting needed changes in the form of police services, and in educating the total community on the importance and complexity of the police function. Among other things, each local bar association should appoint a special committee with which the police administrator can confer as to appropriate means of achieving objectives proposed in these standards.

9.2 Responsibility of educational institutions.
Educational institutions should undertake research and teaching programs which provide understanding of the complex social and behavioral problems which confront urban police.

9.3 The news media.
Public understanding of the police function is heavily dependent upon the coverage given by mass media to the newsworthy events in which the police are involved. Newspaper, radio, and television reporters assigned to reporting on police activities should have a sufficiently thorough understanding of the complexities of the police function to enable them to cover such events (as well as other matters that now go unreported) in a manner that promotes the public's understanding of the police role.

9.4 Openness by police.
Police should undertake to keep the community informed of the problems with which they must deal and the complexities that are involved in dealing with them effectively. Police agencies should cooperate with those who seek an understanding of police operations by affording opportunities for interested citizens to acquaint themselves with police operations and by providing access to the accumulation of knowledge and experience that the police possess.

Part X. Evaluation

10.1 Measure of police effectiveness.
The effectiveness of the police should be measured generally in accordance with their ability to achieve the objectives and priorities selected for police service in individual communities. In addition, the effectiveness of police should be measured by their adherence to the principles set forth in section 2.4. This

means that, among other things, police effectiveness should be measured in accordance with the extent to which they:

(i) safeguard freedom, preserve life and property, protect the constitutional rights of citizens and maintain respect for the rule of law by proper enforcement thereof, and, thereby, preserve democratic processes;

(ii) develop a reputation for fairness, civility, and integrity that wins the respect of all citizens, including minority or disadvantaged groups;

(iii) use only the amount of force reasonably necessary in responding to any given situation;

(iv) conform to rules of law and administrative rules and procedures, particularly those which specify proper standards of behavior in dealing with citizens;

(v) resolve individual and group conflict; and

(vi) refer those in need to community resources that have the capacity to provide needed assistance.

Traditional criteria such as the number of arrests that are made are inappropriate measures of the quality of performance of individual officers. Instead, police officers should be rewarded, in terms of status, compensation, and promotion, on the basis of criteria defined in this section which directly relate to the objectives, priorities, and essential principles of police service.

10.2 Responsibility of society and government generally.

The recommendations made in these standards require particular attention at the level of municipal government. Along with the recommendations relating specifically to police agencies, however, it should be recognized that police effectiveness is also dependent, in the long run, upon:

(i) the ability of government to maintain faith in democratic processes as theappropriate and effective means by which to achieve change and to redress individual grievances;

(ii) the willingness of society to devote resources to alleviating the despair of the culturally, socially, and economically deprived; and

(iii) the improvement of the criminal justice, juvenile justice, mental health, and public health systems as effective ways of dealing with a wide variety of social and behavioral problems, such as improvements in programs to provide assistance to citizens in need of help such as the person who is mentally ill, the chronic alcoholic, or the drug addict.

Notes

NOTES FOR CHAPTER 1

1. F. Berolzheimer, *The World's Great Legal Philosophies* (New York: Macmillan, 1968), p. 35.

2. William Seagle, *Men of Law—From Hammurabi to Holmes* (New York: Macmillan, 1947), p. 27.

3. Chilperic Edwards, *The Hammurabi Code* (Port Washington, N.Y.: Kennikat Press, 1904), p. 11.

4. J. W. Ehrlich, *The Holy Bible and the Law* (Dobbs Ferry, N.Y.: Oceana Publications, 1962), p. 9.

5. George Horowitz, *The Spirit of the Jewish Law* (New York: Central Book Company, 1963), p. 11.

6. Ibid., p. 12.

7. Ibid., p. 166.

8. John M. Zane, *The Story of Law* (New York: Ives Washburn, 1927), p. 101.

9. H. F. Jolowicz, *Historical Introduction to the Roman Law* (Cambridge, Mass.: University Press, 1965), p. 111.

10. Ibid., pp. 180–82.

11. John Crook, *Law and Life of Rome* (Ithaca, N.Y.: Cornell University Press, 1967), p. 69.

12. Jolowicz, p. 88.

13. Rene A. Wormser, *The Law* (New York: Simon and Schuster, 1949), p. 111.

14. Ibid., p. 123.

15. Zane, p. 179.

16. John Henry Wigmore, *A Panorama of the World's Legal Systems,* vol. I (St. Paul, Minn.: West, 1928), p. 422.

17. Wormser, pp. 136–37.

18. Wigmore, p. 444.

19. Zane, p. 207–208.

20. Wigmore, vol. 3, p. 1054.

21. Zane, p. 208.

22. Ibid., p. 209.

23. Wormser, pp. 176–77.

24. Ibid., p. 178.

25. Zane, p. 246.

26. Wormser, p. 250.

27. Zane, p. 243.

28. Lawrence M. Friedman, *A History of American Law* (New York: Simon and Schuster, 1973), p. 17.

29. Wormser, p. 262.

30. Friedman, p. 20.

31. Zane, p. 289.

32. Friedman, p. 22.

33. Zane, p. 302.

34. Wormser, pp. 292–93.

35. Ibid., pp. 310–11.

36. Friedman, p. 125.

37. Ibid., p. 116.

38. Wormser, pp. 300–301.

39. Friedman, p. 135.

40. Bernard Schwartz, ed., *The Code Napoleon and the Common-Law World* (Washington Square: New York University Press, 1956), p. 364.

41. J. W. Bennett and M. M. Tumin, *Social Life, Structure and Function: An Introductory General Sociology* (New York: Knopf, 1948), pp. 45–59.

42. E. Adamson Hoebel, *Anthropology: The Study of Man* (New York: McGraw-Hill, 1972), p. 40.

43. Ibid., p. 222.

44. A. C. Germann, Frank D. Day, and Robert R. J. Gallati, *Introduction to Law Enforcement and Criminal Justice* (Springfield, Ill.: Charles C. Thomas, 1969), p. 40.

45. Thomas F. Adams, *Law Enforcement: An Introduction to the Police Role in the Criminal Justice System* (Englewood Cliffs, N.J.: Prentice-Hall, 1973), p. 55.

46. Ibid., p. 56.

47. Germann *et al.*, p. 47.

48. Ibid., p. 48.

49. Ibid., p. 47.

50. Vern Folley, *American Law Enforcement* (Boston: Holbrook, 1973), p. 40.

51. Germann *et al.*, p. 42.

52. Edward Eldefonso, Alan Coffey, and Richard C. Grace, *Principles of Law Enforcement* (New York: John Wiley, 1968), pp. 43–44.

53. Julian Symons, *Crime* (New York: Bonanza Books, 1966), p. 12.

54. Ibid.

NOTES FOR CHAPTER 2

1. President's Commission on Law Enforcement and Administration of Justice, *The Challenge of Crime in a Free Society* (Washington, D.C.: U.S. Government Printing Office, 1967), p. v.

2. *The Gallup Opinion Index, Political, Social, and Economic Trends,* Report No. 82, April 1972.

3. For a study of robbery as a major crime, see John E. Conklin, *Robbery and the Criminal Justice System* (Philadelphia: Lippincott, 1972).

4. For an account of a mugging and its effects on witnesses, suspects, and police personnel, see Morton Hunt, *The Mugging* (New York: Atheneum, 1972).

5. Edwin H. Sutherland, "White-Collar Criminality," *American Sociological Review 5* (February 1940): p 1–12.

6. See Edwin M. Schur, *Crimes Without Victims* (Englewood Cliffs, N. J.: Prentice-Hall, 1965).

7. For an in-depth analysis of crime data, see Richard D. Knudten, *Crime in a Complex Society* (Homewood, Ill.: Dorsey Press, 1970), pp. 58–86.

8. For a discussion of the limitations of FBI crime statistics, see Ramsey Clark, *Crime in America* (New York: Simon and Schuster, 1970), pp. 44–45.

9. Elmer Hubert Johnson, *Crime, Correction and Society* (Homewood, Ill.: Dorsey Press, 1964), p. 97.

10. Ibid., pp. 101–2.

11. Ibid., p. 125.

12. Gresham M. Sykes and Thomas E. Drabek, *Law and the Lawless* (New York: Random House, 1969), p. 205.

13. Knudten, p. 284.

14. Sykes and Drabek, p. 210.

15. Thomas F. Adams, *Law Enforcement: An Introduction to the Police Role in the Criminal Justice System* (Englewood Cliffs, N.J.: Prentice-Hall, 1973), p. 15.

16. Barbara N. McLennan, ed., *Crime in Urban Society* (New York: Dunellen, 1970), p. 136.

17. Ibid., p. 136.

18. Edwin H. Sutherland and Donald R. Cressey, *Criminology* (Philadelphia: Lippincott, 1970), p. 137.

19. Knudten, p. 76.

20. Adams, p. 4.

21. Ibid., p. 6.

22. Sutherland and Cressey, pp. 124–25.

23. Robert C. Trojanowicz, *Juvenile Delinquency, Concepts and Control* (Englewood Cliffs, N.J.: Prentice-Hall, 1973), p. 64.

24. Ibid., p. 65.

25. For an account of social conditions that contributed to violence, see Robert Conot, *Rivers of Blood, Years of Darkness* (New York: Bantam Books, 1967).

26. For a study of overlegislation, see Norval Morris and Gordon Hawkins, *The Honest Politician's Guide to Crime Control* (Chicago: University of Chicago Press, 1970).

NOTES FOR CHAPTER 3

1. O. W. Wilson, *Police Administration* (New York: McGraw-Hill, 1963), p. 227.

2. John P. Kenney and John B. Williams, *Police Operations* (Springfield, Ill.: Charles C. Thomas, 1968), p. 51.

3. President's Commission on Law Enforcement and Administration of Justice, *The Challenge of Crime in a Free Society* (Washington, D.C.: U.S. Government Printing Office, 1967), p. 55.

4. O. W. Wilson, ed., *Parker on Police* (Springfield, Ill.: Bannerstone House, 1957), P. 55.

5. Wilson, *Police Administration,* p. 353.

6. George Berkley, *The Democratic Policeman* (Boston: Beacon Press, 1969) pp. 21–28.

7. President's Commission, Appendix D. Also see Berkley, P. 22.

8. President's Commission, Appendix D.

9. Alan Williams, "The Optimal Provision of Public Goods in a System of Local Government," *Journal of Political Economy* 74 (1966).

NOTES FOR CHAPTER 4

1. Richard D. Knudten, *Crime in a Complex Society* (Homewood, Ill.: Dorsey Press, 1970), p. 381.

2. Ibid., p. 376.

3. President's Commission on Law Enforcement and Administration of Justice, *The Challenge of Crime in a Free Society* (Washington, D.C.: U.S. Government Printing Office, 1967), p. 148.

4. Knudten, p. 376.

5. Edwin H. Sutherland and Donald R. Cressey, *Criminology* (Philadelphia: Lippincott, 1970), pp. 421–22.

6. President's Commission on Law Enforcement and Administration of Justice, *Task Force Report: The Courts* (Washington, D.C.: U.S. Government Printing Office, 1967), p. 72.

7. Ibid., p. 73.

8. Ibid., p. 75.

9. Sutherland and Cressey, p. 423.

10. John H. Sweet, "Why the Furor over Government Lawyers for the Poor?" *U.S. News and World Report,* January 29, 1973, pp. 46–48.

11. President's Commission, *The Challenge of Crime,* p. 149.

12. A. C. Germann, Frank D. Day, and Robert R. J. Gallati, *Introduction to Law Enforcement and Criminal Justice* (Springfield, Ill.: Charles C. Thomas, 1969), p. 199.

13. Fred E. Inbau and Marvin E. Aspen, *Criminal Law for the Police* (Philadelphia: Clinton, 1969), p. 5.

14. Henry Luce III, "Judging the Grand Jury," *Time,* February 7, 1972, p. 59.

15. Inbau and Aspen, p. 7.

16. Germann, *et al.,* p. 219.

17. Morris J. Bloomstein, *Verdict* (New York: Dodd, Mead, 1968), p. 70.

18. Ibid., p. 52.

19. Hans Toch, ed., *Legal and Crime Psychology* (New York: Holt, Rinehart, and Winston, 1961), p. 55.

20. Ibid., p. 58.

21. Ibid., p. 59.

22. Ibid., p. 71.

23. Ibid., p. 72.

24. Germann *et al.,* p. 222.

25. Toch., p. 77.

NOTES FOR CHAPTER 5

1. Vernon Fox, *Introduction to Corrections* (Englewood Cliffs, N.J.: Prentice-Hall, 1972), p. 4.

2. National Advisory Commission on Criminal Justice, Standards and Goals, *Corrections* (Washington, D.C.: U.S. Government Printing Office, 1973), p. 2.

3. President's Commission on Law Enforcement and Administration of Justice, *The Challenge of Crime in a Free Society* (Washington, D.C.: U.S. Government Printing Office, 1967), pp. 162–63.

4. Ibid., pp. 165–66.

5. Select Committee on Crime, *Reform of our Correctional Systems* (Washington, D.C.: U.S. Government Printing Office, 1973), p. 43.

6. U.S. Bureau of Prisons, *The Jail: Its Operation and Management* (Madison, Wis.: University of Wisconsin Publications, 1970), p. 165.

7. President's Commission, p. 173.

8. Ibid., p. 176.

9. Ibid., p. 180.

NOTES FOR CHAPTER 6

1. A. C. Germann, Frank D. Day, and Robert R. J. Gallati, *Introduction to Law Enforcement and Criminal Justice* (Springfield, Ill.: Charles C. Thomas, 1969), p. 139.

2. "Pennsylvania's State Constabulary," *Nation,* July 20, 1905, p. 49.

3. "I want the State Troopers," *Outlook,* November 21, 1917, p. 451.

4. Ibid.

5. Michigan State Police, *Inventory of State Archives of Michigan State Police* (Detroit: Michigan Historical Records Survey, August 1941), p. 1.

6. "The Question of State Police," *New Republic,* April 1, 1916, p. 231.

7. Germann, *et al.,* p. 139.

8. Michigan State Police, p. 1.

9. Council of State Governments, Iron Works Pike, *The Book of the States, 1972-73* (Lexington, Ky.: n.p., 1972), p. 426.

10. Ibid., p. 427.

11. Harry Soderman and John J. O'Connell, *Modern Criminal Investigation* (New York: Funk and Wagnalls, 1962), p. 463.

12. Attorney General's First Annual Report, *Federal Law, Federal Law Enforcement, and Criminal Justice Assistance Activities* (Washington, D.C.: U.S. Government Printing Office, 1967), p. 184.

13. Germann *et al.,* p. 140.

14. Ibid.

15. Jack E. Gillette, "State Forestry Administration," in Council of State Governments, *The Book of the States,* p. 498.

16. Attorney General's First Annual Report, p. 153.

17. Germann *et al.,* p. 142.

18. Attorney General's First Annual Report, p. 9.

19. Ibid., p. 65.

20. Ibid., p. 287.

21. *United States Government Manual 1973/74* (Washington, D.C.: Office of the Federal Register, National Archives Records Service, and General Services Administration), p. 386.

22. C. B. Colby, *Secret Service* (New York: Coward-McCann, 1966), p. 4.

23. *United States Government Manual,* p. 293.

24. Attorney General's First Annual Report, p. 91.

25. Ibid., p. 51.

26. Germann *et al.,* p. 147.

27. *United States Government Manual,* p. 301.

28. Attorney General's First Annual Report, p. 62.
29. Ibid., p. 89.
30. Ibid., p. 354.
31. *United States Government Manual,* p. 103.
32. Attorney General's First Annual Report, p. 49.
33. Ibid., p. 50.
34. Ibid., p. 343.
35. Ibid., p. 342.

NOTES FOR CHAPTER 7

1. Chicago. Publ. by International City Managers' Association, *Municipal Police Administration,* 5th ed. (1961), p. 44.
2. Ibid.
3. O. W. Wilson, *Police Administration* (New York: McGraw-Hill, 1963), p. 35.
4. Ibid., p. 36.
5. International City Managers' Association, p. 47.
6. Wilson, p. 46.
7. Ibid., p. 48.
8. Ibid., p. 51.
9. N. F. Iannone, *Supervision of Personnel* (Englewood Cliffs, N.J.: Prentice-Hall, 1970), pp. 10–11.
10. Ibid., p. 23.
11. Ibid., p. 15.
12. Ibid., p. 16.
13. Ibid., p. 17.
14. Herbert J. Chruden and Arthur W. Sherman, *Personnel Management* (Cincinnati: South-Western, 1972), p. 322.
15. Ibid., pp. 348–49.
16. Ibid., pp. 397–98.
17. Ibid., p. 402.
18. International City Managers' Association, p. 75.
19. William J. Bopp and Donald O. Schultz, *Principles of American Law Enforcement and Criminal Justice* (Springfield, Ill.: Charles C. Thomas, 1972), p. 345.
20. *The Officer's Guide* (Harrisburg, Pa.: Military Service Publishing Company, 1956), p. 305.
21. Ibid., p. 306.
22. Ibid., p. 308.
23. Wilson, pp. 63–75.
24. Ibid., p. 63.
25. Ibid., p. 67.
26. Ibid., p. 64.

27. Ibid., p. 69.

28. V. A. Leonard and Harry W. More, *Police Organization and Management* (Mineola, N. Y.: Foundation Press, 1971), p. 391.

29. Samuel G. Chapman, ed., *Police Patrol Readings* (Springfield, Ill.: Charles C. Thomas, 1964), p. ix.

30. George T. Payton, *Patrol Procedure* (Los Angeles: Legal Book Corporation, 1967), p. 29.

31. International City Managers' Association, p. 78.

32. Geroge W. O'Connor and Charles G. Vanderbosch *The Patrol Operation* (Washington, D.C.: International Association of Chiefs of Police, 1967), p. 49.

33. Chapman, p. 25.

34. Eugene M. Freeman, *Assigning Patrol Personnel I—Distribution* (Anaheim, Calif.: Litton Instructional Materials, 1966), p. 10.

35. Ibid., pp. 12–13.

36. Ibid., p. 19.

37. Ibid., p. 20.

38. Ibid., p. 46.

39. Eugene M. Freeman, *Assigning Patrol Personnel II—Development* (Anaheim, Calif.: Litton Instructional Materials, 1966), p. 15.

40. Ibid., p. 16

41. *O'Connor and Vanderbosch,* p. 67.

42. Freeman, *Assigning Patrol Personnel II—Deployment,* p. 21

43. Payton, p. 57.

44. *Municipal Police Administration,* George D. Eastman, ed. Washington, D.C.: International City Management Association, 1971. p. 82

45. *O'Connor and Vanderbosch,* p. 181.

46. Eastman, pp. 108–109.

47. Ibid., p. 109.

NOTES FOR CHAPTER 8

1. A. C. Germann, Frank D. Day, and Robert R. J. Gallati, *Introduction to Law Enforcement and Criminal Justice* (Springfield, Ill.: Charles C. Thomas, 1973), p. 87.

2. Joint Anti-Fascist Refuge Committee v. McGrath, 341 U.S. 123 (1951).

3. Germann *et al.,* p. 94.

4. Ex Parte Milligan, 4 Wall 2 (1866).

5. Melvin Zarr, *The Bill of Rights and the Police* (Dobbs Ferry, N.Y.: Oceana, 1970), p. 12.

6. The President's Commission on Law Enforcement and Administration of Justice, *Task Force Report: The Police* (Washington, D.C.: U.S. Government Printing Office, 1967).

7. Ibid., p. 6.

8. Ibid., pp. 10–11.

9. Germann *et al.*, p. 100.

10. Jacob W. Landynski, *Search and Seizure and the Supreme Court* (Baltimore: John Hopkins Press, 1960), p. 13.

11. Germann *et al.*, p. 103.

12. Ibid., p. 103

13. Ibid., p. 107.

14. Zarr, p. 28.

15. Germann *et al.*, p. 83.

16. *Schmerber* v. *California,* 384 U.S. 757 (1966).

17. *Rochin* v. *California,* 342 U.S. 165.

18. *Gideon* v. *Wainwright,* 372 U.S. 335 (1963).

19. *Miranda* v. *Arizona,* 384 U.S. 436 (1966).

20. *Flagg* v. *Michigan,* 40 Mich. 706.

21. *People* v. *Lipsczinska,* 212 Mich. 484.

22. *Edmonton* v. *State,* 72 Ark. 585.

23. *White* v. *State,* 129 Miss. 182.

24. *State* v. *Ellis,* 294 Mo. 269

25. *Jackson* v. *State,* 50 Tex. Cr. 302

26. *People* v. *Barker,* 60 Mich. 277.

27. *Spano* v. *New York,* 360 U.S. 315.

28. *Mallory* v. *U.S.,* 354 U.S. 449.

29. Act 58, Section 13 of the Public Act of the State of Michigan of 1964.

30. *Escobedo* v. *Illinois,* 378 U.S. 478 (1964).

31. *Miranda* v. *Arizona,* 384 U.S. 436 (1966).

32. *Mirana* v. *Arizona,* 384 U.S. 479 (1966).

33. Morton Hunt, *The Mugging* (New York: New American Library, 1973), p. 109.

34. *Harris* v. *United States,* 390 U.S. 234, 236 (1968).

35. *Katz* v. *United States,* 389 U.S. 347 (1967).

36. *People* v. *Superior Court* (Simon), 101 Cal. Rptr. 837, 857, 496 p. 2d 1205 (1972) (Wright, C. J., concurring).

37. Jack H. Wuthrich, "Recent Search and Seizure Development," *Michigan State Police Monthly Review,* no. 183 (February 1974): 1.

38. Ibid., p. 2.

39. *United States* v. *Vita,* 294F 2d530 (1961).

40. President's Commission on Law Enforcement and Administration of Justice, *The Challenge of Crime in a Free Society* (Washington, D.C.: U.S. Government Printing Office, 1967), p. 102.

41. *Harris* v. *United States,* 403 U.S. 573 (1971).

42. Henry Campbell Black, *Black's Law Dictionary* (St. Paul, Minn.: West, 1968), p. 656.

43. *Mapp* v. *Ohio,* 367 U.S. 643 (1961).

44. *Silverthorne Lumber Co.* v. *United States,* 251 U.S. 385 (1920).

45. Gilbert B. Stuckey, *Evidence for the Law Enforcement Officer* (New York: McGraw-Hill, 1968), p. 208.

46. *U.S.* v. *Johnson,* D.C. Circ., May 11, 1973. 475 F. 2d 977.

47. *State* v. *VanBeek,* So. Dakota Sup. Ct., December 7, 1973. 212 N.W. 2d 659.

48. *United States* v. *Perry,* 499 F 2d 1026, 1037 (D.C. Circ, 1971).

49. *Simmons* v. *United States,* 390 U.S. 377 (1968).

50. *State* v. *Jackson,* 269 N.E. 2d 118 (Ohio 1971).

51. *State* v. *Lancaster,* 267 N.E. 2d 291 (Ohio 1971).

52. *United States* v. *Wade, 388 U.S. 218 (6/12/67).*

53. *Walker* v. *Lamb,* 259 A.2d 663 (Del. 1969).

54. *People* v. *Wilkins,* 287 P.2d 555 (Cal. App. 1955).

55. *Davidson* v. *Dill,* supra; Spock v. District of Columbia, 283 A. 2d 14 (D.C. Ct. App. 1971).

56. *Marrow* v. *District of Columbia,* 417 F. 2d 728 (D.C. Cir. 1969).

57. President's Commission, p. 75.

58. *U.S.* v. *McLeod,* 385 F. 2d 734 (5 Cir. 1967).

NOTES FOR CHAPTER 9

1. Wayne R. LaFave, *Arrest* (Boston, Mass.: Little, Brown, 1965), p. 407

2. Ibid., p. 450.

3. James Q. Wilson, *Varieties of Police Behavior* (Cambridge, Mass.: Harvard University Press, 1969), p. 99.

4. Charles G. Howard and Robert S. Summers, *Law, Its Nature, Functions, and Limits* (Englewood Cliffs, N.J.: Prentice-Hall, 1965), p. 46.

5. Michael Banton, *The Policeman in the Community* (New York: Basic Books, 1964), p. 134.

6. Thomas E. Adams, ed., *Criminal Justice Readings* (California: Goodyear, 1972), p. 356.

7. President's Commission on Law Enforcement and Administration of Justice, *The Challenge of Crime in a Free Society* (Washington, D.C.: U.S. Government Printing Office, 1967), p. 447.

8. Charles D. Hale, *Police Community Relations* (Albany: Delmar, 1974), pp. 64-67.

9. Ibid., p. 73.

10. Adams, p. 37.

11. Ramsey Clark, *Crime in America* (New York: Simon and Schuster, 1971), p. 127.

12. William E. Barber, "Polygraphic Screening of Police Applicants," unpublished paper.

13. President's Commission, pp. 274-77.

14. Deborah Anderson and Peter Bloch, *Policewomen on Patrol* (Washington, D.C.: Police Foundation Paper, 1973), p. 47.

15. Ibid., p. 47.

16. President's Commission on Law Enforcement and Administration of Justice, *Task Force Report: The Police* (Washington, D.C.: U.S. Government Printing Office, 1967), p. 125.

17. Anderson and Bloch, p. 47.

18. Ibid., p. 48.

19. Ibid.

20. Richard Blum, *Police Selection* (Springfield, Ill.: Charles C. Thomas, 1964), p. 66.

21. Estelle Ramsey, "Man: The Weaker Sex," *Reader's Digest* (April 1971): 73–75.

22. Ibid., p. 74.

23. Ronald Talney, "Women in Law Enforcement: An Expanded Role," *Police* 14 (1969): 50.

24. Anderson and Bloch, foreword.

25. Ibid., p. 49.

26. Ibid., pp. 31, 35.

27. "Women in Blue," *Time,* May 1, 1972, p. 60.

28. Anderson and Bloch, pp. 44–45.

29. Ibid., foreword.

30. D. X. Fenten, *The Making of a Police Officer* (Philadelphia: Westminister Press, 1972), p. 92.

31. Ibid., p. 90.

32. Anderson and Bloch, p. 12.

33. President's Commission, *The Challenge of Crime,* pp. 653-55.

34. Ibid., p. 283.

35. American Bar Association Project on Standards for Criminal Justice, *Standards Relating to the Urban Police Function* (New York: American Bar Association, 1972), p. 15.

36. Norval Morris and Gordon Hawkins, *The Honest Politician's Guide to Crime Control* (Chicago: University of Chicago Press, 1970) pp. 2-28.

37. Joseph Boskin, *Urban Racial Violence in the Twentieth Century* (Beverly Hills: Glencoe Press, 1969), foreword.

38. Ibid., p. 21.

39. Ibid., p. 28.

40. Ibid., p. 29.

41. Ibid., p. 23.

42. Ibid., p. 30.

43. Ibid., p. 34.

44. Ibid., p. 36.

45. Ibid., p. 59.

46. Otto Kerner, Chairman, *The National Advisory Commission on Civil Disorders* (Washington, D.C.: U.S. Government Printing Office, 1968), pp. 73–74.

47. Ibid., p. 76.

48. Saul Bernstein, *Alternatives to Violence* (New York: Association Press, 1967), p. 35.

49. Ibid., p. 37.

50. Kerner, p. 30.

51. Ibid., p. 31.

52. Ibid., p. 38.

53. John Herbers, *The Black Dilemma* (New York: John Day, 1973), p. 21.

54. Ibid., pp. 22–26.

55. Ibid., p. 27.

56. Ibid.

57. Ibid., pp. 32–33.

58. Ibid., pp. 35–37.

59. Ibid., pp. 44–45.

60. Bernstein, p. 42.

61. William Spinard, *Civil Liberties* (Chicago: Quadrangle Books, 1970), pp. 192–94.

62. Kerner, p. 77.

63. Eugene Methvin, *The Riot Maker* (New Rochelle, N.Y.: Arlington House, 1970), p. 474.

64. Kerner, p. 172.

65. Ibid., p. 174.

66. Ibid., p. 175.

67. Ibid., p. 173.

68. Methvin, p. 487.

69. Ibid., p. 479.

70. Kerner, p. 171.

71. Ibid.

72. John Kenney, *Police Administration* (Springfield, Ill.: Charles C. Thomas, 1972), pp. 202–203.

73. Clark, p. 135.

74. Paul Whisenand and Fred Ferguson, *The Managing of Police Organizations* (Englewood Cliffs, N.J.: Prentice-Hall, 1973), p. 380.

75. Kenney, p. 196.

76. Lee Brown, "Evaluation of Police Community Relation Programs," *Police* 14 (1969): 27.

77. Ibid.

78. President's Commission, *Task Force Report*, p. 175.

79. Donald Black and Albert Reiss, *Studies of Crime and Law Enforcement in Major Metropolitan Areas* (Washington, D.C.: U.S. Government Printing Office, 1968), pp. 79–81.

80. George Savord, "Selling Law Enforcement to the Public," *Police* 13 (1969): 7–9.

81. Whisenand and Ferguson, p. 378.

82. Ibid., p. 379.

83. Report of the *National Advisory Commission on Civil Disorders* (New York: Bantam Books, 1968), p. 280.

84. Ibid., p. 300.

85. Hale, p. 86.

86. Paul Whisenand and James Cline, *Patrol Operations* (Englewood Cliffs, N.J.: Prentice-Hall, 1971), p. 75.

87. *A National Survey of Police and Community Relations* (Washington, D.C.: U.S. Government Printing Office, 1967), p. 34.

88. Ibid., p. 35.

89. Whisenand and Ferguson, p. 380.

90. Ibid., p. 384.

91. Brown, p. 30.

92. Hale, p. 104.

93. Allen Coffey *et al., Police Community Relations* (Englewood Cliffs, N.J.: Prentice-Hall, 1970), p. 64.

94. *A National Survey of Police Community Relations,* p. 115.

95. J. Morche and J. Colling, "Detroit's New Community-Oriented Patrol," *Police* 13 (1968): 94.

96. *A National Survey of Police Community Relations,* pp. 40-43.

97. President's Commission, *Task Force Report,* p. 161.

98. Hale, p. 124.

99. President's Commission, *Task Force Report,* p. 163.

100. Kenney, p. 201.

101. President's Commission, *The Challenge of Crime* (New York: Avon Books, 1972), p. 258.

102. President's Commission, *Task Force Report,* p. 272.

Index